Praise for *The Pashtuns*

'Nobody knows the Pashtuns in Afghanistan and Pakistan the way that Abubakar Siddique knows his own people. He combines his insider knowledge with decades of on-the-ground reporting and academic training. This book is the best available survey and analysis of the interrelations of the wars on both sides of the Afghan-Pakistan border.'
—Barnett Rubin, professor at New York University and author of *The Fragmentation of Afghanistan: State Formation and Collapse in the International System*

'This is the book to read for a comprehensive and definitive understanding of the Pashtuns of Pakistan and Afghanistan, and insight into the roots of Islamic militancy in their borderlands. Siddique's scholarly yet highly readable study offers a much welcomed, often first-hand account of contemporary Pashtuns' troubled history and society, driving ideologies, and radical progeny—the Taliban.'
—Marvin Weinbaum, Middle East Institute

'This is a study of the cultural values and current political affairs of the Pashtuns on both sides of the Durand Line. Siddique, a native of Waziristan, offers a fascinating description not only of his own kinsmen, but of all Pashtuns whom he has visited in various times in their lands. He has interviewed their key figures with the result that the work is rich in valuable information and insights that can not be found elsewhere. All this makes it an outstanding work of its kind. Its appearance at a time when the Pashtun heartland is the focus of special attention will be of great value for all, especially for those who have to deal with this fascinating and still largely misunderstood part of the world.'
—Mohammad Hassan Kakar, former professor of history at Kabul University

'It is one of the best books on Pakistan and Afghanistan.'
—Akbar Ahmed, Ibn Khaldun Chair of Islamic Studies at American University, Washington, DC

Praise for *The Pashtuns* (contd.)

'Abubakar has written a great book. A very elegant job in lining out what a solution will look like in Afghanistan and Pakistan. I have to commend Abubakar for a really impressive job of scholarship. This is seminal work. For anyone who has interest in South Asia, read this book.'—Ryan Crocker, former U.S. Ambassador to Pakistan and Afghanistan

THE PASHTUNS

The Unresolved Key to the Future of Pakistan and Afghanistan

ABUBAKAR SIDDIQUE

PENGUIN
VIKING
An imprint of Penguin Random House

VIKING

USA | Canada | UK | Ireland | Australia
New Zealand | India | South Africa | China | Singapore

Viking is part of the Penguin Random House group of companies whose addresses can be found at global.penguinrandomhouse.com

Published by Penguin Random House India Pvt. Ltd
4th Floor, Capital Tower 1, MG Road,
Gurugram 122 002, Haryana, India

Penguin Random House India

First published in the United Kingdom as *The Pashtun Question* by C. Hurst & Co. (Publishers) Ltd 2014
First published in India by Random House India 2014
Published in Viking by Penguin Random House India 2018

10 9 8 7 6 5 4 3 2

ISBN 9788184006070

Printed at Replika Press Pvt. Ltd, India

This book is dedicated to my parents, a source of wisdom and righteousness in my life.

CONTENTS

LIST OF ILLUSTRATIONS

GLOSSARY

Achakzai	A Pashtun tribe in south-western Afghanistan and south-western Pakistan. Part of the Durrani confederacy.
Afridi	A Pashtun tribe that inhabits regions around the Khyber Pass.
Alizai	A Durrani Pashtun tribe in south-western Afghanistan.
Alokozai	A Durrani Pashtun tribe in south-western Afghanistan.
Amir	'Leader', in Arabic, mostly used by Islamists. Also title of nineteenth-century Afghan kings.
Andiwal/Andiwali	Pashtun equivalent of comrade/camaraderie
ANP	Awami National Party. Secular and moderate Pashtun-based political party in Pakistan.
Ansar	Literally meaning hosts. Refers to Muslim communities who host Muhajireen or refugees.
Amir-ul Momineen	Commander of the Faithful.
Arbaki	Armed volunteers who provide security in Loya Paktia.
Badal	Pashtun concept of reciprocity.
Barakzai	A Durrani Pashtun tribe in south-western Afghanistan.
Bhittani	One of the four main Pashtun tribal groupings. Also the name of a smaller tribe living

	in Waziristan and the neighbouring Tank district of Khyber Pakhtunkhwa Province.
Bid'a	An Islamic concept meaning innovation in religious practice and beliefs.
Dari	Afghan dialect of Farsi or Persian.
Darul Uloom Deoband	An Islamic seminary in the town of Deoband in the Saharanpur district of the northern Uttar Pradesh state of India. Established in the nineteenth century.
Deobandi	Islamic revivalist movement based on strict adherence to Hanafi Sunni Islam as defined by its founders Maulana Mohammad Qasim Nanautavi and Maulana Rasheed Ahmed Gangohi.
Durand Line	Border between Afghanistan and Pakistan drawn in 1893.
Durrani	Pashtun tribal confederation in southern and south-eastern Afghanistan. Most modern Afghan rulers were Durranis.
FATA	In Pakistan, the Federally Administered Tribal Areas.
Fatwa	Religious decree or ruling issued by Islamic scholars or ulema.
Fiqh	Islamic jurisprudence.
Ghilzai	Pashtun tribal confederation in southern and south-eastern Afghanistan.
GWOT	US-decreed Global War On Terrorism.
Ghurghust	One of the four main Pashtun tribal groupings.
Gwand	Pashto for a political party or faction.
Hanafi school	Hanafi, or Hanfiya, is one of the four schools of the Islamic religious law or *fiqh* within Sunni Islam.
Haqqani	An honorific title for the alumni of Darul Uloom Haqqania Akora Khattak in the Nowshera district of Khyber Pakhtunkhwa Province in Pakistan, which is considered a major seat of Deobandi learning.

Hotak	A Pashtun tribe of the Ghilzai confederation.
Hujra	Male quarters that often doubles as a community centre among eastern Pashtuns.
Harakat-e Inqilab-e Islami Afghanistan	Islamic Revolutionary Movement of Afghanistan. One of the seven Pakistan-based anti-Soviet mujahedeen parties in the 1980s. It was led by Mawlavi Muhammad Nabi Muhammadi. Another of its factions was led by Mawlawi Nasrullah Mansur.
Hizb-e Wahdat	Short name for Hizb-e Wahdat-e Islami Afghanistan. An alliance of predominantly Hazara Afghan Shia mujahedeen factions.
ISAF	NATO-led International Security Assistance Force in Afghanistan.
Ishaqzai	Pashtun tribe of southern Afghanistan. Part of the Durrani confederation.
IJU	Islamic Jihad Union.
ISI	Pakistani Inter-Services Intelligence Directorate.
IMU	Islamic Movement of Uzbekistan.
Jirga	Pashto for 'assembly' or council. A dispute-resolution and deliberation forum among Pashtuns. Adopted as a political institution in Afghanistan.
Jizya	A tax early Muslim rulers imposed on their non-Muslim subjects.
Jamiatul Tulaba Harakat	The student wing of Harakat-e Inqilab-e Islami Afghanistan. A precursor of the Taliban movement.
JUI	Jamiat Ulema-e Islam, a majority Pashtun conservative Islamist political party that nominally follows the conservative Deobandi Islamic madrasa in India, it has split into various factions.
JTI	Jamiat Tulaba Islam. Student wing of JUI.
Kafir	Arabic word for 'infidel'.
Kakar	A Pashtun tribe in southern Afghanistan and neighbouring south-western Balochistan province.

Karez	Underground water channels common in arid Pashtun regions.
Karlani	One of the four main Pashtun tribal groupings.
Khalq	'Masses' in Pashto. A faction of the communist People's Democratic Party of Afghanistan.
Khan	A clan leader or notable landowner in some Pashtun communities.
Khateeb	Islamic prayer leader who delivers the sermon during the juma, or Friday afternoon prayers.
Khattak	A large Pashtun tribe in Pakistan's Khyber Pakhtunkhwa Province. Some Khattak communities live in the eastern Punjab Province as well.
Khugiani	A Pashtun tribe mainly concentrated in the eastern Afghan province of Nangarhar.
Lashkar	Armed group organised by tribes to defend territory.
Lashkar-e Jhangvi	Pakistani anti-Shia Sunni extremist group.
Lashkar-e Taiba	Pakistani Salafi jihadist group, the 'Army of the Righteous'. Based in the eastern Punjab Province.
Layeha	Pashto for 'Book of rules'.
Loy Kandahar	Pashto for 'Greater Kandahar', denotes the Pashtun regions of southern and south-western Afghanistan.
Loy Nangarhar (Mashriqi)	Pashto for 'Greater Nangarhar'. An unofficial term for the Pashtun regions of eastern Afghanistan.
Loya Jirga	Pashto for 'Grand Council or Assembly'.
Loya Paktia	Pashto for 'Greater Paktia', denotes the Pashtun regions of south-eastern Afghanistan.
Mehsud (Maseed)	A tribe of Waziristan.
Melmastya	Pashtun concept of hospitality.
Mohmand	A Pashtun tribe in eastern Afghanistan and Pakistan's tribal areas.

Muhajir	Literally a refugee, denotes Muslims who leave their homeland because of oppression or a calamity. Also used in Pakistan to identify the Muslim migrants and their descendants who left India at the time of partition in 1947.
Mullah/Mawlavi/ Maulvi/Maulana	An Islamic cleric who is usually a prayer leader in a mosque.
Murshid	A guide or teacher of Sufism.
Murtad	Apostate.
Nang	Pashtun concept of honour.
Narkh	Pashtun customary laws based on the principles of Pashtunwali.
Noorzai	A Pashtun tribe of south-western Afghanistan. Part of the Durrani confederation.
Panjpir	A village in the Swabi district of Pakistan's Khyber Pakhtunkhwa Province. Known for its madrasa, which propagates a puritanical strand of Sunni Islam close to Salafism.
Panjpiris	Followers of the Panjpir—a distinct sect in the Pashtun regions.
Parcham	'Banner' in Dari. A faction of the communist People's Democratic Party of Afghanistan.
Pashto	The first language of most Pashtuns.
Pashtunwali	Fundamental Pashtun values, which are also codified as customary laws among most Pashtun tribes.
PDPA	People's Democratic Party of Afghanistan. Leftist party in power in Kabul 1978–92.
Pir	Sufi leader.
Popalzai	A Pashtun tribe of southern and western Afghanistan. Part of the Durrani confederation. Tribe of Afghan President Hamid Karzai.
Qazi	Islamic judge.
Quetta Shura	Exiled Taliban leadership council in Quetta, Pakistan.

Safi	A Pashtun tribe of eastern Afghanistan, which extends into Pakistan's Tribal Areas.
Sarbani	One of the four main Pashtun tribal groupings.
Sharia	Islamic law.
Shirk	Shirk is an Islamic concept and applies to people who, while claiming to be Muslims, engage in associating false gods with Allah. Shirk is the first stage of kufar (disbelief in the religion of Allah or Islam) and can be roughly translated as polytheism.
Shura	Council.
Siyali	Competition among relatives or cousins.
Spin	Pashto for white.
Takfir	Takfir is the act of passing the verdict or declaring kuffar (deviation from fundamental Islamic beliefs) on an individual or community whose acts or words openly manifest deviations from, or opposition to, fundamental Islamic beliefs.
Talib	Religious student. Plural: Taliban.
Tarboorwali	Agnatic rivalry, most often among male cousins. A common pattern of animosity and competition in Pashtun society.
Tareen	A Pashtun tribe in Pakistan's Balochistan Province and the adjoining Afghan regions.
Tarun	A declaration issued by a tribal jirga.
Tauheed	Oneness of God, or monotheism. The most fundamental tenant of the Islamic faith.
Taraki	A Pashtun tribe of eastern and southern Afghanistan. Member of the Ghilzai confederation.
Teenga	A binding, or collective, decision by a tribal jirga, particularly in Waziristan.
Tehreek-e Nafaz-e Shariat-e Mohammadi (TNSM)	Pakistani militant group, the Movement for the Enforcement of Islamic Law.
Tehreek-e Taliban-i-Pakistan (TTP)	Umbrella organisation of Taliban groups in Pakistan.

Topakian	Kandahari euphemism for mujahedeen commanders and fighters loyal to them.
Towr	Pashto for black.
Turi	The only Pashtun tribe whose members are Shia. They live in Kurram.
Ulema	Islamic clerics or religious scholars. Plural of maulanas or mullahs.
Ushr	Religious tax usually consisting of 10 per cent of agricultural produce.
Wazir	A Pashtun tribe predominantly living in Waziristan and south-eastern Afghanistan.
Yousafzai	A large Pashtun tribe in Pakistan's Khyber Pakhtunkhwa Province.
Zadran	Pashtun tribe in south-eastern Afghanistan.
Zakat	Religious tax.

ACKNOWLEDGEMENTS

This book is the result of a lifelong quest to understand my people and homeland, and a desire to see lasting peace finally come to our valleys and mountains. Without a doubt, this book is also the result of globalisation, and the co-operation it requires. During the years of research and writing, many people, spread over the continents, from Waziristan to Washington, have assisted me. They have included village mullahs, communists, politicians, immigrants, tribal leaders, scholars, think-tankers, aid workers and journalists. They have shared insights and contributed valuable ideas. It would not be possible to name all of them, but to each one I offer heartfelt thanks for their hospitality, trust and frankness.

I am greatly indebted to my colleagues at Prague-based Radio Free Europe/Radio Liberty (RFE/RL). Patrick Whalen, a writer and editor *par excellence* from California, worked tirelessly to shape and sharpen the manuscript. His speed, diligence and hard work are much admired. Abdul Hai Kakar, a journalist at RFE/RL's Radio Mashaal, made a whirlwind tour of Pakistan in the winter of 2010 to conduct some significant interviews. His contacts with the Taliban, and insights into his native Balochistan, have proved invaluable. Amir Baheer, Mohammad Sadiq Rishtinai and Abdul Hameed Mohmand, all Radio Azadi correspondents, conducted important research in remote regions of Afghanistan. I owe special thanks to Shaheen Buneri for his help in understanding the situation in Swat. Similarly, Rohullah Anwari helped broaden my understanding of the conditions in Kunar and Nuristan in eastern Afghanistan.

I'd also like to extend thanks to many Pashtun friends and mentors. Without their wit, wisdom and insights, I could never have written this book. Tareen Khan Karaykhel, a friend in Waziristan, helped spark my curiosity and was an early coach as I sought to describe the ways of the Pashtuns. Afrasiab Khattak, Rasul Amin, Latif Afridi, Abdul Rahim Mandokhel, Sayin Kamal Khan, Abdul Rashid Waziri, Babri Gul Wazir (Gul Lala) and Azizullah Khan (Aziz Mama) taught me more than anything offered on campuses. I mourn the losses of Rasul Amin, Kamal Khan and Aziullah Khan, all of whom passed away during the writing of the book. Their kindness and acumen will be sorely missed. I also want to thank Hamdullah Sahaf, the Kandahari bookseller in Quetta, and Siyal Kakar and Habibullah Rafi, for introducing me to Pashto literature.

I must also thank friends and mentors in the West. Ahmed Rashid, Barnett Rubin, Marvin Weinbaum, Amin Tarzi, Hassan Kakar and Jon Lee Anderson read the manuscript and made numerous suggestions. Over the years, their friendship, guidance and wise counsel have been a blessing.

This book would have never been published without the support of Nadia Schadlow at the Smith Richardson Foundation. I am grateful for her backing. I must also thank Jeffrey Gedmin for believing in me and encouraging me to accept this challenge when he was RFE/RL's president from 2007 to 2011. Gedmin, who is now president of the Legatum Institute in London, is an inspiring leader. It was an honour to work with him. I owe special gratitude to Martins Zvaners, RFE/RL's communications manager in Washington, for helping me to manage this project.

I want to thank my family for tolerating my long absences from home and the long hours of work during weekends and holidays.

Finally, I'd like to emphasise that the views expressed here are mine alone, as are all the mistakes.

Disclaimer: Other than the official Indian boundaries depicted on Maps 2 and 3, some boundaries are as per the author's own findings and study. The author and publisher do not claim them to be official or legal boundaries. They are for illustrative purposes only.

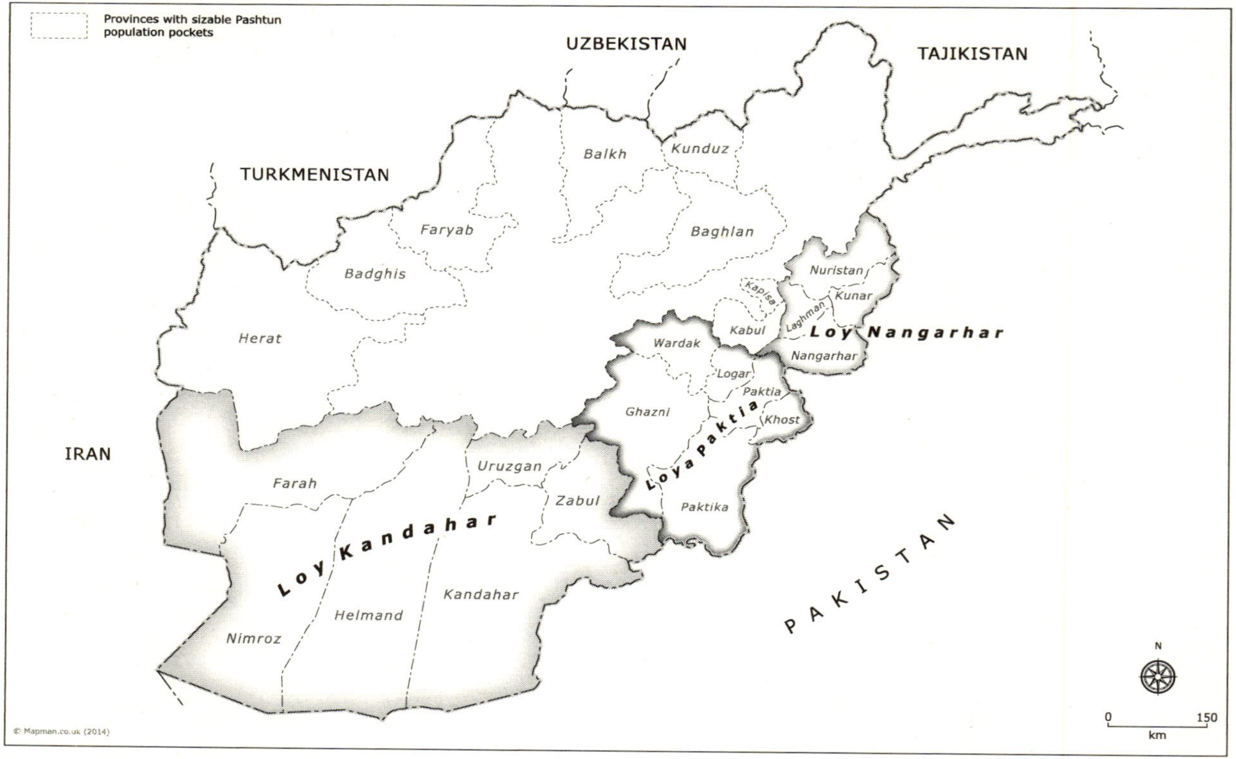

Map 1: The Pashtun Regions of Afghanistan

Map 2: The Pashtun Regions of Pakistan

Map 3: The Pashtuns and Neighbouring Ethnic Groups

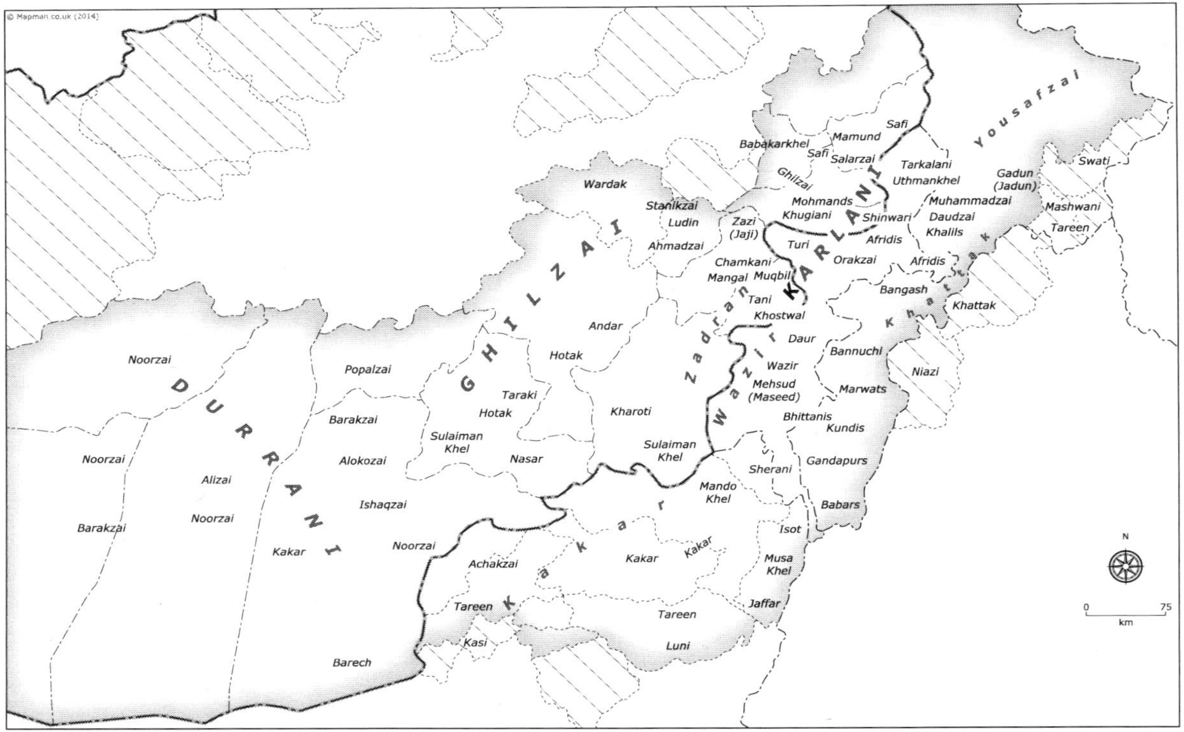

Map 4: The Pashtun Tribes of Afghanistan and Pakistan

INTRODUCTION

ONE of my earliest boyhood memories is seeing the arrival of Afghan refugees to our town. It was 1981 and I had started school in Wana, the administrative capital of South Waziristan in Pakistan's western Pashtun tribal region. Like the local population, most of the refugees were ethnic Pashtuns. Their shambling appearance stung my naïve eyes. Their ordeal had left them shattered. They stood on the streets or huddled on the outskirts of town, no place to go. Their children roamed around without shoes, looking lost. The women had no choice but to cook out in the open.

I was but a youngster and had little inkling of the calamity that had brought them to our doorstep. It was a war we could not see or hear. But it was talked about and felt everywhere. Growing up in that remote corner of Pakistan, I regularly listened to Radio Kabul at night. Much of the talk was of the alleged 'progress' and 'development' that the communist leadership and their Soviet friends were graciously bringing to Afghanistan. There were also frequent condemnations of Pakistan's government, along with the 'imperialist' Western powers that backed Islamabad, and the Afghan guerillas who had sought shelter in Pashtun towns and cities such as Wana.

During the daytime, in classrooms, shops, mosques and on television, I learned the other side. I was told about how the Afghan communist regime and their Soviet backers were killing innocent people. Friday sermons featured excitable mullahs provoking passions with incendiary condemnations. They lamented how communist atheism endangered the survival of Islam. Their talks often ended in a call to arms, or jihad.

Their prayers exhorted Allah to bless the warriors fighting the holy war in Afghanistan.

The war was rapidly changing the world around me. Elder males in my extended family worried about the widespread availability of arms. They regretted how the cheap weapons, and the increasing wealth that the war had brought to some in Waziristan, were changing the norms of Pashtun behaviour. Killing innocents was once considered unthinkable. But the easy availability of small arms and the mushrooming war economy were changing things in ways few could comprehend.

As a child, I went to Azam Warsak many times. This small village, twenty kilometres west of Wana, had become a huge arms market. With enough money, one could easily equip a small army. Soviet Kalashnikovs, Chinese rocket launchers, Dutch hunting rifles and Iranian landmines were all for sale. But these weapons were not bringing happiness. They invited only tears, increasing violence, changing social attitudes and more radicalisation.

One question haunted me then, and it continues to disturb me: why was this happening?

The search for an explanation attracted me to the social sciences. I studied political science and anthropology at college and university. By the time I understood how tribal societies were organised, the Taliban controlled most of Afghanistan. Islamists in Pakistan, meanwhile, were preparing operations to further cleanse the 'land of the pure'—the literal meaning of the word Pakistan. After graduation, I realised it was next to impossible to get funding for serious anthropological research in Pakistan, a country where even some educated folks confused the discipline with the study of ants and related critters. Eventually I moved into journalism, where my academic training has proved an asset.

The idea for this book was suggested by my friend and mentor, the author and expert Ahmed Rashid, during a trip to Balochistan and southern Afghanistan in October 2003. We had witnessed much suffering and privation, and he urged me to write something for a global audience explaining the Pashtun enigma. Years later, a grant from the Smith Richardson Foundation helped me realise this goal. In February 2010, the foundation provided me with funds to develop a fresh understanding of the Taliban by translating the second edition of their rulebook, entitled *Layeha* in Pashto. The aim was to describe the evolution of the Taliban, their organisation, financing and strategic objectives, and to offer a prescription for the challenges posed by their insurgencies to Afghanistan and Pakistan.

The project was originally envisioned as a hundred-page monograph. But as I began my research, it quickly became clear that the topic demanded a more thorough treatment. My publisher, Hurst and Company, agreed that despite the international focus on Afghanistan and Pakistan since 11 September 2001, there were many gaps in the general understanding of the region. We agreed that the book should challenge the 'conventional wisdom', which has held that violent extremism in the Pashtun borderlands is either rooted in Pashtun history or finds willing hosts among its tribes and clans.

Some fifty million Pashtuns have paid a steep price over the past thirty years due to such flawed analyses. The Taliban and allied extremist movements, as well as regional states and Western powers, have used violence in a bid to mould the Pashtun lands to their liking. Their attempts have left behind a legacy of misery and mistrust, and contributed to the creation of a resourceful and committed enemy, the Taliban. The West's political goals for the region, meanwhile, have remained unfulfilled.

In this book, I have attempted to show that the failure of both Islamabad and Kabul to incorporate the Pashtuns into state structures and the economic and political fabric has compromised the security of both countries. I have sought to show that the often extraordinary great power interventions in the Pashtun borderlands—and their focus on the Taliban as primarily a military threat—have only prolonged the crisis. I have tried to show how regional states have fallen short in making the Pashtun homeland a bridge for transnational co-operation. And I have sought to demonstrate that religious extremism, mainly manifested in the Taliban and allied movements, is to a large degree a product of all these critical failures. Above all, however, I have tried to show that the main factor behind the rise of Islamic radicals such as the Taliban is the lack of development and stability in the Pashtun homeland.

This work explains the rise of the Taliban, their contemporary behaviour, strategic vision and potential future. I have come to my conclusions after repeated visits to the region and a deep immersion in the literature of the Taliban in its original language and format. I have focused on the suffering of ordinary Afghans and Pakistanis. I have attempted to relate their views on extremism and terrorism, and explain how they have coped with some of the most hard-line ideologies of the twentieth and twenty-first centuries.

The first part of this book consists of three background chapters. Chapter One is a survey of contemporary Pashtuns, from their mountain ranges to their towns and cities. Some of these places will be familiar to those who have paid more than glancing attention to the news since 11 September 2001. The second chapter is a précis of the last five centuries of Pashtun history, including the complex relations the Pashtuns had with various empires and states, some of which they founded and sustained. Such relations continue to influence the way conflict is played out today. Since European colonialism, great power interventions have altered both the geography and politics of the region, while sabotaging indigenous modernisation campaigns. The third chapter concerns more recent history—that of the Taliban movement's rise and fall from power in Afghanistan. Again, the aim is not merely to recount events, but to decipher and interpret key issues.

The second part of the book focuses on Pakistan. Chapter Four covers the fighting in Waziristan. It describes the rise of the Pakistani Taliban and analyses their ideology and relations with Al-Qaeda, Central Asian extremists and the Afghan Taliban. The chapter addresses the conglomerate of international jihadists who have sheltered in the region since losing their Afghan sanctuary in late 2001. It examines the impact of Pakistani military operations and US drone strikes, and documents the breakdown of tribal and social solidarity. The fifth chapter covers the rest of Pakistan's Federally Administrated Tribal Areas (FATA), including flashpoint regions such as the Khyber, Kurram, Bajaur and Mohmand tribal districts. This chapter presents a critical appraisal of reforms in the FATA, which has been treated as an economic, legal and political backwater by Pakistani rulers and their British predecessors for more than a century.

Chapter Six focuses on the north-western Khyber Pakhtunkhwa Province. It looks at the uphill political struggle of moderate Pashtun politicians to rid their society of messianic radicalism. It documents the rise and fall of Taliban power in the alpine Swat Valley. It also evaluates the role played by Pakistan's most powerful institution, the army, in both endorsing and fighting militancy. Chapter Seven focuses on the Afghan Taliban's sanctuary in Pakistan's south-western Balochistan Province. It has been reported frequently for years that the Taliban leadership council has been based in Quetta (the Quetta Shura), but there have been few serious attempts to understand this important region. The chapter also highlights the cauldron of sectarian, separatist and political conflicts in impoverished Balochistan.

Part Three covers Afghanistan. Its three chapters investigate the three major Pashtun-dominated regions of the country. Chapter Eight covers the east, which local Pashtuns refer to as Loy Nangarhar. It probes the various Islamist currents in the region and their impact on contemporary Afghanistan. Chapter Nine describes the Pashtuns of Loya Paktia, in south-eastern Afghanistan, which shares much with the FATA regions of Pakistan across the Durand Line. Pashtun tribes in this region have largely preserved their makeup and the elaborate customary law that regulates society and mediates disputes. I have looked at the region's evolving social relations, its strategic significance and how continued instability in the region could cause further trouble for Kabul. Loya Paktia had a significant role in shaping the major communist factions in Afghanistan, and has been home to some of the most diehard jihadists.

Chapter Ten examines the rise of the new Taliban in their home base in south-western Afghanistan: the historic and politically decisive Loy Kandahar. The chapter explains the ideology, worldview, organisation and strategy of the Taliban. It also considers the Taliban's potential for reconciliation with other Afghan factions and society at large. The concluding chapter is dedicated to charting a roadmap for peace. I have argued that crafting a sustainable peace in the Pashtun homeland is the key to peace and development in the region as a whole. The West and other powers will continue to fall short of their ambitions in the region, so long as their focus remains only on short-term security goals and not an overall policy of development and co-operation. Importantly, however, I have regarded the people of Pakistan and Afghanistan as the principal drivers of their future.

Abubakar Siddique November 2013

PART ONE

THEATRE OF CONQUEST

1

TWENTY-FIRST CENTURY PASHTUNS

CONTINUITY AMID CATASTROPHE

It was International Literacy Day, and a group of Afghan cabinet members, lawmakers, foreign dignitaries, teachers and students had assembled in Kabul for an address by President Hamid Karzai. He was expected to announce appointees to his High Peace Council. This was a new, seventy-member body seen by Karzai and his team as an important step towards implementing one of the president's key election promises: reconciling with the Taliban.

Karzai did not pander to his audience with bromides about progress in the country since the end of Taliban rule in late 2001. Instead, the president began his speech by lamenting the persistent backwardness of Afghanistan, a country where two-thirds of the people cannot read or write. He recalled the memoirs of a Russian doctor who, visiting Kabul during Amir Sher Ali Khan's reign in the mid-nineteenth century, failed to save the monarch's ill son, Abdullah Jan.

Afghanistan's dependence on outsiders was not much different today, Karzai said. He noted that Afghans were collectively spending about $100 million per month to travel to foreign countries to receive better medical care than they could obtain in Afghanistan. 'Our education and the development of our people remains the same as 130 years ago,' Karzai somberly told the September 2010, gathering at the formerly German-sponsored Amani High School. Speaking in the Afghan language of Dari,[1] Karzai showed no hesitation in blaming foreigners for Afghanistan's current miseries. 'First,' he said, 'the Soviets came [in the 1980s], claiming that they would turn us into communists. They failed and destroyed us in the process. Then our neighbours came [Pakistan and Iran in the 1990s] and said, "We are going to administer you."' That effort also didn't succeed, the president said.

'Now,' he continued, 'NATO has come here in the name of fighting the war against terrorism. But this war has been going on for ten years and we still don't know its result.' Karzai went on to deliver an impassioned appeal to the Taliban, 'Remember, every bullet you fire hits the heart of this land. And it only benefits the enemy.' He described the Taliban as his 'countrymen', and told the militants that, if they considered themselves Afghans and Muslims, they should not destroy their country just to appease their sponsors in neighbouring Pakistan. 'Do not kill your people for the interest of others, and do not force the closure of your schools for the interest of others,' the president said.

Building his speech to an emotional climax, Karzai warned that Afghans risked losing their identity if fighting continued. With tears forming in his eyes, the president said he wanted his people to become educated and self-reliant. Karzai spoke of his desire to see his three-year-old son, Mirwais, grow up and live in Afghanistan instead of in a foreign country where conditions were better.

'Feel the pain in my heart,' Karzai said. 'Oh, people! Please understand me. I am concerned that my own son, Mirwais, could be forced to go abroad.' He paused for a moment as the crowd broke into applause. 'I don't want him to become a foreign citizen. I want him to go to school in Kabul and to be educated in Afghanistan by an Afghan teacher. So he can grow up here, can become a doctor, serve this land and be buried here.'[2]

The president's address had come shortly after US intelligence officials were quoted, in a book by the American journalist Bob Woodward, as describing Karzai as 'manic-depressive'.[3] Perhaps to an outsider, the Afghan president's public display of emotion suggested evidence of this alleged disorder. Inside Afghanistan, however, his words resonated strongly. Afghans are well aware of their troubled history and the role violence has played in bringing them to their current state.

Indeed, a student of the school where Karzai was speaking murdered an Afghan king, Mohammad Nadir Shah, in 1933. All males in the assassin's adopted Charkhi family had been eliminated by Nadir a year earlier because of their support for Amanullah Khan, the monarch who had abdicated a few years earlier. And fourteen years before Karzai's speech, outside the presidential palace, the last socialist president of Afghanistan was dragged out of the United Nations compound and hanged by Taliban fighters. Dr. Mohammad Najibullah's murder on 27 September 1996 continues to stand as a fearsome symbol of the Taliban takeover of Kabul.

Seen through the lens of Afghan history, the fate of the twice-elected Karzai was itself uncertain. Many Afghan rulers have either been assassinated or forced into exile—casualties of a political culture that has yet to see a peaceful transfer of power. Like Karzai, most Afghan leaders—whether kings, communists or Islamist ideologues—have been ethnic Pashtuns. The fate of these leaders cannot be understood without first understanding the people they tried to govern, sometimes through brute force. In the modern era especially, Pashtun national identity has been intimately tied to the large number of Pashtuns living to the east—brethren who were forcefully separated and occupied by the British, and then bequeathed to Pakistan.

Who are the Pashtuns?

Pashtuns are identified by several related names. 'Afghan', which denotes a citizen of Afghanistan in the juridical sense, is interchangeable with 'Pashtun'. Many Pashtuns in north-western Pakistan are very much conscious of their ethnic identity and still identify themselves in official documents as 'Afghan'—a practice that originated in the raj. 'Pathan', a corruption of the native 'Pakhtun' used in the subcontinent, identified the Pashtuns in British colonial ethnography. This term of usage has been declining.[4]

Many Pashtun leaders and intellectuals view their people as among the most maligned of the twenty-first century. This is because their lands have been transformed into a staging ground for a global conflict that has entangled some of the world's most powerful regular and private armies. But little attention is paid to understanding the modern Pashtun, in his own environment. Most contemporary journalistic and scholarly accounts of the instability gripping the Afghan and Pakistan borderlands have sought to demonstrate that violent Islamic extremism, including support for the Taliban and related groups, is either rooted in Pashtun history and culture, or finds willing hosts among Pashtun communities on either side of the Durand Line.[5]

Since the 11 September 2001 terrorist strikes inside the United States, Pashtun communities in both Afghanistan and Pakistan have paid a heavy price for such erroneous descriptions. A vast majority of Pashtuns have almost become mere adjuncts, watching from the sidelines as the local and foreign Islamist extremists and the outsiders who came to fight them fundamentally alter the existing order through violence.

While accurate current census data is lacking, it can be estimated that at least forty million—and perhaps as many as fifty million—Pashtuns live in Afghanistan and Pakistan. Pashtuns are estimated to constitute nearly half of Afghanistan's population of 25.5 million. They are Pakistan's largest minority, making up about 15–20 per cent of the country's 174 million citizens in 2010.[6] The original Pashtun homeland was situated between the Hindu Kush mountains in central Afghanistan and the Indus River that bisects Pakistan, but Pashtun communities are now scattered over a vast territory. In northern Afghanistan, the Pashtun population extends to the Amu Darya (Oxus River) border with Central Asia, where Pashtun communities have grown substantially over the past century.[7] The southern Pakistani port city of Karachi, on the Arabian Sea, is today home to one of the region's largest urban Pashtun populations, the result of massive economic migration. Some four million Pashtuns live among Karachi's twenty million people.[8]

For at least the past six centuries, Pashtun history has been shaped by war, invasion and endemic local violence. These ordeals have shown that the Pashtun identity is resilient. While former nemeses such as the Mughals exist today only in history books, the Pashtuns have survived to constitute a nation in the archetypal sense. But Pashtuns, as a whole, have never been fully integrated into a single empire, state or political system—though they have formed empires of their own. Twentieth-century Afghanistan, before the Soviet invasion, was a Pashtun-dominated state where the elite attempted to advance a cosmopolitan national identity and culture. The alpine highlands of Swat in north-western Pakistan were a modern Pashtun princely state before the region's accession to Pakistan in 1947 and its administrative absorption into Pakistan in 1969. Ironically, the historic pattern of political instability and outside interference in the region has helped to preserve and reinforce the tribal nature of Pashtun society, particularly in the countryside, where most Pashtuns live.

The Great Tribal Maze

Elaborate genealogies have been woven around Qais Abdul Rashid (Abdur Rashid), who is assumed to be the primal ancestor of all Pashtuns.[9] Pashtun genealogies originated in seventeenth-century Mughal courts and were written by court scribe Naematullah. These genealogies eventually found their way to British colonial ethnographies and are sometimes mentioned in modern books on the region. Their only relevance today is that they sketch a very rough chart of the relationship of different tribes to each other, or different lineages within tribes.[10]

Under the prevailing classifications, Pashtuns are divided into four main tribal groupings: the Sarbani, Bhittani (Bitan), Ghurghust and Karlani. The first three were considered to be the sons of Qais, while the fourth, Karlani, was an adopted son. The Sarbanis are divided into two branches: the Sharkbun and the Kharshbun. The most significant tribes of this branch today are the Sherani, the Tareen, the Urmer (an adopted tribe), the Durranis,[11] Khalils, Mohmands, Daudzai, Chamkanis, Yousafzai, Shinwari, Kasi and Tarkalani.

The second branch, the Bhittani, consists of the Bhittanis, Niazis, the Lodhis, Marwats, Babars, Gandapurs and Kundis, and the Ghilzai confederacy. The Ghilzais are one of the largest nomadic populations in the world, known for their seasonal migratory herders called *kuchis*. The Hotak, Sulaiman Khel, Kharoti, Ali Khel, Nasar and Taraki are the main Ghilzai tribes.[12]

The Ghurghust branch includes the Kakar, Mando Khel, Musa Khel and Panri tribes, who inhabit districts of Balochistan Province in Pakistan. The Safi and Gadun (Jadun) tribes are found in Pakistan's Khyber Pakhtunkhwa Province, the Tribal Areas and in eastern Afghanistan.

The fourth major grouping was little known to Mughal scribes. The Karlani preserve aspects of pristine tribal organisation, supplemented by intricate traditional laws. Its members live today on both sides of the Afghan-Pakistan border. The Karlani include some of the most famous Pashtun tribes, among them the Afridis, the Khattaks, Mangal, Zadran, Muqbil, Zazi (Jaji), Bangash, Mehsud (Maseed), Orakzai, Khugiani, Daur, Bannuchi, Wardak, Turi and Wazirs.[13] This great tribal maze makes the Pashtuns the world's largest tribally organised society.

An Evolving Social Tapestry

Pashtuns live in two neighbouring and sometimes hostile states, and under markedly different political arrangements. They engage in a wide variety of economic activities that have exposed them to both the bright and dark sides of globalisation. The social make-up of Pashtun communities varies according to whether they are rural or urban, the degree of their inclusion or separation from surrounding societies, the extent of their embrace of modernity and development, and the intensity of the pressures they have faced during the past three decades of turmoil. The nomad Pashtun herders, or *kuchis*, for example, have been dealt a severe blow from the fighting, as it has disrupted their traditional cyclical movement between the plains and the highlands.

The mother tongue of most Pashtuns is Pashto, an Indo-European language. In rapidly growing urban areas and regions with mixed ethnic populations, bilingualism among Pashtuns is common. In regions that border other ethnic groups, significant acculturation, including the adoption of regional languages and cultures, is common. Many small groups, even if they speak a different first language, identify themselves as Pashtuns based on ethnic heritage. One example is the former royal family of Afghanistan and Kabul's Muhammadzai elite. They adopted the Dari language by the early twentieth century, but have retained a strong degree of Pashtunness. Pashto, nevertheless, remains the foremost identity-marker of Pashtuns. 'Doing Pashto', or observing the behaviour code of the *Pashtunwali*, is closely tied to speaking the language.

Rooted in a tribal organisation of society, *Pashtunwali* embraces values that are shared with the larger surrounding civilisation. But, importantly, it includes a set of fundamental ideals of individual and collective behaviour that are seen as specific to Pashtuns. The Western writer is often guilty of reducing *Pashtunwali* to a handful of behaviours that serve to perpetuate a stereotype. These include: honour (*nang*); hospitality (*melmastya*); and the concept of reciprocity, or *badal* (this is often confused with mere revenge, but is actually something more complex).[14] *Tarboorwali*, or agnatic rivalry, most often among male cousins, and *siyali*, or competition within an extended family, has made Pashtun society intensely competitive at a core level. *Pashtunwali* also includes the values of forgiveness, equality and egalitarianism, and chivalry. The institution of the *jirga*, or council of elders, is summoned to resolve local disputes and to deliberate on how to respond to threats and challenges.

Over the centuries, some Pashtun tribes have developed their own peculiar *narkh*, or sets of customary laws based on the principles of *Pashtunwali*. Most often, these are unwritten codes that compensate for the lack, or inefficiency, of state institutions. In short, the best way to understand *Pashtunwali* is to understand that it incorporates many universal values, but is subject to local tradition.

The overwhelming majority of Pashtuns are Sunni Muslims of the Hanafi school. The Turi tribe in the Kurram Valley of Pakistan, some clans of the neighbouring Bangash and Orakzai tribes, and small communities in Afghanistan are Twelver Shia. Some Sufi orders, too, have considerable followings among Pashtun tribes. Many Pashtun clerics in both Pakistan and Afghanistan consider themselves Deobandis, or the followers of the Deoband Islamic movement, which originated in the second half of the nineteenth century in British India. Over the past three decades, Pashtun regions in Afghanistan and Pakistan have also become home to a range of radical Islamic political ideologies and sects that preach global jihadism. Jihadist ideology is now entrenched in the region. The rise of radical Islamic ideologies has often come at the expense of traditional religious orders and the clerical establishment, and has been backed by sustained funding and strategic guidance from outside.

Pashtuns were not the primary actors in bringing this change to their society. Their land, near the centre of the Eurasian landmass, has for centuries been both a contested zone and a crossroads of cultures and civilisations. The latest transformation began when the Cold War became a hot war with the Soviet invasion of Afghanistan in December 1979. What had begun as an indigenous nationalist resistance to a domestic communist coup was, upon the arrival of Soviet troops, swiftly transformed into a religious struggle, or jihad. Leaders in neighbouring Pakistan encouraged the jihad—partly over fears that the perpetuation of unfettered Afghan nationalism could lead to renewed irredentist Afghan claims to Pakistani territory. Islamabad also feared a surge of ethno-nationalism among Pakistani Pashtuns.

Three decades of war in the Pashtun borderlands has created new classes, alliances and leadership structures. Mass violence gained new legitimacy as rival ideologies and political systems struggled for control of territory and jockeyed for the hearts and minds of ordinary people. For the first time, networks of puritanical Sunni clerics and Islamist militant commanders became more powerful than the traditional secular tribal and political leadership. Years of external patronage and billions of dollars of covert and overt funding for armed factions culminated in the rise of radical political Islam. The Taliban in both Afghanistan and Pakistan are one manifestation of this process. The rise of the Taliban, in turn, cleared the way for Al-Qaeda, whose leadership and core is largely Arab, to come to the Pashtun regions and set up 'safe havens' in which to strategise and regroup. Without its Pashtun sanctuaries, the global jihadist movement would be deprived of a region that has become central to its survival.

More than one million Pashtun lives have been lost to the conflicts that have convulsed their homeland over the past three decades. Pashtuns now constitute one of the world's largest populations of displaced persons. The violence has undermined or destroyed most Pashtun social and political institutions. While massive sums of money have been invested in war in the region (estimates range from $50 to $100 billion in the 1980s alone), there has been relatively little investment in human and economic development.[15] The Soviet Union in the 1980s, and NATO in the first decade of the twenty-first century, have overwhelmingly dealt with the plight of the Pashtun people as a military problem, not an economic and political challenge that requires a multi-dimensional resolution.

As a result of successive wars, Pashtuns today are among the most underdeveloped people in the world. Key human development indicators, such as life expectancy, literacy, employment, food security and rule of law, invariably place Pashtuns near the bottom of global rankings. War, which had virtually wiped out the Afghan state by the early 1990s, has done much to assist in the establishment of a huge criminal economy based on opium cultivation, drug smuggling and the proliferation of small arms. Pashtun farmers understand that they pocket only a tiny fraction of the proceeds from the cultivation of poppies used to produce heroin. But that has not stopped them from making their lands available to drug cartels. The criminal economy has created new classes of businessmen, who have gone on to claim major stakes in the legal economy. The stature of these criminal classes has risen alongside the glass shopping malls of Kabul and Peshawar that cater to their material desires and provide outlets for their ill-gotten wealth. Traditional agriculture has been decimated by insecurity, a lack of global market access and unfamiliarity with modern farming techniques. In its place, the trade of imported goods and transport has become the backbone of the Pashtun economy.[16]

Globalisation has influenced Pashtun society primarily through the millions of Pashtun workers who form a large share of the expatriate underclass in the oil-rich Gulf states. While remittances from the diaspora serve as one of the few sources of wealth for those remaining in the Pashtun homeland, the money is a mixed blessing. It can alter traditional village power relationships, or provide the wherewithal for the use of force to settle feuds. Few of the funds sent home from Dubai and Kuwait are funnelled towards generating economic growth in the homeland, or for contributing to the general good by helping, for example, to construct schools and clinics.

Despite the stereotype of Pashtuns as culturally disposed to violence and disorder, and the very active involvement of some Pashtun leaders and militants in conflict, a vocal—and sometimes politically dominant—peace camp exists. Elections and *jirgas* held in both Pakistan and Afghanistan since 2001 demonstrate that many Pashtuns are weary of conflict and are seeking a peaceful and emancipated future. These are a people who, since the early 1980s, have seen their remote mountain villages, fertile agricultural valleys and bustling cities repeatedly targeted by Soviet MiGs, American 'daisy cutter' bombs and Al-Qaeda suicide bombers.

The Soviet-Afghan war, one of the last major wars of the twentieth century, is today viewed as a conflict that wounded Moscow's authority and hastened the breakup of the Soviet Union in 1991. The United States' declared campaign against Islamist extremists, usually referred to as the War on Terror, has been centred on the Pashtun regions. The outcome of this conflict may well play a key role in determining the shape and contours of the global twenty-first century.

A Shattered Homeland

In 2010, the 150,000 NATO troops that remained deployed in Afghanistan were mainly concentrated in the eastern, south-eastern, and southern Pashtun regions.[17] An equal number of Pakistani troops were stationed in Pakistan's north-western Khyber Pakhtunkhwa Province, the Federally Administered Tribal Areas (FATA) and the northern districts of Balochistan Province—all Pashtun regions along the Durand Line.

Perched high in the Hindu Kush Mountains,[18] Kabul showcases the transformation Afghanistan has undergone since the arrival of the Americans and the infusion of hundreds of millions of dollars of foreign aid. Home to 400,000 people in the late 1970s, this city of wide avenues, vast residential neighbourhoods and narrow ancient bazaars has changed profoundly since the demise of the Taliban regime in late 2001. Traffic jams clog Kabul's roads, frequently cloaking the capital in a blanket of dust and smog. The opening of new boutiques, hotels, apartment buildings and restaurants is a regular occurrence. Government offices, foreign embassies and international organisations, meanwhile, barricade themselves behind high blast walls, cordoned-off streets and checkpoints.[19]

Kabul has been a stage for Afghan political drama for more than two centuries. Over the past forty years, it has witnessed several coups—some bloodless affairs within the ruling elite, others involving air strikes and gun battles. The Afghan government that was installed after the fall of the Taliban has established reminders of its existence across Kabul. The executive, the legislature and the judiciary are visibly present in the presidential palace, ministries, parliament and the Supreme Court. But beyond their reconstructed buildings, these organs of government have so far failed to provide basic services to ordinary Afghans or to assure them they are working for a better future.

Kabul is connected to Mashriqi, Afghanistan's eastern zone, through the narrow Tang-e Gharu gorge. The eastern region—called Loy Nangarhar or Greater Nangarhar—spans the provinces of Nangarhar, Kunar, Laghman and Nuristan and is home to Ghilzai and Karlani Pashtuns.[20] Jalalabad, the centre of Nangarhar Province, is the regional capital. The low-lying Jalalabad Valley has informally served as the winter capital of Afghanistan since the mid-nineteenth century loss of Peshawar, first to the Sikhs and then to the British. Located at the gateway of the Khyber Pass, Jalalabad is an important connecting point between South Asia and Central Asia. The region's proximity to Peshawar, the de-facto headquarters of the anti-Soviet mujahedeen in the 1980s, transformed it into a front line. The cover provided by the region's forests were a great aid to the guerillas who fought Moscow's troops. A relatively high literacy level led to the region having considerable representation in the Afghan bureaucracy before the Soviet invasion of 1979.

Tora Bora, part of the Safed Koh (Dari for Spin Ghar, or White Mountain) south of Jalalabad, came under intense US bombing in late

2001 after it was suspected of being the hiding place of Al-Qaeda leader Osama bin Laden.[21] Since 2001, Islamist insurgency and economic development have surged in parallel in Greater Nangarhar. The insurgency is led by Hizb-e Islami[22] and various Salafi groups, and the violence there is considerably less than that seen in Pashtun regions in the south-east and south.

The Safed Koh separates Loy Nangarhar from Loya Paktia, the Greater Paktia region to the south. Many recent writings have described the region as being composed of the south-eastern mountainous provinces of Khost, Paktia and Paktika.[23] But tribal ties suggest Greater Paktia should also rightfully extend into the provinces of Logar, Ghazni and Wardak. The region, it could be argued, is home to Afghanistan's most robust tribal social formation, encompassing the Zadran, Mangal, Jaji, Tani, Wazir and Muqbil tribes. The region is also home to Ghilzai tribes such as the Sulaiman Khel and the related Ahmadzai tribe. In the absence of a regular army, the tribes of Loya Paktia served as the surrogate army for Afghanistan until the second part of the twentieth century, when the Afghan government established the country's first professional conscripted army.

In 1929, the tribes of Loya Paktia were instrumental in restoring the Durrani throne to Mohammad Nadir Shah, a distant cousin of deposed King Amanullah Khan. A reformist, Khan had been ousted in a revolt led by the Tajik guerrilla leader Habibullah Kalakani, who was supported by conservative clergy. Nadir Shah, commonly called Nadir Khan, responded by organising a tribal *lashkar* composed of Loya Paktia and Waziristan tribes from both sides of the Durand Line. The new alliance was successful in overthrowing Kalakani and returning Nadir Shah to leadership.[24] He demonstrated his appreciation by granting the tribes maximum autonomy, including exempting them from taxation and conscription, under the assumption they would again mobilise *lashkars* in the future if necessary. In the twentieth century, the tribes of Loya Paktia, including those in the Tribal Areas of Pakistan, contributed many men to the Afghan military's officer corps. Men from the region also predominated among the Soviet-trained military officers who went on to join or sympathise with Afghan communist groups.

Jalaluddin Haqqani, a Zadran cleric, became a favourite of the Pakistani military and wealthy private Arab donors due to his military successes against the Red Army. His reputation was built on feats including resistance to Operation Magistral, the 1987 offensive aimed at clearing the road between the Greater Paktia towns of Gardez and Khost. The operation is considered the largest Soviet ground offensive of the nine-year war. Khost was the first city to fall to the mujahedeen in 1991 under the leadership of Haqqani. He joined the Taliban in 1995 and was instrumental in helping the militants drive to Kabul in September 1996.

Takur Ghar and the surrounding ridges of the Zurmat district of Paktia were the scenes of the US military's Operation Anaconda in the spring of 2002. In intense battles that lasted days, Washington and its allies suffered some of their first casualties while engaging Taliban and Al-Qaeda forces on the ground. The militant forces involved in the battle were allies of Haqqani.[25]

From Kandahar to Swat

While the majority of Afghanistan's Pashtuns live in south-eastern and eastern Afghanistan, it is southern Afghanistan where they are most significant politically. Loy Kandahar, or Greater Kandahar, was the centre of the Afghan empires and states that grew out of the Pashtun revolt against Iranian Safavid rule in the early eighteenth century. The region became the capital and political seat of Durrani power under Ahmad Shah in 1747. He changed his tribe's name from Abdali to Durrani, and it went on to rule Afghanistan until 1978, first as an empire and then as one of the first independent Muslim countries in the twentieth century.

The region was marginalised by communist cadres and mujahedeen leaders during the Soviet war. But Kandahar regained its political significance with the rise of the Taliban in the 1990s, when it served as the de-facto Taliban capital. Greater Kandahar is still central to the political clout of the Durrani tribes. Pre-war Kandahar City was a Pashtun melting pot, mixing Ghilzai tribes to the east and Durranis in the west. It was an environment where tribal affiliations were replaced by an urban Kandahari identity. Greater Kandahar includes the provinces of Kandahar, Helmand, Uruzgan, Zabul, Farah and Nimroz.[26] The Taliban first emerged in Loy Kandahar, and their key leaders and many foot soldiers have come from this region.

The extensive agriculture of Greater Kandahar is sustained by the Helmand and Arghandab rivers, which deliver snowy waters from the southern slopes of the Hindu Kush. The region yields a significant wheat harvest, but is most famous for its grapes and pomegranates. Over the past two decades, however, poppy cultivation for heroin production has replaced or supplemented much traditional agriculture. Located between Kabul and the western city of Herat, with access to the Pakistani port city of Karachi via the border town of Chaman, Kandahar is also a business hub. In recent years, an Indian-funded road has linked Kandahar to the south-eastern Iranian port of Chabahar. The region has seen significant fighting in recent years, with US-led forces attempting to stymie Taliban influence with a counterinsurgency strategy.

Over the past two decades, politics in Greater Kandahar have been skewed by the largely undocumented trade and transport business, including trafficking in contraband. In the winter of 1998, I went to Wesh, an informal market town between the border towns of Spin Boldak on the Afghan side and Chaman on the Pakistani side. There, in the middle of the desert, one could buy late-model Toyota sport utility vehicles, second-hand Taiwanese computers, cheap crockery made in Iran and, if one had the money and spoke to the right person, perhaps even Chinese-made weapons.[27] The market is emblematic of the transitory and undocumented nature of the borderland economy. It also sheds a light on the enterprising spirit of Pashtuns.

The short drive from Spin Boldak to Chaman crosses an international border, but the marker is only a bureaucratic transition within a seamless society. Many of the Pashtuns in the region, mainly from the Achakzai and Noorzai tribes, have maintained kinship ties, even while living on opposite sides of the Durand Line. People with businesses in Chaman often reside in Spin Boldak, and vice versa. A similar phenomenon is at work in other Pashtun regions of Pakistan's Balochistan Province. There, the soft southern dialect of Pashto is the same as that spoken in southern Afghanistan, thanks to the presence of the Ghilzai and Durrani tribes that span the border.[28]

Contacts between the two regions have intensified over the past forty years, in part because thousands of Baloch rebels went into exile in southern Afghanistan in the 1970s. But it was the mainly Pashtun migration from Afghanistan in the aftermath of the Soviet invasion that cemented the modern relationship. In a few cases, the entire population of an Afghan southern district resettled in Balochistan, bringing with them expertise that contributed greatly to horticultural development in the semi-arid region. Just as in southern Afghanistan, *karez*, or traditional underground water channels, have given way in Balochistan to mechanical water pumps that continually deplete the underground water tables.

Chaman is connected to Balochistan's capital Quetta, to the south, through the Khojak Pass. The pass served as a supply line for anti-communist mujahedeen guerillas in the 1980s, and today it is a key supply route for both NATO and the Afghan Taliban. Ringed by high, dry mountains, Quetta resembles a miniature Kabul. With Pashtuns forming a majority, it is perhaps Pakistan's most ethnically diverse city, on a par with the megalopolis of Karachi to the south. Quetta is also an example of the transformation that Pakistan's western Pashtun border region has undergone since the onset of global conflict in the region. Once home to a British sanatorium and a garrison town of a few thousand residents, Quetta now claims half a million residents. Its neighbourhoods are haphazardly constructed, but nevertheless form an invisible ethnic boundary between the Baloch and the Pashtun, with the former living in territories stretching to the Arabian Sea in the south, and the latter extending almost to the Pamirs in the north.

The recent history of Balochistan, Pakistan's biggest but least populated province, has been dominated by successive ethnic Baloch insurrections against the Pakistani military's stranglehold on the resource-rich region. Most Pakistani soldiers and officers are ethnic Punjabis, and it is common to hear Baloch refer to Punjabi domination.[29] The northern Pashtun regions of Balochistan have generally been indifferent to the Baloch rebellions. The Pashtun regions are a key constituency for Jamiat Ulema-e Islam (JUI), a majority Pashtun Islamist political party that nominally follows the conservative Deobandi Islamic madrasa in India.[30]

Several key Taliban leaders, as well as many foot soldiers, have emerged from Balochistan's JUI madrasas. After being ousted by US-led forces in late 2001, major remnants of the Taliban regime retreated to Balochistan and reorganised under the Quetta Shura, or leadership council. The Quetta Shura, led by Mullah Mohammad Omar, dominates the leadership of the Afghan Taliban.

The Pashtun districts of northern Balochistan take up nearly 40,000 square kilometres. The districts are surrounded by the Toba Kakar range and the Sulaiman mountains, which gradually turn hilly before disappearing into the Indus plains. These features make the region virtually indistinguishable from the Afghan provinces of Kandahar and Zabul.

Compared to neighbouring Khyber Pakhtunkhwa Province and the FATA, northern Balochistan has generally been spared the carnage of the Islamic militant wars.

There is little in the desolate landscape of Balochistan's Zhob district[31] that would obviously differentiate it from neighbouring South Waziristan in the FATA. But there is not a single asphalt road linking the regions—a legacy of the nineteenth-century British 'frontier of separation' policy.[32] This policy attached the regions to different administrative regimes within British India and later on in Pakistan. To this day, they continue as formally disconnected entities, subject to separate ruling structures.[33]

The FATA and Khyber Pakhtunkhwa, formerly called the North West Frontier Province, have a combined area of 100,000 kilometres—larger than Hungary or Portugal, and slightly smaller than the US state of Colorado. The regions run along the Indus River from north to south, and Pashtun communities spill over into Attock and Mianwali in Punjab. Most Pashtun communities—from the northern mountainous Indus Kohistan region to the plains of Dera Ismail Khan in the south—live west of the Indus. The regions close to the river are often fertile, but turn into arid hills and desolate plains. Beyond the hills lie the Sulaiman, Himalaya and Hindu Kush mountains. Khyber Pakhtunkhwa features stunning contrasts of scenery. If Swat in the north can be compared to alpine Switzerland, then parts of Karak, Lakki Marwat and Dera Ismail Khan in the south are the Gobi Desert.

The Peshawar plain is economically significant. Irrigated by the waters of the Swat and Kabul rivers, it is the breadbasket of the region and produces a bumper tobacco crop. The valley is home to the provincial capital Peshawar and towns such as Nowshera, Swabi, Mardan and Charsadda. In terms of per capita income and industrialisation, it is perhaps the richest of all Pashtun regions. The valley is ringed by mountains on three sides, hemmed in by the Indus River to the east, and connected through the Khyber, Darra Adam Khel and Malakand passes to other parts of the province.

Only two of Khyber Pakhtunkhwa's twenty-four districts, Dir and Chitral, border Afghanistan. The rest border FATA.[34] The region is home to some of the most famous passes connecting Central Asia with South Asia: the Gomal and Tochi passes in Waziristan in the south, Pewar in Kurram, Nawagai in Bajaur and Gandhab in Mohmand. The

Khyber Pass is famous, of course, used throughout history as a supply line or invasion route. FATA shares a 600-kilometre border with Afghanistan. As in northern Balochistan, most of the tribes of FATA span the Durand Line. The larger tribes of FATA, from south to north, include the Waziris, Mehsuds, Daurs, Jajis, Turis, Bangash, Orakzais, Afridi, Shinwaris, Safi and Mohmands.

FATA is an awkward administrative, political and economic entity, unique among Pashtun regions.[35] But, like Khyber Pakhtunkhwa, it possesses an array of frequently stunning natural features. The bleak foothills on the edge of the plains turn gradually into alpine valleys and rolling oak forests. The forests and freshwater streams of central Waziristan, the willow trees of Parachinar and the peaks of the Tirah Valley hold great tourism potential.

In late 2001, Al-Qaeda's top leaders sought refuge in Waziristan. Since early 2004, the region has seen little but misery and destruction. Tens of thousands of Pashtuns have died in military operations, extremist suicide bombings and US unmanned drone strikes. Millions of people have been displaced. Assassinations of clerics and political and tribal leaders have deprived communities of the wisdom and guidance that could help them navigate the uncertainty. While many senior Al-Qaeda figures have been killed or captured, ordinary civilians have borne the brunt of the violence. A decade into the twenty-first century, the region is still home to Al-Qaeda and affiliated extremist networks that threaten regional and global security.

2

FROM PEACEFUL BORDERLANDS TO INCUBATOR OF EXTREMISM

Pashtun historiography has many blank chapters—a result of the foreign invasions and internal fragmentation that have for centuries stymied the development and social evolution of this people. Adversaries of the Pashtuns have proven skilled at providing a skewed or outright biased reading of events that continues to colour the understanding of Pashtuns. Historical narratives of twentieth-century Afghanistan, each emphasising a perception of Pashtun antiquity and uniqueness, have all employed some degree of mythmaking.

The development of the Pashtun identity, inspired heavily by Islam, has defined or helped shape political movements, empires and states over the course of five centuries. A greater understanding of the prominent figures and events in the history of the Pashtuns is key to comprehending the contemporary problems in Afghanistan and Pakistan—including how the Pashtun regions have been transformed into incubators of extremist movements mobilised in the name of Islam.

The Enlightened Teacher

The population of most Pashtun regions had largely become Muslim by 1,000 A.D. The first predominantly Pashtun patriotic movement, woven around a moderate Sufic vision of the faith, came much later, in the sixteenth century. It arrived via the Roshnya, or 'enlightened' movement, pioneered by Pir Roshan, 'the enlightened saint'. Pir Roshan—whose real name was Bayazid Khan or Bayazid Ansari—was born in Jalandhar, in present-day northern India. But he was raised in Waziristan, in present-day Pakistan, after his family returned to its ancestral lands early in his childhood. He was born into an age where he would have been able to witness the decline of Pashtun power on the subcontinent.

The Pashtun Lodi dynasty (1451–1526) met its demise at the hands of invading Mughals. Zahiruddin Babur (1483–1530), founder of the Mughal dynasty, was a Chagatai from the Fergana Valley, which is located in today's Uzbekistan. He was a descendent of Tamerlane and Genghis Khan. Repeated failures to capture Samarkand and other regions in Central Asia pushed him to move east and south. He occupied Kabul in 1504 and Kandahar in 1522, using the conquests as stepping stones to move into India. He exploited internal squabbling among the Lodis and used an invitation from Daulat Khan, the Lodi governor of Punjab, to invade India. He defeated the last Lodi ruler, Ibrahim Khan, in a major battle outside Panipat, near Delhi, in April 1526.[1]

The Pashtuns challenged Mughal rule. Sher Shah Suri, an able general and administrator, defeated Babur's son and successor Nasirruddin Muhammad Humayun. The Mughal emperor subsequently sought refuge in Iran in 1540. Sher Shah died in the mid-1540s. The death of his son and successor, Islam Shah Suri, in 1554 effectively ended this Pashtun dynasty. With considerable Iranian help, Humayun recaptured the throne in 1555, amid feuding among the successors of the last Suri king. Hymayun's son and successor, Jalaluddin Muhammad Akbar, would go on to lead one of the most stable periods of Mughal rule.

The suffering that resistance to the Mughal Empire brought upon the Pashtuns had a lasting influence on Pir Roshan, and ultimately defined his writings and political struggle. It was a time when, it has been argued, the word 'Mughal' represented 'calamity' or 'enemy' in the Pashto language. Such metaphors first emerged in folklore, and later gained currency in spoken language and literary traditions.[2] Amid the Pashtun liberation struggle, Mughal ruler Akbar founded a new religion: Din-e Ilahi, or 'heavenly faith,' which combined elements of Islam, Hinduism, Catholicism, Jainism and Zoroastrianism. At its core, Din-e Ilahi was a personality cult. Pir Roshan's movement launched an open rebellion, which eventually grew into a Pashtun national uprising. Pir Roshan travelled from Waziristan to other regions to inspire and instruct the masses.

In a radical departure from the established practices of religious leaders of his age, Pir Roshan developed a body of work that was republican in spirit, but that also adhered to moderate Sufi interpretations of Islamic *sharia* law. Based on extensive research and readings of Pir Roshan's original writings, Saifur Rehman Masud has concluded that he sought to ultimately unite all Pashtuns under a single national ideology combining religion and politics.[3]

Pir Roshan wanted all Pashtuns to follow a dignified way of independent existence that he called *tariqat*, or path of Sufi thought. A crucial element of this involved educating the Pashtuns about their perpetual body-politic—*haqiqat*, or reality, in Sufi parlance. During his decades of influence, Pir Roshan attempted to heal tribal divisions. He brought together Pashtun tribes from Kandahar in the south to Nangarhar in the north under the banner of *wahdat*, *qurbat* and *waslat*—or oneness, unity and nearness. His vision was to see the Pashtuns live peacefully (*sakunat*) and independently in their homeland.[4]

Pir Roshan is considered the first writer of prose in Pashto. His first work, *Khair-ul-Bayan*, a compilation of religious writings, remains his most influential. It emphasised spirituality and moderation, while advocating adherence to an Islam rooted in Pashtun tradition and identity. He later wrote *Halnama*, an autobiographical work. Two other volumes, *Maqsood-ul-Momineen* and *Sirat-ul-Tauheed*, flesh out his religious and political ideas.

Mir Wali Khan Mahsud, an expert on Pir Roshan's writings, offered this conclusion:

> In Bayazid's (Pir Roshan's) opinion, *shaykh kamil* (a perfect guide) is one who guides people to *tauheed*,[5] enjoining them to seek Allah. *Saykh naqis* (the imperfect guide), according to him, is the one who misleads people and bids them to seek other than Allah. Man's superiority to other creatures is because of his knowledge and recognition of the Unity of Allah.... The object and action of *shari'at*, *tariqat*, *haqiqat*, *qurbat*, *wasalat*, *wahdat*, *sakunat* and the object of all obedience, worship, asceticism and self-mortification, is '*Ilm al-Tauheed*' (knowledge of the Unity of Allah). Bayazid saw that the *khalifa* (vicegerent) was the embodiment of the call of Allah; also an embodiment of His revelation, in the form of a missionary and guide who invite people to the abode of peace.[6]

The Roshnya movement would spearhead Pashtun resistance against the Mughals for nearly a century. The family's involvement was not just philosophical and theoretical; Pir Roshan's sons and grandsons led troops against the Mughals on the battlefield. Roshnya functioned like a modern political organisation, seeking to use knowledge and ideology to organise resistance. The movement also gave the Pashto language its first script and introduced thirteen new alphabets. This script, still in use with modifications, was adopted from Arabic. The movement produced several notable Pashto language poets and writers.

The Rigid Mullah

Roshnya had its detractors; chief among them the sixteenth and seventeenth century cleric Akhund Derweza. He, too, employed Pashto prose—but to oppose Roshnya and to re-label Pir Roshan *pir tareek*, or the 'dark teacher'. By some accounts, Derweza was a propagandist bankrolled by the Mughal court. Derweza wrote *Makhzan al-Islam*, which is ranked among the pioneering works of Pashto prose dealing with Islamic themes. *Makhzan al-Islam*, which has remained popular among Pashtun clerics for centuries, is a compilation of various debates and discussions on religion, spirituality, *hadith* (narrations from the Prophet Muhammad's words and deeds) and Islamic jurisprudence (*fiqh*).

The movement spawned by Derweza was, like Roshnya, rooted in the religious traditions of the time. It stressed the importance of the *pir* or *murshad* (spiritual guide or teacher). Like Pir Roshan's *Khair-ul-Bayan*, Derweza's works helped shape future Islamic philosophies and movements that continue to resonate in contemporary Pashtun society. For centuries, Derweza's followers have adhered to Hanfai Islam—the largest and oldest school of jurisprudence in Sunni Islam. Derweza's followers were staunch supporters of the Mughal court—putting them starkly at odds with Roshnya. Whereas *Khair-ul-Bayan* emphasises spiritualism and moderation, *Makhzan al-Islam* preaches strict obeisance to *sharia* law. Derweza condemned Pir Roshan as a heretic and called for his books to be burned.

The two writers helped forge a division that has only grown stronger over the centuries. Pir Roshan advocated a patriotic, moderate Sufism inclined towards rationalism. Derweza promulgated the primacy of a rigid Sunni mullah. The split continues to reveal itself through the Sunni clerical establishment's opposition to reforms, development and modernity in Pashtun society. Its influence can be felt in how religious movements and personalities continue to define themselves—up to and including those involved in the wars of the 1980s and in the conflicts in Afghanistan and Pakistan of the early twenty-first century.

The Warrior Poet

Khushal Khan Khattak, who would go on to be regarded as a great Pashtun luminary, attempted to move away from the infighting of his intellectual predecessors. Khushal (1613–1691) was born into a wealthy Pashtun family that was closely tied to the court of Mughal Emperor Shah Jahan. Khushal first served the Mughals as a tribal leader, a position he inherited from his father. But he soon had a falling out with Mughal Emperor Aurangzeb, who imprisoned him for seven years. The experience altered his worldview and impacted his poetry. He spent the rest of his life fighting the Mughals and trying to inspire unity among Pashtuns. At a time when Western Europeans were struggling to define nationalism and the nation-state, Khushal was busy outlining the contours of Pashtun patriotism. Many of his verses continue to be used as slogans by modernist and traditionalist Pashtun nationalists in both Afghanistan and Pakistan.

Da Afghan pa nang me wathrala toora
Nangyalay da zamaney Khushal Khattak yam

(I bound on the sword for the pride of the Afghan name,
I am Khushal Khattak, the proud man of this day).[7]

Khushal's voluminous, mostly poetic, works marked a departure from Roshnya and its critics. Khushal dealt with the pragmatic realities of the life in his times. He urged unity among tribally fragmented Pashtuns, and championed what in modern times would be considered a national liberation struggle against the Mughals. Khushal's secular concepts endear him to modern scholars, who consider him a visionary—a warrior-poet who served the Pashtuns with pen and sword. His poem 'Dey Pashtun Na Gilla', or 'Displeasure With the Pashtuns', is exemplary.

The whole of the other Afghans from Kandahar unto Attak,
In honour's cause, both secretly and openly, are one.

For this state of things, no other termination can be seen,
Than that the Mughals be annihilated, or the Afghans undone.

There is no deliverance in anything, save the sword:
Afghans who nourish any other idea than this are lost, indeed.

The Afghans are far superior to the Mughals at the sword,
Were but the Afghans, in intellect, a little discreet.

If the different tribes would but support each other,
Kings would have to bow down in prostration before them.[8]

Afghan Empire

Imperial decline in the early eighteenth century provided the Pashtuns the opening to form a homeland. But the seeds of this opportunity were planted much earlier. The death in 1707 of the puritanical Mughal Emperor Aurangzeb Alamgir offered an early hint of the possibilities for political union. After Aurangzeb's death, the once-mighty Mughal dynasty fragmented and was unable to counter rising Hindu Maratha power in southern India. By the beginning of the eighteenth century, the influence of the three Muslim empires that had divided South and Central Asia—the Mughals, the Iranian Shia Safavid and the Uzbek Astrakhanid (or Janid)—was on the wane. The Mughals and the Safavids struggled for control over Pashtun regions, Kandahar in particular.

In 1709, Mir Wais, a leader of the Hotak tribe of the Ghilzai Pashtuns, led a rebellion against Giorgi XI. The rebellion against the Georgian mercenary and Safavid governor of Kandahar faltered, however, and Giorgi exiled Mir Wais to the Safavid court in Isfahan. The Ghilzai chief used his exile to visit Mecca to perform the *hajj* Islamic pilgrimage. While there, Mir Wais secured a *fatwa*, or religious edict, that legitimised a revolt against the apostate Safavid governor. Mir Wais and his successors, Shah Mahmud and Shah Ashraf, succeeded in conquering most of Iran. But the empire lasted only until 1729. That year, Nadir Shah Afshar, a Turkmen general and tribal leader, drove the Ghilzais out of Iran and subsequently established his own empire in 1739.

But it was another short-lived empire. Returning with booty from a trip to Mughal India in 1747, Nadir Shah Afshar was assassinated near Mashhad. An ensuing nine-day Pashtun tribal *jirga* in Kandahar chose a young charismatic commander in the imperial army, Ahmad Shah Abdali, to be ruler of the Afghans. He changed the name of his tribal confederation from Abdali to Durrani, the traditional rivals of the Ghilzais. At the invitation of the Indian Muslim cleric Shah Waliullah, the Durranis crushed the Marhatta Hindus, a rising power, in 1761.[9]

Ahmad Shah ruled until 1773—a quarter-century that saw the expansion of the Afghan Durrani Empire. His son, Taimur Shah, and grandsons Shah Zaman, Shah Shuja and Shah Mahmud, continued the Saddozai dynasty until 1826. But the reigns of the latter three were undermined by intrigues and infighting. Timur Shah moved the capital away from the Pashtun heartland of Kandahar to the ethnically mixed zone of Kabul in 1776. He also concluded a treaty with the Uzbek Khanante of Bokhara, which for the first time recognised Afghan authority south of the Oxus river. The Europeans first came in contact with the Pashtuns during this period. Mountsturat Elphinstone, the first envoy of the British East India Company, visited Shah Shuja's court in Peshawar in 1805.[10]

The Durrani Empire, until 1793, enjoyed cohesion. At its peak, the realm of the Durranis extended from Central Asia to Sirhind near Delhi, and from Kashmir to the Arabian Sea. It was the second-largest Muslim empire of the eighteenth century, behind the Ottomans. But internal disunity and tribal rivalries led to collapse. The Durrani Empire had broken up by 1818, when Afghanistan fragmented into four fiefdoms. Dost Mohammad Khan, governor of Kabul, was elected *amir* in 1834. With his accession to the throne, power moved from the Saddozai clan to the Barakzai clan within the Durrani tribal confederacy.

Internecine conflict among the Durranis aided the rise of a brief but powerful Sikh empire in Punjab, which had become a prized colony because of its fertile plains. The first significant Sikh victory came in the Battle of Attock in 1813. In the following years, the Afghans lost Multan, Kashmir, Dera Ghazi Khan and Dera Ismail Khan to the Sikh ruler Mahraja Ranjit Singh. But the loss of Peshawar in 1833 proved the most devastating blow. The Durranis never recovered the valley, which had served as their winter capital. The Durrani failure to attempt to reclaim Peshawar may have been part of a strategy by Dost Mohammad Khan to not provoke the British. The Sikhs would suffer a decisive defeat in the 1837 Battle of Jamrud.[11]

Frontier Jihads

Popular militant resistance movements in the wake of the rise of the Sikhs, and throughout the century of British rule, contributed much to shaping the Pashtun border region. At times, resistance was a local affair involving a single clan or tribe. On other occasions, tribes launched wider movements, sometimes coordinating with the broader Afghan and Indian struggles against European colonialism. Charismatic tribal leaders or clerics, many of them non-Pashtuns, were sometimes involved in leading such rebellions. Successes were rare, however, as the Sikhs and British were capable of deploying overwhelming military force to suppress revolts. Bribes, diplomacy and economic development initiatives were also used as incentives to sustain imperial influence.

The first ideologically driven militant movement in the Pashtun regions was *Tariqa-yi Muhammadiyya*, better known as the *wahhabi* movement, led by Sayyid Ahmed, who hailed from Rai Bareilly in north-eastern India. Its followers were called 'Hindustani fanatics' or Indian mujahedeen, depending on whether Indian Muslims or the British were writing about them. Inspired by the teachings of Shah Waliullah, the movement was militant in outlook and ostensibly aimed at fighting the rise of the Sikhs in the Peshawar Valley and its environs.

The movement's downfall came when followers attempted to forcefully impose their vision on the Pashtuns, whose social structure and hierarchy resented such intrusions from outside. The movement called for strict adherence to the teachings of the Quran and *hadith*. It also advocated strict observance of Islamic prayers, or *salath*, and *Ramadan*, or fasting.[12] The movement's attempt to transfer leadership from tribal leaders (khans) to clerics (mullahs) backfired.[13] A Pashtun revolt forced the Indian zealots to abandon the Peshawar Valley.

In 1831, Sayyid Ahmed and key followers were killed by the Sikhs in a decisive battle in Balakot, a mountainous valley 200 kilometres north of Peshawar in the alpine Hazara region. During the 1857 Indian soldier mutiny, also known as the Indian War of Independence, the Afghans under Dost Muhammad remained neutral. But in a tactic that would be used later to deal with Pashtun rebellions, Britain raised 35,000 soldiers from among Pashtun tribes. These troops proved instrumental in putting down the Indian rebellion, which had been mainly instigated by Muslims and Hindus.

A significant religious personality emerged during this period among the Yousafzais of Swat. Akhund Abdul Ghaffur, also known as Saidu Baba, was an ally of the Indian *wahhabis* who gradually built his own power base in Swat and the adjacent Buner Valley. He led local resistance to the British attempt to encroach into Swat in 1863. In one of the bloodiest episodes of the conflict, some 900 British troops were killed in a clash at the Ambela Pass. Akhund, a shrewd manipulator of the local political scene, was reluctant to implement literalist interpretations of Islamic dictates. He succeeded in building a political base in Swat that eventually resulted in his grandson forming a state. This entity was recognised by the British in 1926 as Swat State, and was merged into Pakistan nearly a half century later.

Perhaps the most significant of the Pashtun revolts came in 1897, when border tribes from Swat in the north to Waziristan in the south rose in an uncoordinated uprising, known as the 'great tribal revolt' by the British historians. It was the first major Pashtun rebellion in which Indian *wahhabis* had no major role. Sadullah of Malakand—remembered as the 'Mad Mullah'[14] by British historians—and Mullah Najmuddin (Hadda Mullah)[15] were among its main leaders. The British crushed the uprising by mobilising 70,000 troops. The British also used indirect counterinsurgency methods, such as dividing the rebellious population by providing aid to rival tribal militias. While historians have credited holy men with inciting the rebellion, the demarcation of the Durand Line in 1893 is now seen as the immediate cause.

Waziristan would remain a military headache for the British until their departure in 1947. Wazir and Mehsud, the major tribes of Waziristan, often fought under the leadership of Mohiudin Mullah Pawinda and Haji Mirzali Khan, or the Faqir of Ipi. The 1919 Battle of Ahnai Tangi in South Waziristan was among the most ferocious, leading to the decimation of an entire British brigade and 2,000 dead or wounded. The dead included forty-three British officers. Casualties among the Mehsud were almost twice as many, but the effort resulted in victory. During the Second World War, the British maintained 50,000 soldiers and camp followers in Waziristan—more troops than on the rest of the subcontinent.[16] British casualties ran into the thousands during the 1930s and 1940s, as Waziristan remained the scene of some of the bloodiest fighting the British ever engaged in South Asia.

The Great Game

Centuries of resistance, rivalries and great power empire building led to the political and legal structures that continue to the present day in Pashtun regions.[17] In the nineteenth century, the weakness of the Durrani Empire and the ambitions of European imperialism set the stage for the Great Game. The Pashtun territories of today's Afghanistan and Pakistan were the Game's central arena. The British East India Company conquered Delhi in 1804, and British forces invaded Afghanistan in 1839. But the first Anglo-Afghan war, which lasted until 1842, proved a disaster. The British invading force, called the Army of the Indus, was defeated by an uprising in Kabul. The entire British force was annihilated as it retreated east towards Jalalabad.[18]

By the late 1820s, the British had become concerned about tsarist expansion. Russian advances in Central Asia reached Afghanistan's borders by 1876. For the first time in history, the tsar controlled all territories north of the Amu Darya, the river that constitutes Afghanistan's northern border. Afghan Amir Sher Ali's efforts to establish friendly relations with his powerful northern neighbour led the British to launch the second Anglo-Afghan war in 1878. The British deposed Sher Ali and forced him to leave Kabul. The war marked the peak of the Great Game.

After occupying Kabul, the British forced Sher Ali's son Amir Yaqub Khan to sign the Treaty of Gandamak in 1879. The *amir* agreed to let the British open an embassy, and gave up control of several frontier districts, including most of today's FATA in Pakistan and parts of Balochistan.[19] The treaty guaranteed British support to Afghanistan against external aggression. The Raj also provided an annual subsidy of money and arms. However, most Afghan governments since then have repudiated the treaty because it was signed under duress.[20] In a further show of imperial control, Russia and Britain demarcated the country's northern and western borders with Central Asia, Iran and China between 1870 and 1896.[21]

Following the Second Anglo-Afghan War, British administrators created new mechanisms to control the territories and peoples under their domination. The border regime they designed included separate legal statuses and governance mechanisms for Afghanistan, the Pashtun borderlands, and Pashtun and Baloch regions adjacent to the territories under the administration of British India. In Afghanistan, the British needed an autocrat. They invited Abdul Rahman Khan, a nephew of Amir Sher Ali Khan living in exile in Central Asia, to assume the throne in 1880. During his twenty-year reign, the 'Iron Amir' brutally suppressed dissent. He decreed the country's administrative institutions and laid the foundation of modern Afghanistan. Crucially, he agreed to the demarcation of the Durand Line. In his defence, many historians have pointed out that the *amir* contended that excluding the Pashtun tribal territories from Afghanistan was a mistake.

After the 1893 Durand Line demarcation, the British placed five Pashtun tribal regions under the direct control of the central government in Delhi. A political officer was appointed for Khyber in 1878. Kurram became an agency (the official parlance for a tribal district) in 1892, while the Malakand and Waziristan agencies were created in 1895–96. In 1901, Lord Curzon, the British viceroy of India, created the North West Frontier Province (NWFP). Mohmand, Bajauar and Orakzai were carved out of other tribal districts after the creation of Pakistan in 1947.[22] The British devised an oppressive legal regime called the Frontier Crimes Regulations (FCR) to administer these regions. The FCR is still the law of the land in FATA.

The British rout in the First Anglo-Afghan War put an end to the 'forward policy', which envisioned British India separated from Russia along the Amu Darya. Instead, Delhi settled for a 'closed border policy', which established a frontier buffer zone. The border region was eventually shaped into what British officials called a 'threefold frontier'. Directly administered territories constituted the first zone of this frontier.[23] The second zone was the Pashtun tribal territories between Afghanistan and the settled districts of NWFP. This region was placed under indirect rule. Nepal and Afghanistan, both British protectorates, comprised the outer edge. The three rings of the arrangement ensured that the borderlands remained a 'frontier of separation', as opposed to a 'frontier of contact'. British administrators defined the frontier as a 'wide tract of border country, hinterland or a buffer state'.[24]

The 1907 convention between Imperial Britain and Tsarist Russia formally ended the Great Game. The deal divided Persia into respective zones of influence, and formally protected Afghanistan's western borders from Russian penetration. The two sides agreed to recognise Chinese control over Tibet. St Petersburg conceded Afghanistan to the British sphere of influence, but London was supposed to stay out of Afghan internal affairs and refrain from occupying or annexing any part of the country. The Afghan suzerain, Amir Habibullah, declared the convention illegal because Kabul was not party to the agreement. The great powers paid little attention to his protests.

With Afghanistan lacking a modern army, the rulers of Kabul often mobilised Pashtun tribes to fight their wars. In 1919, the nationalist and modernist King Amanullah Khan declared a jihad to end British control over Afghanistan's foreign affairs. The month-long war that followed was fought by Pashtun tribal *lashkars* composed of volunteers from both sides of the Durand Line. This was the Third Anglo-Afghan War, which ultimately led to Kabul obtaining full sovereignty. The British Empire, exhausted after the First World War, formally recognised Afghan independence in the 1919 Treaty of Rawalpindi.

In 1929, King Amanullah was ousted from the throne in a revolt led by Tajik guerrilla leader Habibullah Kalakani, who was supported by conservative clergy and an alliance of influential Pashtuns. Under the leadership of Nadir Khan, the king's distant cousin, a *lashkar* of Pashtun volunteers—again, from both sides of the Durand Line—eventually put an end to the rule of Habibullah II, the proclaimed title of Habibullah Kalakani. Nadir Khan consolidated his rule by slowing down the pace of reform and modernisation. In return for their military services, he promoted self-rule for the tribes of south-eastern Afghanistan. He also encouraged institutional ties with Pashtuns in British India by granting some of their leaders lands close to Kabul. He exempted the Pashtuns of Loya Paktia from taxation and conscription. Throughout the twentieth century, Afghanistan's rulers used honorary and material rewards, including recruitment into the officer corps, to maintain a significant number of tribal sympathisers east of the Durand Line.[25] Members of tribes that fought for Nadir Khan predominated among military officers who trained in the Soviet Union. They would eventually join or sympathise with Afghan communist groups.

Parallel to these developments, a non-violent Pashtun patriotic movement emerged in the NWFP in 1930, after British troops killed unarmed protestors in Peshawar. The victims were members of an organisation called the Organisation for Promoting Reforms Among Afghans, headed by Khan Abdul Ghaffar Khan. It was later known as the Khudai Khidmatgars, or Servants of God. The organisation allied with the Indian National Congress and won the 1937 and 1946 elections in the NWFP. The Khudai Khidmatgars ended their alliance with the Congress in 1946, after the Congress accepted the British partition plan calling for a plebiscite in NWFP on whether to join India or the new Muslim state of Pakistan. The Khudai Khidmatgars demanded the inclusion of a third option creating an independent state for Pashtuns called Pashtunistan. The movement boycotted the referendum of July 1947, when a majority of voters opted for joining Pakistan. The turnout in the referendum was a mere 51 per cent.[26]

The Cold War and Pashtunistan

Kabul voted against Pakistan's admission to the United Nations in 1947. Afghanistan argued that Pakistan should not be recognised before the 'Pashtunistan' issue was resolved. Kabul, however, withdrew its objection after one month. In February 1948, it became one of the first governments to establish diplomatic relations with Pakistan.[27] After the partition, the Khudai Khidmatgars moderated their stance and accepted Pakistan as a *fait accompli*. Ghaffar Khan took the oath of allegiance to Pakistan in February 1948. Faqir Ipi was among the tribal leaders in FATA who continued to maintain militias in hopes of a future Pashtunistan. These leaders viewed the new Pakistan as a continuation of British imperialism. They challenged the claims of the new state's founders, who touted it as a Muslim homeland. Pakistani leaders failed to befriend Ghaffar Khan and other ethnic minority leaders. Khan was imprisoned in June 1948, and his organisation was banned. Successive Pakistani administrations attempted to suppress Pashtun nationalism by bankrolling a loyalist alternative leadership.

Pakistan withdrew army units from the Tribal Areas in late 1947. The government, however, was soon relying on Pashtun *lashkar*s from both sides of the Durand Line to fight as its surrogate army. Pashtun fighters were deployed in the battle for control of Muslim Kashmir after the Hindu Maharaja Sir Hari Singh declared Kashmir's accession to India in 1947. Pakistan rejected the declaration; sporadic clashes between Pakistani and Indian forces occurred for fifteen months until early 1949. Pakistan characterised the struggle as a holy war and won the loyalty of Pashtun volunteers by distributing arms and money. Although tribal forces made a determined march, they failed to capture Srinagar, Kashmir's capital.[28]

Since 1947, Pakistan and India have occupied separate parts of Kashmir. The territory today remains divided by the Line of Control, a de facto border which, however, has never been internationally recognised. Skirmishes between Pakistani and Indian troops in Kashmir are common, and the conflict has shown little sign of resolution. New Delhi insists that what it calls the state of Jammu and Kashmir is an integral part of India. Islamabad, on the other hand, has demanded implementation of United Nations Security Council resolutions calling for a plebiscite on whether Kashmir should join India or Pakistan. Some Kashmiri Muslim movements have demanded independence.

Chronic instability spawned by the Durand Line brought the Cold War to the Pashtun homeland. After a Pakistani bombing raid on an Afghan border village in July 1949, the Afghan government convened a *loya jirga* in Kabul. The meeting resulted in decisions that have clouded Afghan-Pakistani relations ever since. The *jirga* declared support for Pashtunistan and affirmed Kabul's position that Pakistan was a new state, rather than a successor state, to British India. This, the *jirga* declared, made all past treaties with the British pertaining to the status of the border null and void. Agreements included in this renunciation were the 1879 Treaty of Gandamak, the 1893 Durand Agreement, the Anglo-Afghan Pact of 1905, the Treaty of Rawalpindi of 1919 and the Anglo-Afghan Treaty of 1921. Afghanistan next moved to align with the Soviet Union to secure military aid. Kabul's position on Pashtunistan made it impossible to receive aid from Washington and its Western allies, who were aligned with Pakistan.

Afghan leaders and Pashtun nationalist figures in Pakistan were never able to unite behind a single vision of Pashtunistan. Some factions said it should become an independent country. Others sought to make it an autonomous province of Pakistan. Some individuals and factions asserted it was an integral part of Afghanistan. Successive Afghan rulers manipulated the question to strengthen Pashtun support for the Afghan state. But Kabul's championing of a Pashtun ethnic cause inadvertently intensified an ethno-linguistic rivalry between Pashtuns and non-Pashtuns.

During the decades of the Cold War, the Soviet Union and India paid lip service to Pashtunistan while pursuing their own interests. Moscow's aim was to prevent Afghanistan from joining a Western military alliance. New Delhi wanted to divert Pakistani military resources from Indian borders by stoking fears of an unstable western border. Most of Afghanistan's allies in the second half of the twentieth century exploited the insecurity of its rulers, who were well aware of the losses the country had sustained during a century of European meddling. It was standard for Afghan leaders to view themselves and their country as very vulnerable.

Diplomatic ties between Afghanistan and Pakistan were broken when Pakistan closed the border in 1961, in the aftermath of a botched

Afghan cross-border raid the previous year. With its principal trade artery cut, the Afghan economy suffered a severe contraction. Turmoil in the royal family led to the resignation of Prime Minister Daud Khan in 1963. Elderly Afghans recall with irony the 'decade of democracy' that followed when the king became a constitutional figurehead. The often quarrelling parliament dissolved the government three times, ultimately leading to a palace coup in 1973. Daud Khan accused Zahir Shah's government of neglecting Pashtunistan in a bid to improve relations with Washington and Islamabad. Daud also accused the king of failing to respond forcefully to the sacking of Pashtun and Baloch ethno-nationalist administrations in Pakistan's NWFP and Balochistan. These governments were headed by the National Awami Party—a coalition of predominantly Pashtun and Baloch leftists who were considered by Pakistani Prime Minister Zulfiqar Ali Bhutto to be his primary political rivals. Bhutto later appointed a senior tribal figure, Nawab Akbar Khan Bugti, as governor of Balochistan.[29]

The sacking of the democratically-elected provincial administration was prompted by Pakistani insecurity. In Islamabad's view, Pashtun and Baloch ethno-nationalist movements posed an active secessionist threat. Pakistani rulers had been severely shaken by the trauma of 1971, when Bangladesh broke free from Pakistan after a violent struggle and emerged as an independent country. To achieve its security goals, the 1972–77 Bhutto administration employed a carrot-and-stick approach. It launched a crackdown on nationalists while also carrying out development projects. To win support in FATA, Islamabad backed a limited programme of economic development. The region saw the building of roads, hospitals and a few factories in the 1970s. The government also gave jobs in the federal bureaucracy to educated tribal youth.

Islamabad kept the region isolated by denying any prospect of political reform. Bhutto's administration even incorporated the colonial-era border regime into the 1973 constitution. Islamabad unveiled another destructive policy by supporting Islamists opposed to President Daud's secular ethno-nationalism and the rising power of Afghan communists. Islamabad had begun to favour Afghan Islamists after they publicly opposed the creation of Bangladesh. The Islamists were seen as reliable allies because of their opposition to the West and Soviet Union. Islamabad was already sensing that the movement could serve as a bulwark against Afghan irredentist claims and domestic Pashtun ethnic nationalism. The Afghan Islamists were also seen as a potential bridge to Muslims globally who could be recruited to support the proclaimed Islamic ideals of Pakistan.

With each offering sanctuary to the other's opponents, bitterness and mistrust between Kabul and Islamabad spiked in the 1970s. Kabul extended shelter to some 30,000 Marri Baloch tribesmen after they escaped a Pakistani military crackdown. Though fighting for a nationalist cause, the Marri guerillas cast themselves ideologically as Marxists. In response, Islamabad sheltered and provided military training to Afghan Islamists such as Ahmed Shah Massoud and Gulbuddin Hekmatyar. With Islamabad's backing, they staged an abortive uprising in 1975.

Pakistani interference in Afghanistan escalated dramatically in the 1980s. Pakistan hosted the Afghan mujahedeen, while Afghanistan became a safe haven for Pakistani dissidents. Kabul's pro-Soviet regime hosted al-Zulfiqar, a militant offshoot of the Pakistan People's Party. The group intended to destabilise General Muhammad Zia-ul Haq's military regime, which had overthrown and hanged Zulfiqar Ali Bhutto, the founding leader of the People's Party. The group was headed by Zulfiqar Ali Bhutto's son, Murtaza Bhutto.[30]

The Globalisation of Jihad

In April, 1978, military officers loyal to the Khalq faction of the communist People's Democratic Party of Afghanistan (PDPA) launched a coup against President Daud Khan. They killed him, along with his entire extended family. The overthrow ended the Durrani ruling dynasty and opened Afghan political space to a new kind of competition. It shattered the relative peace and stability in the Pashtun borderlands and marked the beginning of a new generation of conflict. Some twenty months later, the 1979 Christmas Eve Soviet invasion was the first major act in the modern globalisation of war in Afghanistan. The international jihad in Afghanistan would materialise in the coming years. It is not without irony that many of the jihad's original sponsors were not Muslim, nor had they any abiding interest in the long-term goals of the jihadis.

The Soviet invasion of Afghanistan transformed Pakistan into a frontline ally of the United States. With Washington's blessing, Islamabad's military rulers had virtually a free hand to shape the Afghan resistance. To prevent the establishment of nationalist guerillas, Islamabad refused to recognise parties and exiles associated with the nationalist mainstream. Pakistani agents controlled supplies intended for the Afghan Islamists that had been sent by the United States, Saudi Arabia, Western Europe and China. The Islamists were also generously funded by wealthy private donors in the Gulf. The regime of General Muhammad Zia-ul Haq promoted the jihad to legitimise Pakistani military rule. Pashtuns were major victims of this policy, as it radicalised and militarised their homeland.

By funding thousands of Islamic madrasas, or seminaries, and arming Islamist organisations, Pakistan underwent an extraordinary metamorphosis that eventually proved a disaster. Islamabad hoped to use engagement in successive wars in and around Afghanistan as a means of dealing with its root national security threat: India, a country with more than eight times Pakistan's population and far greater economic resources. Pakistan's engagement in the Cold War, the post-Cold War civil conflict in Afghanistan and the US-led War on Terror must be seen as being broadly motivated by Islamabad's competition with New Delhi.

In Pakistani perceptions, Indian elites have never fully accepted the legitimacy of Pakistan's existence. By supporting Islamists, Pakistan has sought to block the possibility of India gaining influence in Afghanistan and being able to threaten Pakistan's western border. During the 1980s and 1990s, Pakistani generals described securing the western border—or gaining 'strategic depth', as they call it—as among their highest priorities. In practical terms, Islamabad wanted to be able to rely on a client regime in Kabul that could provide territory and airspace to accommodate the retreat and recuperation of Pakistani troops in case of a confrontation with India.

Pakistan has shown itself to be skillful at exploiting extremist networks in both Afghanistan and Kashmir to wage asymmetrical warfare targeting India. But these provocations have several times veered close to nuclear escalation. One major incident occurred over the 1999 intrusion by Kashmiri Islamic insurgents and Pakistani troops in Kargil, in Indian-occupied Kashmir. Another occurred following the December 2001 attack on the Indian parliament by a Pakistan-based terrorist group.[31] Tensions were again raised over the November 2008 attacks by armed gunmen on high-profile sites in the Indian commercial hub of Mumbai. New Delhi and many Western powers have held Lashkar-e Taiba—a Pakistani Salafi organisation based in Punjab—responsible for the Mumbai bloodshed, which killed and injured more than 160 people, mostly Indians but at least twenty-eight foreigners as well, including Americans, Israelis, Germans and Australians.

Arab Revolutionaries

In the 1980s, thousands of Islamist radicals from across the Arab world, and a lesser number from Southeast Asia, came to Pakistan to fight and assist the anti-Soviet jihad in Afghanistan. They established support networks in the NWFP and bases along the Afghan side of the Durand Line, in areas such as the Jaji district of Khost Province and in the Tora Bora mountains in Nangarhar Province. These camps had Arabic names such as al-Masada, or 'lion's den'.[32]

The concept of Al-Qaeda as a global jihadist conglomerate was formulated in Peshawar, Pakistan in the late 1980s. By 1998, Al-Qaeda had adopted a formal organisational structure that sought to recruit extremists from around the world. That year, Osama bin Laden and Ayman Al-Zawahiri announced Al-Qaeda's aim and objectives to the world from Khost, Afghanistan. These outsiders changed the orientation, meaning and goals of jihad in the Pashtun borderlands. Their first objective was to harm the 'far enemy', whom they held responsible for propping up the 'near enemy'—the name Al-Qaeda gave to the predominantly pro-Western rulers in the Arab and Islamic world and Israel.

Despite being founded in the borderlands, Al-Qaeda has never had a Pashtun leader. But the wars in the Pashtun homeland have undoubtedly nurtured the leaders and ideologues of modern global jihad. Palestinian scholar Abdullah Azzam, Zawahiri and bin Laden have gained prominence because of their role in these wars.[33] The Arabs were so engrossed in the Afghan jihad that many stayed behind in the Pashtun regions after the Soviet withdrawal. They eventually attracted a second wave of jihadis during the 1990s. Volunteers and converts to diehard jihadism from Chechnya, Central Asia, Chinese Turkistan, Southeast Asia and Europe formed a truly global conglomerate under an overall Arab leadership.

Pashtuns were the main losers in the globalisation of jihad. Pashtun society and politics on both sides of the Durand Line underwent structural changes. Modernist, secular Pashtun nationalism had been associated with tribal leaders, the intelligentsia and the royalist elite. These nationalist cadres joined Islamic conservatives in opposing British colonialism. But they differed over the adoption of Western social and political values. Afghan and Pakistani radical Islamists opposed liberal institutions. They attempted to craft an Islamic political system by redefining concepts and institutions such as the nation-state, revolution, political ideology, political parties and development.

The wars caused one of the largest human displacements in recent history—and Pashtuns, again, were the main victims. Pashtuns are no more or less prone to extremism than members of any other ethnicity. In the case of the borderlands, however, radical movements and intelligence agencies collabourated to spread extremism. In Pakistan in the 1980s and 1990s, such policies were an obsession with the security establishment. Generals and spymasters such as Muhammad Zia-ul Haq, Aslam Beg and Hamid Gul advocated them publicly.[34]

Many Pashtun leaders have told me they believe the Pakistani military's myopic view of Pashtuns is the core problem. The war in Afghanistan provided Pakistan with a golden opportunity to act on its longstanding desire to weaken Pashtun nationalism. However, Islamabad's support for pan-Islamism resulted in a new movement that could be described as Pashtun Islamism. This new mindset gained traction during the Taliban's ascent to power in Afghanistan, when pan-Islamist solidarity surpassed the imperatives of tribal relations and ethnic cohesion.

Decades of Pakistani investment transformed Pashtun Islamism into a formidable political force and reduced the Pashtun nationalist threat. But several built-in contradictions in the policy backfired on Islamabad and its goal of enhancing Pakistani security and prestige. Indeed, these contradictions have become so onerous they now threaten Pakistan's survival. The country's existence as a nation-state directly clashes with the pan-Islamism of Al-Qaeda and radical elements of the Taliban. Strengthened and emboldened over recent decades, these groups have demanded a complete Islamic overhaul of the state and society.

The Geneva Accords set the terms for the Soviet withdrawal from Afghanistan, which was completed in February 1989. In the wake of the pullout, Washington and Moscow opened talks on an agreement to form a transitional Afghan government to preside over elections. Had they been fully implemented, the Geneva Accords would have resulted in a weak Afghan government, still close to the Soviet Union, but with Soviet troops no longer in the country. In effect, Afghanistan would have become a de facto buffer within the Soviet sphere.

Washington and Moscow, however, failed to reach a deal. The war continued, eventually resulting in the collapse of the Afghan state. The United States and Pakistan pursued an anti-Soviet 'rollback' policy, aimed at wiping out any lingering Soviet influence, by continuing to aid the Afghan guerrillas. During this period, when many Afghans believed the jihad had already ended with the departure of Soviet troops, the rollback policy increasingly relied on Salafi Arab fighters who had joined the jihad for very different reasons than most Afghans had. This US-Pakistani policy eventually led to the total destruction of a century of modernisation in Afghanistan.

Representative rule was restored in Pakistan following military ruler Zia-ul Haq's death in an air crash in August 1988. Pashtun nationalist parties participated in the Pakistani national and provincial elections and moderated their demands. They backed replacing the name 'Pashtunistan' with 'Pakhtunkhwa' to denote a new name for the NWFP.[35] The change to a superficially civilian government in Pakistan between 1988 and 1999, however, hardly affected Islamabad's Afghan policy, which remained in the purview of the military.

During the early 1990s, Afghanistan became an international pariah as the United States walked away from the Cold War's last battleground. Fighting raged, while levels of education, health and wealth declined. Hundreds of thousands of people fled. Successive US administrations did not view the collapse of Afghanistan as a threat to the United States. Not until the attacks of 11 September 2001 did Washington recognise warnings that, in the absence of legitimate law and order, a multinational terrorist opposition had been using the borderlands to consolidate its links and sharpen the skills of its followers.

3

THE TALIBAN IN POWER

On a sunny afternoon in autumn, 2010, I arrived at a modest house on a rubbish-strewn street in western Kabul. It was the innocuous abode of Wakil Ahmed Muttawakil, the former Taliban foreign minister. Muttawakil had been a key part of the Taliban government, serving until the regime collapsed during the American bombing campaign of late 2001. I was welcomed to the house by uniformed Afghan intelligence agents. The agents, who lived in a wooden shack outside the residence, were ostensibly tasked with protecting Muttawakil. In reality, their job was to keep tabs on him.

Our meeting involved few formalities. Muttawakil's son ushered me into a small room ringed by sofas. Golden calligraphic inscriptions gleamed on the spines of religious books lined up along wall shelves. The room was filled with the scent of burning oil.

In a country where hardships are often written in wrinkled faces and grey hair, Muttawakil appeared younger than his forty-two years. It was difficult to imagine that the black-bearded, turban-wearing cleric sitting in front of me once participated in talks about the fate of fugitive Saudi millionaire Osama bin Laden, and had negotiated pipeline deals with global energy giants. But the soft-spoken man's relaxed appearance concealed several lives' worth of pain and suffering.

As a youth, Muttawakil lost his father during the Communist Revolution. Abdul Ghaffar Baryalai was a leading Kandahari cleric and poet. He was arrested after returning from the Islamic hajj pilgrimage in the months after the April 1978 coup that overthrew nationalist President Daud Khan and established a socialist republic. Muttawakil's family had been permitted to visit him in prison, where he was detained without charge or a court proceeding. One day, Baryalai disappeared, never to be seen again.[1] Muttawakil was not yet a teenager.

The young Muttawakil inherited his father's library, as well as the responsibility of looking after his mother, five siblings and two stepmothers. The family did not own their modest mud house in Panjwai, close to Kandahar. Muttawakil had no uncles to assume responsibility for the family, as is the norm among rural Pashtuns. The family initially tried to survive in rural Kandahar by living with relatives, but soon joined an exodus to the outskirts of neighbouring Pakistan's southwestern city of Quetta. 'The dual responsibilities of studying and looking after my large family at a young age made my life really miserable,' Muttawakil has written of those trying days.[2]

As the jihad against the Red Army reached its zenith in the mid-1980s, Muttawakil began climbing the clerical hierarchy. The core of his studies revolved around the Quran, the Islamic holy book. His areas of emphasis included the sayings and biography of the Prophet Muhammad, Islamic jurisprudence and the Arabic language.[3] After a few years, Muttawakil became the administrator of a madrasa on the outskirts of Quetta. It was a time of tectonic political shifts for Pashtun clerics in Afghanistan and Pakistan.

For generations, clerics had been economically impoverished and inhabited the lower rungs of the social hierarchy (apart from a few charismatic leaders who headed political or militant movements). But the jihad in Afghanistan opened the floodgates to foreign funding and exposed clerics to foreign influence, from Arabs in particular. It also brought Pashtun mullahs into much closer contact with each other and compelled them, for political reasons, to build alliances with Islamists around the world.

Muttawakil became one of a new generation of Afghans to be trained in the Deobandi madrasas of Pakistan. Such schooling contributed to the development within this generation of a markedly different worldview from that of previous Afghan clerics. It would be a legacy whose impact would be felt for decades.

With war raging across the border in Afghanistan, Muttawakil enjoyed participating in long debates with predominantly Pashtun fellow students in Quetta's Noorul Madaris seminary. Tales of mujahedeen war heroics and Red Army brutalities interested everybody. But the young students also often engaged in polemics over which jihadi groups and leaders were superior to others. While they professed to be followers of Sunni Hanafi Islam,[4] almost all declared their adherence to the worldview and teachings of Darul Uloom Deoband.[5]

After the creation of Pakistan in 1947, some Pashtun Deobandi clerics became followers and leaders of various factions of the JUI political party. They contested elections and, in some cases, became coalition partners. They justified their political involvement by describing it as part of a quest to implement an Islamic system. Muttawakil, like many young Afghan religious students, was inspired by the political culture he found in the JUI-sponsored madrasas in Balochistan. Stimulated by the example of his forebearers, Muttawakil decided to deepen his commitment to Islamist activism by becoming leader of the jihadi group Jamiatul Tulaba Harakat.[6]

Muttawakil lost a brother in a battle with the Red Army and its socialist allies in the late 1980s. 'The sight of the first aggressor planes in the skies left an indelible mark on my heart,' he would write. 'That pain changed into pleasure when I heard about the mujahedeen victory over Kabul years later.'

The majority of mujahedeen, however, had priorities beyond victory over Moscow: they hoped to establish an Islamic utopia. But the mujahedeen leadership was an ostentatious and often-quarrelling bunch. Years before they declared victory over the last Afghan socialist president, Mohammad Najibullah, who left power in April 1992, they had been engaged in disputes which sometimes broke out into open hostilities. The splits were aggravated by the presence of rival socialist factions who had joined opposing mujahedeen groups, mostly along ethnic lines. Their plan to bring Islamic harmony to Afghanistan thus deteriorated into anarchy, violence, mounting ethnic and sectarian rivalries, and ultimately the destruction of the modern Afghan state built by Amir Abdul Rahman Khan and his successors.

Student Militias Ascendant

Conflicting and varying accounts of the origin of the Taliban have helped lend the group a certain mystique. Most observers agree that the rise of the 'student militia' was both a reaction by Kandahari clerics to the anarchy of the mujahedeen and an effort by Pakistan to create an Afghan leadership that would do its bidding.

Mullah Abdul Salam Zaeef, among the best-known Taliban figures because of his media appearances, was a founding member of the movement when it was launched in the autumn of 1994. He told me in a 2010 interview that Taliban aspirations were initially limited to the Panjwai and Maiwand districts of Kandahar Province.[7] A first attempt to organise a militia failed because of tribal differences, he said. But a second attempt, under Mullah Mohammad Omar, began to gain popular support after a small group—numbering no more than forty—took action to confront former mujahedeen. He said local people had reached out for help after the former mujahedeen—known as *topakian*, or gunmen—set up checkpoints around Kandahar to harass residents.

'Each one of these check posts used to demand money from people,' Zaeef said. 'They would steal and even kill people. Some of them would kill people to take away their motorcycles or cars. The worst were those who would violate the honour of the people [by raping women and boys]. This is what motivated us to rise up against those people and disarm them. We never imagined we would transform into such a huge movement.'

Zaeef said the movement's supporters quickly swelled into the hundreds as word spread of the successful action against the mujahedeen. 'Everybody wanted to support somebody who would stand against the [mujahedeen's] criminality and corruption,' Zaeef said. 'We had no constitution, organisational structure or a proper name. The names Taliban, Taliban movement and Taliban Islamic Movement were all given to us by the people.'

Pakistani intelligence officers took note of the movement after Kandahar fell under the movement's influence, Zaeef said. He said these officers soon asked the Taliban to help recover a Pakistani truck convoy that had been looted by former mujahedeen as it travelled via Kandahar and Herat to Turkmenistan. Zaeef said the Taliban succeeded in seizing what was left of the convoy from mujahedeen commanders.

'This laid the ground for establishing Islamabad's contacts with the Taliban,' Zaeef said. 'Pakistan also sensed that its strategic interests could be best served under the Taliban, because they could be instrumental in bringing peace to the region. That's why they supported the

Taliban. But Iran, on the contrary, concluded the Taliban were a creation of Pakistan. They stuck to this conclusion as long as the movement remained in power.'[8]

The story of the thirty-truck Pakistani convoy figures prominently in all accounts of the Taliban's rise. What is not clear, however, is whether fighters of the budding movement captured a major arms depot before launching the operation to recover the convoy. The Taliban are said to have seized the arms depot from Gulbuddin Hekmatyar's Hizb-e Islami in the border town of Spin Boldak in early November, 1994.[9] The lack of clarity has contributed to the debate about whether the militia is an independent Afghan movement or a Pakistani proxy.

For Muttawakil, the creation of the Taliban was the culmination of 'various waves' of activism around Kandahar. 'Media has wrongly portrayed it to have begun in Spin Boldak,' Muttawakil told me. 'The movement was a mix of the jihadi Taliban who had gained substantial military mettle against the Soviet occupation [in the 1980s], and a younger generation of Afghan madrasa students who had substantial political exposure in Pakistani madrasas. But over time, people from all kinds of backgrounds joined. People welcomed them because they needed such a movement. When they controlled Loy Kandahar, neighbouring states took interest. It was natural for Sunni Pakistan to succeed over Shia Iran in reaching out to a Sunni movement [in Afghanistan].'[10]

Muttawakil said early Taliban members included both veterans of the anti-Soviet war and Afghan students who had studied in the madrasas of Balochistan. 'Some of them were organised under *jamiatul tulaba*, or student unions, of various jihadi parties,' he said. 'Most prominent among them was Jamiatul Tulaba Harakat, which was very similar to Jamiat Tulaba Islam (JTI) because both followed the Deoband school of thought.[11] The movement first appeared in Maiwand. Haji Bashar Noorzai handed over the control of his district to them.[12] From there, they came down to Kandahar and controlled it.'

By early 1995, the Taliban had succeeded in taking control of three predominantly Pashtun-populated provinces in southern Afghanistan. Kandahar, Zabul and Uruzgan were captured without much fighting. In some instances, such as in Zabul, former mujahedin commanders like Mullah Abdul Salam 'Rocketi' recruited hundreds of fighters into the Taliban fold. Nimroz to the east and Farah to the west also fell under the movement's control in early 1995. The Taliban failed, however, in an initial attempt to take the western province of Herat. But by the time it began to advance northwards towards Kabul, it had largely cemented its control over Loy Kandahar. Taliban fighters seized Ghazni and most Hekmatyar-controlled regions in Wardak and Logar, including Hekmatyar's headquarters in Charasyab. After Jalaluddin Haqqani and other commanders in Loya Paktia threw their allegiance behind the Taliban, the militia was able to claim control over most territories in Khost, Paktia and Paktika.

The Taliban's offensive was not without setbacks. After the Hazara leader Abdul Ali Mazari was captured and executed in March 1995, the militia earned the permanent animosity of the Shia minority. The movement also suffered repeated battlefield debacles against the forces of Ismail Khan around Herat. But in early September, the Taliban finally succeeded in seizing the province. With each victory, Taliban ranks expanded. The movement could count 25,000 fighters by the end of 1995.[13]

In April 1996, a *shura* of 1,000 *ulema* in Kandahar made Mullah Mohammad Omar the *Amir-ul Momineen*, or Commander of the Faithful. The *shura* also declared jihad against Afghan President Burhanuddin Rabbani's government in Kabul. Most former mujahedeen factions appeared to be uniting under the threat of growing Taliban power.

Hekmatyar had joined his former foes Ahmad Shah Massoud and Rabbani in June 1995 to bolster the defence of Kabul. But momentum was clearly on the side of the Taliban. Jalalabad and other mujahedeen strongholds in eastern Afghanistan fell to the movement in September 1996, securing their control of all geographically contiguous Pashtun regions of Afghanistan. After over-running Hekmatyar's headquarters in Sarobi on 24 September—the headquarters had been described as the 'linchpin' of Kabul's defence—the government was forced to devote most of its resources to organising a coordinated retreat towards Massoud's base in the Panjshir Valley.[14] The Taliban failed in multiple attempts to take the valley. It was one prize that would continue to elude the Taliban's grasp, remaining beyond the movement's control throughout the regime's rule.[15]

Nearly two years after their emergence in southern Afghanistan, the Taliban captured Kabul. One of the militia's first acts was the torture and killing of former socialist President Mohammad Najibullah and his brother.[16] According to Waheed Mozhdah, who served as a senior aide in the Taliban's Foreign Ministry, the Taliban justified the killing of Najibullah, an ethnic Pashtun, as an act to please Allah—not an act of murder motivated by ethnic and tribal differences.[17]

Melting snows and warm springtime weather heralded a new fighting season in 1997. The Taliban had shifted its focus north of the Hindu Kush. However, the Taliban capture of the northern metropolis of Mazar-e Sharif in May of that year proved elusive. The movement's nominal regional ethnic Uzbek ally General Abdul Malik Pahlawan, a former second-in-command to Abdul Rashid Dostum, ended up leading the Taliban into a collision with Shia ethnic Hazaras. Pahlawan had encouraged the Taliban to disarm the Hazaras, while at the same time instigating the minority to oppose control by the hard-line Sunni Taliban.[18]

Hundreds of Taliban were killed in an intense couple of days of fighting in Mazar in May 1997. Thousands more Taliban were taken prisoner. The United Nations later discovered mass graves close to Mazar containing the remains of some 2,000 Taliban prisoners who were tortured before being shot. There are also reports of atrocities carried out by the Taliban. But the alliance of ethnic Uzbek and Hazara militias that drove the Taliban out of Mazar-e Sharif began to crumble after the Taliban's withdrawal. Dostum's return to Mazar in October 1997 divided the Uzbeks into pro-Dostum and pro-Pahlawan factions, and ultimately resulted in Pahlawan's flight to Iran. Dostum would go on to fight bloody but inconclusive battles with the Hazaras. The conflict weakened the Hazaras and exposed them to annihilation by the Taliban.

In the summer of 1998, the Taliban launched a lightning attack in northern Afghanistan, using Herat as a base. The ostensible objective was to sweep through the provinces of Badghis, Faryab and Jawzjan and eventually link up with Taliban strongholds in the north-eastern province of Kunduz. The militia overran Dostum's headquarters in Sheberghan in July and recaptured Mazar-e Sharif on 8 August 1998, after a week of fighting with the Hazara Shia militia Hizb-e Wahdat. The Taliban appeared to have vengeance in mind. The United Nations and the International Committee of the Red Cross accused the movement of committing atrocities and killing thousands of people, including noncombatants. During the conquest of Mazar, Taliban fighters also killed nine Iranian diplomats, escalating tensions with Tehran.

Reacting to the murders of its diplomats, Iran sent significant numbers of troops to the border. Reports at the time suggested the Taliban mustered nearly 200,000 fighters to respond to the Iranian challenge, but the real number is probably closer to 20,000. The standoff eased by the end of the year thanks to behind-the-scenes diplomacy by the United Nations and Islamabad-based Western diplomats. In August, the Taliban released some two dozen Iranian truck drivers who were detained during the capture of Mazar-e Sharif in August.

The Taliban conquest of Mazar-e Sharif and Bamiyan, which was captured in September, extended the movement's control to most of Afghanistan. Ahmad Shah Massoud and his predominantly Tajik followers were now limited to a narrow sliver of territory in the high mountains of the north-east.

Beginning in 1999, the Taliban's focus on military matters receded as the movement's leaders increasingly focused on consolidating their political system. During this period, the movement rejected and sometimes sabotaged any efforts by Afghans to negotiate a more equitable power-sharing system. Relatives and sympathisers of murdered Afghan political leaders blamed the Taliban or Pakistani intelligence services. Taliban figures, reflecting on their time in power, argue that the militia prevented Afghanistan from disintegration, which they portray as a remarkable achievement.[19]

Ruling by Decree

The Taliban movement went through several evolutions between its first appearance in the autumn of 1994 to its demise in late 2001. The rural clerical roots of the movement, for example, emphasised that governance decisions should be made through consensus-building in the *shura* of top leaders. Mullah Omar, however, would eventually emerge as both the spiritual leader and chief executive of the movement.[20]

After the capture of Kabul in 1996, the Taliban embarked on forming a Sunni clerical regime. Over the years, this regime would become increasingly hard-line. The systematic elimination of the nationalist mainstream of royalist supporters and communist bureaucrats, and the movement's military defeat of mujahedeen remnants, left an open field for the Taliban to consolidate power, particularly in the Pashtun south. The Taliban's association with Islam, its rural background, simple lifestyles and imposition of harsh order, initially gave the movement legitimacy in the eyes of the public. Clerical networks opened the way for the Taliban to penetrate villages and clans.

The Kandahar *shura*, which consisted of close associates of Mullah Omar, remained a key decision-making body, although the process of its inner workings has never been made clear. The Taliban did form a Kabul *shura*. All members of this *shura* were also in the cabinet. But they lacked any real powers, and most major tactical and strategic powers remained in the hands of the Kandahar *shura*. A separate military *shura*, similarly, had no real powers.

With most of its prominent members moulded by fighting, the Taliban never excelled at governance. The structure of the regime was such that government officials could be removed at the snap of a finger. Although the movement did retain some government bureaucrats from past regimes, the appointment of large numbers of barely literate Taliban members created resentment and hindered the development of coherent institutions. According to Waheed Mozhdah, Taliban cadres always received preferential treatment over non-Taliban professionals. Such professionals were discriminated against in terms of salaries and had little influence. *Andiwali*, a Pashto equivalent of camaraderie, or group solidarity, was a hallmark of Taliban organisation.

> When someone replaced a minister [or] a governor, he would transfer all his *andiwals* to the new department. The negative effect of this practice was that those who worked and gained experience in an office for some time had to leave their jobs and hold a new position in a different branch of the government that they had no knowledge of. The same applied to their successors. The *en masse* departure of *andiwals* meant that the successors have to begin from scratch. It clearly indicated that they lacked an unambiguous transparent plan for a government system. During their five-year rule they made no efforts to correct and improve that situation.[21]

Hassan Kakar, an elderly Afghan historian now living in California, made an extensive tour of Afghanistan in the spring of 2001 and met hundreds of Afghan leaders, including Taliban cabinet ministers and advisers in Pakistan and Afghanistan. He notes that Taliban leaders claimed to be implementing the civic laws of Daud Khan's secular republican era that were in place before the communist coup. But he says that in reality, they were increasingly obsessed with the distinction between Muslims and *kufar*, an Arabic word adopted into Pashto and Dari meaning 'infidels'. Kakar observed that despite many *shura* meetings, decision-making ultimately remained in the hands of a few individual advisers around Mullah Omar in Kandahar.

Kakar, a Pashtun with a broad range of contacts, says he was shocked by the skewed worldview of the Taliban. He could not believe the Taliban actively tried to prevent Afghans from developing relations with non-Muslim countries. The Taliban 'do not want the Afghans to live among people they call "infidels"', he wrote. 'They are convinced about dividing people in the name of religion.'[22] Kakar notes that one of the key structural changes the Taliban introduced to Afghan society was the empowerment of rural clerics, who were given one-third of the *usher*, or tithe, collected on agricultural produce. He wrote that many Taliban were so obsessed with power that, while on holidays or visiting the front lines, they would often leave behind close relatives to informally look after their official affairs instead of relegating responsibilities to subordinates.[23]

One Taliban governance innovation was the creation of the Department of Promotion of Virtue and Prevention of Vice. Modelled on a Saudi government body, the institution served as *de facto* morality police. It was the government's arm of social control and an informal intelligence service, whose tentacles eventually extended to most urban Afghan homes. Thousands of baton-wielding, Kalashnikov-toting young madrasa graduates made up the much-feared cadres of the Munkirat.[24] Their appetite for harshly implementing the Taliban's moral rules—which, in fact, frequently changed—was felt across Afghanistan. This was particularly true in multiethnic major cities such as Kabul, Mazar and Herat, where the crackdown by the young zealots of the Munkirat was seen as ethnic discrimination against non-Pashtuns. In 2001, years after first launching the Vice and Virtue Department, the Taliban Justice Ministry formally published the regulations the department was created to enforce. They included:

> Any woman who goes out of her house without the appropriate veil should be promptly identified. Her husband should be appropriately punished, or else the woman should be warned not to do so again. If such a woman is seen in public transport, the driver should be immediately imprisoned from one to five days.
>
> If somebody is caught listening to music cassettes or watching video films in a shop or a hotel, the persons who own such materials should be punished by imprisonment from one to 20 days. If the owner of the shop or hotel is responsible for the playing of such materials, he should be imprisoned from one to 20 days. His business should be forced to close for five days.'[25]

For the Taliban, Islamic *sharia* law was not merely the inspiration behind a complicated tradition subject to differing interpretations. To the militants, *sharia* law meant a set of specific, iron-clad rules. As punishment, the regime relied on *hudood*, a strict Islamic criminal code which stipulates a series of punishments including amputations of limbs for theft, stoning to death for adultery and lashes for alcohol consumption.

In 1998, Taliban officials wrote a constitution called *Dastur*. It was never formally published, and it is not clear how much of it was ever implemented. But the governing structure outlined in the document roughly corresponds to what was in place in Afghanistan in the later part of 1998. Similar to other Afghan constitutions in the twentieth century, the Taliban constitution envisaged a centralised state where *sharia*, as interpreted by the Hanafi school, was the supreme law and all other laws were subservient to it. Put together, its provisions outline the vision of a purist Islamist society.

Taqwa, or piety, was the first condition for awarding state jobs on merit, according to Article 7 of the supreme law. Reliance on the promotion of virtue and the prevention of vice was the duty of the entire nation and government. Promotion of Arabic and Islamic studies was also considered the duty of the state. Most executive authority rested in the hands of Amir-ul-Momineen, the Commander of the Faithful, who was the commander-in-chief and chief executive. The Amir was granted sweeping powers over the judiciary and the legislature, most of whose senior members were appointed by him. According to the charter, the customary sermon during Friday prayer congregations was supposed to be read in the name of Amir-ul-Momineen to grant him added legitimacy.

Islam was also the guiding principle in foreign policy. Article 99 of the constitution reads: 'The Islamic Emirate of Afghanistan backs the charters of the United Nations, Organisation of the Islamic Conference, and the Non-Aligned Movement. It also backs the Universal Declaration Of Human Rights and other principles and guidelines as long as they are not in contradiction with Islamic principles and our nation's interests.'[26]

Pashtun Nationalists?

The Taliban were never correctly understood after their appearance on the Afghan stage. Many observers have allowed their own interests to colour their view of the movement. When the Taliban confronted powerful non-Pashtun Islamist warlords and militias, for example, Afghan analysts and observers sympathetic to these forces tended to describe the movement as being composed of Pashtun nationalists who wanted to revive a centralised Pashtun-dominated state.

The Taliban failed to please any segment of Afghan society. Most Pashtuns, in particular, eventually came to detest the movement's rigid policies. The Taliban were opposed to the Pashtun political elites who had preceded them. They opposed the nationalist mainstream of the old royalist regime and, unlike the communists, had no worldly focus on material development as a means to progress. The mujahedeen, the majority of whose leadership and foot soldiers were Pashtuns, also suffered. Many Pashtun mujahedeen commanders fought against the Taliban for years. Many Kandahari mujahedeen joined Ismail Khan to fight against the Taliban, and senior Pashtun commanders from southern and eastern Afghanistan allied themselves with Massoud during the Taliban's stint in power. Some Pashtun mujahedeen commanders, however, joined the Taliban.

Although the majority of the Taliban came from the southern Pashtun tribal confederacies of the Ghilzai and the Durrani, engaging in tribal politics remained anathema to them. While they were seen as adhering to *Pashtunwali* by outside observers, the Taliban opposed important aspects of local *narkh*, or customary laws. Implementing *sharia* law and bringing their own vision of peace to Afghanistan were their central objectives, and they largely remained loyal only to them.

Though small in number, ethnic Tajiks, Uzbeks and even Hazara were also members of the Taliban. Many Pashtuns who welcomed and joined the Taliban in hopes of restoring peace were bitterly disappointed in later years because of the Taliban preference for ideological affinity over kinship ties. Notoriously, Arabs and Pakistanis often received better treatment from the movement compared to fellow Afghans. This is one reason why the Taliban attracted few exiled Pashtun technocrats from the West.

Many Pashtun exiles in the West may have initially supported the Taliban's military sweep against the Pashtun warlords, and eventually against militia factions dominated by ethnic Uzbeks, Tajiks and Hazaras. But they soon became alienated over the Taliban's focus on hard-line Islam as the movement's ultimate goal. There was opposition to the Taliban's drive to Islamise the Afghan identity. But this dissatisfaction was never transformed into a vibrant opposition movement. Assassination and intimidation in both Afghanistan and Pakistan served as an effective deterrent to dissuade anti-Taliban Pashtuns from mobilising.

One curious aspect of the Taliban era was the movement's promotion of the Pashto language. This was also rooted in the utilitarian needs of the southern clerics, who only understood Pashto, unlike the bilingual Pashtun elites of earlier eras. The Taliban's promotion of Pashto, the language with which it conducted most of its official business, led many to conclude that the movement supported ethnic Pashtun hegemony. However, the reality on the ground was more complicated. Pashtuns were, in fact, bitterly divided over perceptions of the Taliban's motives. Many continued to suspect that the movement was an Arab-financed effort by Pakistan to colonise Afghanistan in the name of Islam. Roy Gutman cites Afghan scholar Rasul Amin to explain this process of 'Arabization'.

> From the country's cemeteries to its greatest works of antiquity, from its schools to its libraries, and from the battlefield to the national calendar, the Taliban made a series of decisions to diminish the role of national history and tradition in culture and social practice in favor of Arab tradition and mores. This never-colonized country with a proud history as a receptive crossroads of Asia, was now a magnet for Islamist militants from around the world, a center for intolerance and a hub for revolution. Bin Laden did not start the process of Arabization, but he certainly spurred it on.[27]

For Pakistani leaders, the prospect of organised nationalist Pashtuns—in both Afghanistan and Pakistan—represented the most significant threat to Pakistan's national unity since the creation of Bangladesh in 1971.[28] In Islamabad's view, support for the Taliban—who always put pan-Islamist solidarity before national interests—was a crucial bulwark against a potential Pashtun ethno-nationalist rising. Pakistan also believed the Taliban could be relied upon to block Pakistani rivals such as India, or regional powers such as Russia and Iran, from gaining influence in Afghanistan.

Divisions among Pashtuns along tribal and geographic lines have long offered openings for ideological intervention by outsiders. Such interference eventually went a long way towards devastating the modernist, secular Pashtun nationalism that had been advocated by Afghanistan's royalist elite and a broad spectrum of tribal leaders and intellectuals. It shattered old Pashtun alliances, in which Islamic conservatives had joined nationalists to oppose British colonialism. It exploited already existing tensions in Afghan society between conservative Islamists and modernists who supported the adoption of Western, or liberal, social values and political institutions.[29]

The new Islamists who emerged on the Afghan scene attempted to Islamise, rather than reject, institutions and concepts such as modernity, development, the nation-state and political ideology. They found a generous patron in Pakistan's ruling establishment. Unprecedented Western support to Pakistan after the Soviet occupation of Afghanistan provided Islamabad with a prime opportunity to realise its longstanding desire to weaken Pashtun nationalism. Pakistan thus supported hard-line pan-Islamist factions among Afghans, as well as Islamist parties in its western border region. Islamabad imagined it could both strengthen and control these forces. But Pashtuns do not have a greater liking or affinity for Islamic extremism than other Muslims. Islamabad's investment resulted in the unexpected ascendency of Pashtun Islamism, as exemplified by the Taliban. The Taliban have always claimed that their passion for pan-Islamist solidarity surpasses the imperatives of tribalism and ethnic cohesion. But the movement has never turned its back on its Pashtun roots.[30]

Taliban rule in Afghanistan bitterly divided Pashtuns in Pakistan. Support for the movement by the Islamist JUI party was universally opposed by secular Pashtun ethno-nationalists, who aggressively competed with the *mullahs* for votes. To the Pashtun ethno-nationalists, the Taliban represented the climax of the Pakistani military's imperial overreach. Although the nationalists failed to convince Islamabad to change its security calculations, their public opposition carried weight. 'The Taliban were a demolition squad,' Pashtun politician Afrasiab Khattak told me.[31] 'Their aim is to replace the *Afghaniyat*, or "Afghanness", in the Afghan identity and promote *Islamiyat*, or Islamic identity, instead. The renaming of Radio Kabul as the Voice of *Sharia*, banning the national flag and national anthem, the destruction of the Bamiyan Buddhas and vandalism of cultural heritage were all part of a strategy to re-engineer Afghan society along Islamist lines.'

Pakistani Proxies?

Pakistan's influence in Afghan affairs reached its zenith during the Taliban's era in power. The Pakistani rupee virtually replaced the devalued Afghani as the currency of choice. Islamabad's annual aid paid the monthly salaries of Taliban government workers.[32] The only working telephone lines in Kabul and Kandahar were extensions from Pakistan's telephone grid in Peshawar and Quetta. Many, if not all Taliban, had grown up in Pakistani refugee camps or studied in Pakistani madrasas. Although Pakistani intelligence services manipulated the Taliban, the movement also maintained independent links to Pakistani Islamist political parties, sectarian extremists, cross-border trade and transport networks, government departments and even secular politicians. The scope of influence occasionally allowed Taliban leaders to ignore pressure from Pakistani diplomats and even the military and ISI on some issues. It was a markedly different time than in the 1980s, when the mujahedeen was exclusively dependent on the ISI for survival.[33]

Pakistan's Afghan policy was riddled with contradictions. In 1994, Pakistani forces were deployed to crack down on a revolt by the Tehreek-e Nifaz-e Shriat-e Mohammadi, or Movement for the Enforcement of *sharia*, in the western Malakand region. But this did not deter Islamabad from supporting a similar movement in Afghanistan, the Taliban—despite the scars this would eventually leave on Pakistan. The influence of the Taliban, unlike the mujahedeen, reached deep into Pakistani society. Many Pashtun mullahs in the borderlands were energised by the Taliban's governance model and enforced a similar vision of regulating public morality by enforcing a ban on television and music. These figures also sometimes meted out *hudood* punishments. Pakistani state institutions were oblivious to the rising domestic threat.

Many anti-Shia Sunni extremists found refuge in Afghanistan during the time of Taliban rule. Many of these extremists topped the list of Pakistan's most-wanted criminals and were responsible for hundreds, perhaps thousands, of murders across Pakistan, particularly in the provinces of Sindh and Punjab.

If the rise of the Taliban marked the high point of Islamabad's quest for 'strategic depth', or having access and control over Afghan soil in the case of a confrontation with India, the extremists succeeded in carving out their own strategic depth inside Pakistan. Islamabad's decades of investment in Pashtun Islamism achieved the goal of countering the Pashtun nationalist threat, but it had turned Pashtun Islamism into a formidable political force that created its own cross-border realities. The Islamists were not married to the Pakistani state's security agenda. Indeed, they remained committed only to their ideology. After the onset of the Taliban and Al-Qaeda insurgency in Pakistan in 2002, Pakistani leaders soberly began to realise that 'Talibanisation' clashed with the Pakistani state's strategic vision. Pro-Taliban forces were demanding a complete overhaul of the Pakistani state and society, as part of a broader Islamist union of Pakistan, Afghanistan and Central Asia.[34]

In the 1990s, Islamabad's model for a Taliban-controlled Afghanistan was inspired by the indirect control exercised by Pakistan over its western FATA. Colonel Imam, the *nom de guerre* of former Brigadier General Amir Sultan Tarar, acted as Pakistan's vice-regent in Afghanistan. As the Pakistani consul general in Herat, Colonel Imam served as a mentor to Taliban leader Mullah Omar. He claimed to have trained a young Omar in the 1980s.[35] He was a prominent member of ISI's Afghan cell, which accumulated huge resources and regarded itself as the ultimate winner of the war against the Soviet Army and Afghan communism.

Colonel Imam, an ethnic Punjabi, was closely aligned with the Pakistani military's thinking on Afghanistan, which envisioned Islamised Pashtuns as a fortification against India to the east and secular Afghan nationalism to the west. Some authors have credited ethnic Pashtun military officers in the Pakistani Army for supporting the Taliban—but given that more than 80 per cent of the military's rank and file comes from the eastern Punjab province, it is not feasible for officers of other ethnicities to chart an independent line to support a militant movement in a neighbouring country. The go-between role of Islamabad between the Taliban and the international community led many internationally to conclude that Pakistan was the ultimate benefactor of the Taliban.

But the Taliban, or at least some leaders within its ranks, were sceptical of Pakistani intentions. Despite some perceptions, Islamabad's control over the Taliban was rather flimsy. The Taliban leadership ignored repeated requests by Pakistani leaders to formally sign an agreement recognising the Durand Line as the international border between the two countries. All previous Afghan governments also resisted recognising this demarcation.

'Pakistan formally approached us about the Durand Line three times,' former Taliban diplomat Mullah Abdul Salam Zaeef told me.[36] 'We always told them that we are not a national government and we see ourselves as an emergency transition, which cannot decide on such important issues.' In response to pressure from the US administration in 2001, Pakistani dictator General Pervez Musharraf advised the Taliban to heed international demands.[37] In reply, Mullah Omar recommended that Musharraf implement Islamic law and give Pakistan an Islamic government. '[Pakistan's religious parties] would be contented and avoid raising a hue and cry,' Omar wrote in a letter dated 16 January 2001. 'This is our advice and message based on Islamic ideology. Otherwise you had better know how to deal with it.'[38]

Bridge to Extremism?

Arab radicals set up bases in Afghanistan long before the Taliban emerged. The 'Afghan Arabs'—a misnomer referring to thousands of Islamist zealots from Morocco to Muscat—played only a minor role in combat against the Red Army in the 1980s. They instead focused on charitable operations and providing resources to individual Afghan commanders. They also made valuable contacts and gathered experience for their future extremist activities. Many of the Afghan Arabs lived in Pakistan, particularly the north-western city of Peshawar and the tribal town of Miram Shah.

The Arabs made occasional forays across the border into Afghanistan's Pashtun regions, where they established bases in areas such as the Jaji district of Khost and in Nangarhar. The al-Masada, or 'lion's den' camp in Khost, and a similar tunnel complex in the Khugyani district of Nangarhar, were the most notable. But most Afghan Arabs had a very superficial understanding of Afghan culture and little genuine support for the political ambitions of mujahedeen leaders. They publically said the jihad in Afghanistan was a stepping stone for a greater jihad against Israel and its Western backers. The concept of Al-Qaeda was formed in Peshawar in the late 1980s, but none of its leaders were ethnic Pashtuns or more broadly Afghans or Pakistanis. Fostering peace among the Muslims of Afghanistan, or easing the miseries of Pashtuns in Pakistan, never appeared on Al-Qaeda's agenda.

Among the Arab jihadists, Abdullah Yussuf Azzam, a Muslim Brotherhood-inspired Palestinian scholar, can perhaps be considered a figurehead and founding leader of Al-Qaeda. A leading proponent of global jihad in the 1980s, Azzam outlined his thinking in his book *Join the Caravan*. To Azzam, the single greatest cause of Muslim misfortune was their 'abandonment of jihad'. He declared the Afghan and Palestinian jihads to be the individual obligation of each Muslim. 'Jihad is the most excellent form of worship, and by means of it the Muslims can reach the highest ranks,' he wrote. 'According to our modest experience and knowledge, we believe that jihad in the present situation in Afghanistan is individually obligatory (*fard 'ayan*), with one's self and wealth, as has been confirmed by the jurists of the four schools of Islamic jurisprudence, without any exception. Along with them, the same opinion has been given by the majority of exegetes (*mufassirin*), hadith-scholars and the scholars of religious principle (*usul*).'[39]

However, jihad in Palestine was his ultimate objective. He wrote:

> Whoever can, from among the Arabs, fight jihad in Palestine, then he must start there. And, if he is not capable, then he must set out for Afghanistan. For the rest of the Muslims, I believe they should start their jihad in Afghanistan. It is our opinion that we should begin with Afghanistan before Palestine, not because Afghanistan is more important than Palestine, not at all, Palestine is the foremost Islamic problem. It is the heart of the Islamic world, and it is a blessed land... The battles in Afghanistan are still raging and have reached a level of intensity.... The situation in Afghanistan is still in the hands of the mujahedeen. There are more than 3,000 kilometres of open border in Afghanistan and regions of tribes not under political influence. This forms a protective shield for mujahedeen. However, in Palestine the situation is entirely different.'[40]

Although the majority of these predominantly young international Muslim radicals were Arabs, the Afghan jihad in the 1980s attracted recruits from Morocco to Mindanao. Many were connected through the Makataba Al-Kidamat or Bureau of Services, run by Abdullah Azzam. Many of these fighters left for their own countries after the Soviet withdrawal in 1989 and the demise of the communist regime in 1992. A handful, however, stayed behind and even fought in the civil war. But they were left leaderless after the 1989 killing of Azzam in a bomb blast outside a Peshawar mosque. Most were considered dangerous criminals in their home countries and lacked an overarching organisation that could unite them for a common cause back in their homeland or internationally.

Among the thousands of Arab volunteers for jihad was a tall, lanky and shy Saudi who considered Azzam a mentor. Osama bin Laden was the son of Muhammad bin Laden—a Yemeni migrant to Saudi Arabia who turned his small business into a construction conglomerate thanks to his connections to the House of Saud. Osama bin Laden's role in the Afghan jihad was minimal, but he rose to prominence because of his family's name. He helped build tunnels for the Afghan mujahedeen in south-eastern Afghanistan and financially aided Arab volunteers.

Bin Laden returned to Saudi Arabia, but fell out bitterly with the House of Saud when it opted to have American forces oust Iraqi dictator Saddam Hussein's troops from Kuwait in 1990. Bin Laden had proposed that he himself would lead a jihadist brigade that would expel the Iraqi forces. Enraged, bin Laden left Saudi Arabia for Sudan, where he bankrolled the Islamist government. He later decided to move to Afghanistan to evade growing Saudi pressure on his activities.[41]

Bin Laden flew to Jalalabad in eastern Afghanistan in May 1996, and lived under the protection of the local mujahedeen shura. He fell into the Taliban's hands when they overran the city in September of that year. Bin Laden moved to Kandahar in the winter of 1996. He soon endeared himself to the Taliban's leaders, particularly Mullah Mohammad Omar, who were enthralled by his talk of grand construction projects, very few of which were actually undertaken. Some reports have suggested that the Pakistani and Saudi intelligence services might have facilitated bringing bin Laden together with the Taliban. In any case, in a move aimed at winning the favours of the movement, bin Laden pledged a personal oath of loyalty, in the Islamic tradition of *bayat*, to Mullah Omar.[42]

Bin Laden's presence in Afghanistan was not opposed by the Saudis. Riyadh even rejected a Taliban offer to hand him over for prosecution over a November 1995 bombing in Riyadh, which killed six people, including five Americans. Bin Laden, in turn, succeeded in converting some key Taliban leaders to his cause. His success in forging a close relationship with Mullah Omar spared him from questioning by other Taliban leaders, some of whom privately criticised him. Mullah Omar provided residential compounds for bin Laden's family and close associates.[43] It was also in Afghanistan that bin Laden struck up an alliance with Egyptian radicals under the leadership of Ayman al-Zawahiri. During the 1990s, waves of Islamists from Chechnya, Central Asia, Chinese Turkistan, Southeast Asia and Europe joined the Arabs to form a truly global conglomerate.

The rise of Al-Qaeda coincided with the peak of Taliban military victories in Afghanistan in the summer of 1998. The Taliban had captured most of the north and central regions of Afghanistan by August of that year—the same month that Al-Qaeda carried out bombings of the US embassies in Kenya and Tanzania. Those attacks revealed a new aspect of the globalisation of Afghan wars to Western policymakers. They announced the consolidation of Osama bin Laden's international network of anti-Western Islamist militants, then widely known as Al-Qaeda. Bin Laden did not inform Taliban leaders about the plans to bomb the embassies or other major plots, but he did bankroll foreign jihadists who fought against the forces of Taliban nemesis Ahmad Shah Massoud.

A decade later, after being conceived in a sleepy Peshawar neighbourhood, Al-Qaeda had a somewhat formal organisational structure whose aims and objectives bin Laden and Zawahiri announced to the world from Khost, Afghanistan, in 1998:

> On that basis, and in compliance with Allah's order, we issue the following fatwa to all Muslims: To kill the Americans and their allies—civilians and military—is an individual duty for every Muslim who can do it in any country in which it is possible to do it, in order to liberate the al-Aqsa Mosque and the holy mosque [Mecca] from their grip, and in order for their armies to move out of all the lands of Islam, defeated and unable to threaten any Muslim. We—with Allah's help—call on every Muslim who believes in Allah and wishes to be rewarded to comply with Allah's order to kill the Americans and plunder their money wherever and whenever they find it. We also call on Muslim *ulema*, leaders, youths, and soldiers to launch the raid on Satan's US troops and the devil's supporters allying with them, and to displace those who are behind them so that they may learn a lesson.[44]

Although Al-Qaeda was based in Afghanistan, the Taliban had no control over the strategic and tactical direction of the group. In a September 1998 meeting with Prince Turki al-Faisal, the head of Saudi intelligence, Taliban leaders refused to surrender bin Laden. According to a Pakistani diplomat who was present, the meeting ended with the two sides exchanging accusations.[45] Soon afterwards, Riyadh recalled its ambassador from Kabul, but did not withdraw its recognition of the Taliban government. In the ensuing years, Washington pressured Pakistan's military—the ISI in particular—and the country's civilian leaders to roll back Al-Qaeda's activities, but little was delivered. The Taliban eventually became a target for American wrath, but Washington was still hesitant at the point of publicly declaring the movement an enemy of Washington. Even by early 2000, Omar reportedly wanted to 'get rid' of bin Laden because of the trouble he caused, but 'did not know how'.[46]

The Taliban and Al-Qaeda leaders were not of the same cloth. Indeed, the rural Pashtun mullahs of impoverished southern Afghanistan were polar opposites of the Arab leaders of Al-Qaeda, who came from wealthy backgrounds, were well-travelled and had secular educations. Senior Kandahari Taliban leaders had little contact with Arab jihadists, most of whom lived in Peshawar. Many of the Arabs had long-standing friendships with mujahedeen leaders, many of whom became the arch-foes of the Taliban. The Taliban sought to control Afghanistan—but the fate of the country was not even a secondary concern for Al-Qaeda, whose leaders were focused on revolution in their home countries.[47] The Taliban practised an extreme interpretation of Hanafi Islam inspired by Deobandism. Most Al-Qaeda leaders were followers of Takfiri Salafism.

The Taliban, however, extended moral and perhaps material support to various jihads outside Afghanistan. They recognised the independence declared by the Muslim separatists of the Russian republic of Chechnya in 2000. Due to their connections to the ISI, the movement also welcomed Pakistan-based militant groups fighting the Indian Army in Kashmir. These militants would use stints in the Afghan theatre to gain combat experience. However, contrary to Islamabad's wishes, Sunni extremists involved in anti-Shia attacks in eastern and southern Pakistan also found refuge with the Taliban. To counter Uzbekistan's support for the Afghan-Uzbek warlord Rashid Dostum, the Taliban offered an invitation to the leadership of the radical Islamic Movement of Uzbekistan in 1999, allowing it to set up bases in the northern Kunduz Province on the Tajik border.

Former senior Taliban leaders tell a nuanced story of their relationship with Al-Qaeda and foreign jihadists. Former Taliban envoy Mullah Abdul Salam Zaeef told me that bin Laden and other international jihadists had links with Afghan mujahedeen factions going back years. He said Islamists from Chechnya, Tajikistan and Uzbekistan, as well as from China and Pakistan, all had connections inside Afghanistan that predated the emergence of the Taliban.

Zaeef added that the Taliban accepted bin Laden's request for refuge after Jalalabad fell to the militants in 1996. 'Our major problem was that nobody, including Mullah [Mohammad Omar] Sahib, knew what the world's problem was with Osama bin Laden,' he said. 'We had no idea about his aims and objectives.' He added that most Taliban believed that because bin Laden had participated in the Afghan jihad, he was free to live in Afghanistan as a mujahid. 'The Taliban were simple people and had little understanding of the game being played on the global stage, so they accepted these people [as guests]. Once accepted, they became a cultural problem. Once you accepted somebody [as a guest], it is impossible to force him out of your home.'[48]

Muttawakil, the former Taliban foreign minister, had somewhat tenuous relations with many foreign jihadis. In thinly-veiled criticism of bin Laden, he wrote about how the Saudi fugitive known as 'Sheikh Osama' befriended the Taliban leadership by promising infrastructure, agricultural development and other reconstruction projects. 'When the Saudi authorities repeatedly requested controlling his activities, he was brought to Kandahar, but he never engaged in reconstruction and development activities,' he wrote. 'He talked about Islamic solidarity and always praised Afghan hospitality. He would elaborate on the popular anti-American themes in the Arab world.'[49]

According to Waheed Mozhdah, Muttawakil, after becoming foreign minister, ordered that Osama bin Laden's activities be curtailed. But his attempts to limit bin Laden's media statements divided the Taliban and earned him oppsition from the Arabs. 'Muttawakil was of the thinking that the Taliban took Osama and his followers as guests, but now they want to destroy the entire domicile [Afghan nation],' he wrote. 'Yet others, such as Tayeb Agha, special secretary of Mullah Omar, and [Mullah] Abdul-Hai Mutameen, supported Osama until Mullah [Amir Khan] Muttaqi went to Kandahar and tried to end the feud between Osama and Muttawakil.' The pragmatic Taliban camp ultimately lost the argument about the dangers of hosting Bin Laden and his jihadist brigade.[50]

Muttawakil engaged in numerous talks to negotiate the fate of bin Laden. He told me the Taliban floated numerous proposals, none of which were accepted by Washington, which demanded the handover of bin Laden. 'We proposed that an Islamic court of three Muslim countries should be formed to hear his case,' Muttawakil said. 'If convicted in that court, he should be punished. Another proposal was to put him under the supervision of the Organisation of Islamic Countries.'

But Muttawakil said that the Americans continued to insist that bin Laden be surrendered only to them. 'This was complicated because the Taliban government had no agreement of exchanging criminal suspects,' and was not even formally recognised by Washington, Muttawakil explained. 'The lack of relations between Afghanistan and the United States allowed this issue to linger and turn into a major problem.' Muttawakil said Taliban leaders found it impossible to expel bin Laden without solid grounds, because he and other Arabs had made sacrifices against the Soviet occupation. 'They were Muslims and never violated the laws of the Islamic Emirate,' he said.[51]

The gulf between the Taliban and the international community widened and ultimately led to the movement's demise as ruler of Afghanistan. The Taliban and its Northern Alliance enemies repeatedly ignored United Nations Security Council pleas and resolutions for a negotiated settlement of the conflict. Despite its battlefield victories and consolidation of control over most of Afghanistan, the UN never recognised the Taliban as a legitimate government, and the administration of President Burhannuddin Rabbani continued to occupy Afghanistan's seat at the UN. In addition, the Taliban's lack of diplomatic acumen, its controversial governance policies and frequent problems with UN and Western humanitarian aid agencies did not win the regime many friends.

A key turning point was UN Security Council Resolution 1193, passed on 28 August 1998. It reiterated that the international community was 'deeply concerned at the presence of terrorists in the territory of Afghanistan'.[52] Resolution 1214, adopted in December, singled out the Taliban. It said the Security Council was 'deeply disturbed by the continuing use of Afghan territory, especially areas controlled by the Taliban, for sheltering and training of terrorists and the planning of terrorist acts'.[53]

After failing to persuade the Taliban to change its behaviour, the UN Security Council imposed sanctions. In Resolution 1267, adopted in October 1999, the Security Council demanded the Taliban hand over Osama bin Laden over his role in the August 1998 US embassy bombings in Africa. The resolution established a committee, which is still functioning, to maintain a list of hundreds of individuals and entities associated with Al-Qaeda and the Taliban and to monitor sanctions against them. The resolution called on all member states to freeze the assets of, and deny travel and transit to, individuals named in the list. It also called for a complete ban on selling arms or providing technical assistance to them.[54]

In Resolution 1333 of December 2000, sanctions were further tightened. The resolution called for a complete ban on selling weapons to the Taliban. In a thinly-veiled message to Islamabad, it also called on foreign governments to 'withdraw any of their officials, agents, advisers and military personnel employed by contract or other arrangement present in Afghanistan to advise the Taliban on military or related security matters'. The resolution banned all flights to and from Afghanistan and called on all states to 'close immediately and completely all Taliban offices in their territories'.[55]

The 11 September 2001 attacks in the United States sealed the Taliban's fate. In a televised address, US President George Bush promised to punish the 'evil' behind the attacks. Referring to the Taliban, he said,

'We will make no distinction between the terrorists who committed these acts and those who harbor them.'[56] In Kandahar, the Taliban reaction was subdued. An official statement called for investigation of the attacks and urged Washington 'not to put Afghanistan into more misery because our people have suffered so much'.[57]

The United States began bombing Afghanistan on 7 October 2001, and the Taliban's grip on power soon began to waver. In mid-November, Mazar-e-Sharif was the first major city to fall to US-backed forces. By early December, the Taliban had been routed across Afghanistan.

Resolution 1378, adopted by the Security Council on 14 November 2001, called on all Afghan factions—excluding the Taliban—to form a 'broad-based, multiethnic and fully representative' government.[58] An agreement on a transitional post-Taliban administration was reached during UN-sponsored negotiations in Bonn, Germany. Soon thereafter, the Security Council authorised 'an International Security Assistance Force to assist the Afghan Interim Authority in the maintenance of security in Kabul and its surrounding areas'.[59] The transitional administration led by a southern Pashtun tribal leader, Hamid Karzai, took an oath of office in December. The Taliban, it seemed, had been relegated to history.

PART TWO

PAKISTAN

4

WAR IN WAZIRISTAN

Summer lingers through September in Wana, the major town in western Pakistan's South Waziristan Agency, or tribal district. Waziris live much like their ancestors did hundreds of years ago. Farmers, small traders and their families rise early with the first *azan*, or call to mandatory Islamic prayer. The morning is filled with routines, with residents conducting business or performing manual labour inside high-walled mud houses or the region's vast apple orchards. Then it is time for afternoon prayers.

A favourite activity for men is to visit the Adda Bazaar, located at the opening of the narrow gorge at the eastern entrance of the valley. It is a place of square shops built of mud, irregular rubbish-strewn streets and haphazardly-built concrete shopping centres. It's what passes for modernity in this remote Pashtun region. The hustle and bustle of the bazaar reflects the economic transformation of the region's Wazir Pashtun clans, who began to make money from their agriculture production only a generation ago.

On 10 September 2001, I went to Adda Bazaar to search for a local mullah who had just returned from fighting with the Taliban in Afghanistan. Local conversations were dominated by the previous day's attack in Takhar Province on Ahmad Shah Massoud, the Afghan mujahedeen commander whose resistance in northern Afghanistan had prevented the Taliban from extending control over the whole of the country. Massoud's condition was still unclear on 10 September but most people understood he had been severely wounded in a suicide bombing. After asking a few shopkeepers, I was directed to the Taliban mullah I was searching for. Let's call him Mullah Manan.

A tall, well-built figure with a lion-like mane of hair, Manan sported a pistol holster and bandolier under his waistcoat. We sat in the back of a darkened shop, sipping milky tea. After a suitable interval, I asked for his help with a research project. He seemed sceptical about my motives, but—after I pledged to keep the information private—he offered the name of a contact to help with my project. That task out of the way, we then discussed the situation in Afghanistan. In a warning of things to come, he told me, 'We have taken care of Massoud, and we will soon come to Pakistan to implement true Islam there.'

Manan's words continue to haunt me when I look back at the events that would soon overtake Waziristan and other Pashtun regions.[1]

Rise of the Pakistani Taliban

As the Taliban regime collapsed under American bombing in late 2001, senior Kandahari Taliban leaders and the bulk of the Afghan Taliban regime headed to Quetta, the capital of Pakistan's south-western Balochistan Province. During the war against the Soviets in the 1980s, Quetta and other Pashtun regions in the province had served as sanctuaries for the mujahedeen.

Wounded Al-Qaeda members, their organisation in disarray, were directed by the Taliban leadership and Pakistani sympathisers to shelters in Pakistan's FATA. Al-Qaeda had battled US forces in the mountains of Tora Bora, in eastern Nangarhar and Shahi Kot in south-eastern Paktia Province, before streaming into Waziristan through the Tochi and Gomal passes. Contrary to perceptions that the Pakistani Taliban movement emerged after the 11 September attacks, the movement was in fact already active in Afghanistan and only returned home after the demise of the Kabul regime. A few budding Taliban commanders were natives of Waziristan. Most were members of Pakistani Islamist political parties and extremist organisations, or had joined the Afghan Taliban movement as individuals.

Waziristan received many of Al-Qaeda's Arab leaders, as well as members of allied extremist movements from the former Soviet Union and China. Some Taliban commanders who hailed from the region had already laid the groundwork for welcoming their comrades and their

Al-Qaeda guests. The remote, nearly 12,000-square-kilometre region is administratively divided into the South Waziristan and North Waziristan tribal districts. The militants found it easy to hide among the region's more than 1.5 million residents, most of whom lived in small villages spread out among deserts, oak and pine forests, towering mountains and deep ravines. The extremists also saw great potential among its residents as recruits.

Pakistan's government failed to deploy troops to block or arrest Al-Qaeda and Taliban fighters as they retreated into Waziristan. Pakistani forces were deployed in the Khyber and Kurram tribal districts, across the border from Tora Bora, and locals helped troops arrest hundreds of Al-Qaeda members in Kurram. But the lack of a significant Pakistani military presence left open a back door for extremists to establish themselves in the FATA. Some Al-Qaeda leaders crossed undetected into the Mohmand tribal district, travelling north of Tora Bora and across the Kabul river in the Lal Pur district into Pakistan.

Pakistan's government publically accepted praise for being a 'frontline ally' of Washington, and denied turning a blind eye to Al-Qaeda's recuperation in its own backyard. But the military regime never made a genuine effort to persuade the Pakistani people that it was serious about its proclaimed alliance with the US. Its policy can be described as a classic game of doubletalk, in which it sent out different messages to different audiences in hopes of capitalising on the ignorance of both, and gambling that its deception would not be noticed by anyone in a position to do anything about it.

By early 2002, South Waziristan, the largest and most populous of the seven tribal districts, had become a refuge for thousands of Arabs and Central Asian militants. These regions, called agencies in the official parlance, were familiar to the Afghan Taliban. Years of migration, cross-border tribal ties and the fact that most Taliban cadres had been educated in Pakistani madrasas since the 1980s, meant that Afghan Taliban networks were deeply enmeshed in the social fabric. Madrasa networks in the FATA, the Pashtun regions and the rest of Pakistan provided a constant stream of recruits during the years the Taliban held power in Afghanistan. The relatively meagre international military presence in Afghanistan, combined with Islamabad's deliberate blind eye to extremist safe havens on its soil, helped Al-Qaeda recover in the Pashtun borderlands.

Islamabad's policy of denial, however, would eventually collapse under intense international pressure, and Pakistan would be forced to confront the extremists militarily. The first sizeable military operation began in the spring of 2004, after two failed assassination attempts on Pakistani President General Pervez Musharraf in December 2003.[2] Pakistan's initial military operations only galvanised local support for the extremists. The militants were becoming more powerful than the tribes and the local administration, and a new kind of order was on the rise in the tribal areas.

For most of 2004, fighting was limited to villages around Wana and the Shakai Valley to the north.[3] The population of these areas is dominated by the Ahmadzai Wazir tribe. Fighting intensified and expanded after the June 2004 killing of Nek Muhammad, the leader of the Taliban in Wana. Pakistani military pressure around Wana eventually forced a significant number of foreign militants to flee to the neighbouring Mehsud region. By the end of 2004, the war had moved into this mountainous region mainly populated by the Mehsud tribe.

The shift of the battle theatre opened the door for Abdullah Mehsud and Baitullah Mehsud to emerge as the new leaders of the Pakistani Taliban. Like Nek Muhammad, they had gained notice fighting for the Afghan Taliban. Abdullah Mehsud, the *nom de guerre* of Noor Alam, had even spent twenty-five months in the US military prison at Guantanamo Bay, Cuba, after being detained on the battlefield in Afghanistan in late 2001. In an apparent blunder, American authorities had decided to release him from Guantanamo without even establishing his real identity.

In 2006, fighting moved into North Waziristan. By this time, Hafiz Gul Bahadar and Maulana Sadiq Noor had taken over as leaders of the Pakistani Taliban. Like their comrades in South Waziristan, both men had fought for the Taliban in Afghanistan. These new Taliban leaders had not been central to politics and social life in Waziristan before the beginning of the Pakistani offensive.

In the initial days of the conflict, the objectives of the Taliban were straightforward: to secure the region as a base camp for the war in Afghanistan and protect the mujahedeen—a euphemism for the Al-Qaeda-linked Arabs and affiliated Central Asians. However, the rapid pace of events, an increased international focus on the region, regional affinities and Islamabad's policies combined to ultimately divide the

Pakistani Taliban into two distinct currents. Personal differences, economic interests and turf battles also played a role, as did declared or discreet alliances with Al-Qaeda, the Islamic Movement of Uzbekistan, and the Pakistani intelligence services.

The split resulted in a majority of Pakistani Taliban groups uniting in late 2007 in a formal organisation, the Tehreek-e Taliban Pakistan (TTP), Urdu for Movement of the Pakistani Taliban. Its leadership and majority of its cadres were from Waziristan, but it attracted followers and allies from across FATA, the neighbouring Khyber Pakhtunkhwa Province, the eastern Punjab Province and the southern Sindh Province. The TTP, while not hostile to the Afghan Taliban, dissociated itself from the battle there against NATO-led forces and the internationally-backed government. It absorbed cadres of anti-Shia Sunni extremists groups, such as Lashkar-e Jhangvi from the eastern Punjab Province, and adopted a strategy of attacking Shia.[4] It also struck an alliance with the Islamic Movement of Uzbekistan (IMU), which it began sheltering after IMU members were driven out of Wana in the spring of 2007.

At the zenith of its power, the TTP's extended network sometimes controlled large swaths of territory in north-western Pakistan. Baitullah Mehsud, the founding leader of the TTP, appeared on *Time* magazine's 'Time 100' list of the world's most influential people in 2008. But his August 2009 death in a US drone strike precipitated the TTP's decline. It began losing territory and increasingly faced the wrath of the Pakistani state and public for carrying out attacks against military and civilian targets.

Outside observers have argued that tribal divisions are the key factor behind splits among militant factions in Waziristan and elsewhere. But a faction's ties to Islamabad and non-Pakistani militant groups are often more decisive. Maulvi Nazir Ahmad, for example, began to distance himself from other IMU-allied militants in Wana in 2006. In the spring of 2007, his group launched a bloody confrontation with the IMU, aided by Pakistani special forces who helped drive the Central Asians into central Waziristan. Similarly, the Pakistani military encouraged Zianuddin Mehsud, Taseel Khan and Turkistan Bhittani to organise a network against the TTP in South Waziristan in 2008. The group was instrumental in driving the TTP back from the Tank and Dera Ismail Khan districts on Waziristan's border, despite the assassination of Zianuddin Mehsud in 2009. Many more members of this network were killed in subsequent years.

In North Waziristan, Hafiz Gul Bahadar and his deputy Sadiq Noor ostensibly honour peace accords and have avoided confronting the Pakistani military. Attempts to reconcile these groups with the TTP, or to forge an alliance of all Taliban groups in Waziristan and the tribal areas, have so far failed. In early 2009, the TTP attempted to join up with Hafiz Gul Bahadar and Maulvi Nazir. 'Allah Almighty directs all Muslims to unite against the infidels,' read a pamphlet widely distributed in Waziristan in the spring 2009. 'Ordinary Muslims and the commanders whose leaders are the Commander of the Faithful Mullah Mohammad Omar and Sheikh Osama bin Laden should unite to humiliate the infidels whose leaders are Obama, Zardari and Karzai.' The alliance fell apart after a few months.

Maulvi Nazir Ahmad and Hafiz Gul Bahadar did not raise a gun against the military when Islamabad's troops moved into central Waziristan to counter the TTP in the autumn of 2009. By the end of the year, the Rah-e Nijat (Path of Salvation) operation had expelled the TTP from most regions of Mehsud that it had controlled. But the operation also forced nearly 400,000 Mehsud residents to leave their homes and move into neighbouring districts of Khyber Pakhtunkhwa. The Pakistani military consolidated its control over Wana and the surrounding Ahmadzai Wazir regions by adopting a policy of tolerance toward Maulvi Nazir Ahmad's faction. The group co-operated with local elders to establish a modicum of peace in Wana. The Pakistani military also fulfilled a long-standing demand of the Ahmadzai Waziris by building a new road connecting Wana to the neighbouring district of Tank, bypassing Mehsud territory.

Ideology and Paths of Action

Many leaders of the Pakistani Taliban began their careers as members of the Jamiat Ulema-e Islam, Fazlur Rehman Group (JUI-F). This Deobandi Islamist political party has had a mixed record of electoral success and failure in western Pakistan's Pashtun regions. But it has consistently stayed away from violence, unlike other Deobandi groups such as Sipah-e Sahaba Pakistan (Army of the Companions of the Prophet in Pakistan), which has exploited sectarian divides to rise in influence.

In North Waziristan, Hafiz Gul Bahadar headed the student wing of the JUI-F in 2000. Wali-ur Rehman Mehsud, head of the TTP in South

Waziristan, was also affiliated with the party before he joined the Taliban in 2004. When they joined up with the Taliban, both men and many of their fellow leaders embraced the anti-Shia Deobandi extremism that had been advocated by radicals in the eastern Punjab and southern Sindh provinces, where some of these leaders were educated in hard-line madrasas. Significantly, many Pakistani Taliban have also enthusiastically embraced Al-Qaeda's Takfiri-Salafism—something the Taliban in Afghanistan always resisted. A TTP pamphlet from 2010 reads:

> With Allah's blessing, the hereafter of the Taliban will be blessed because who can be better devoted to Allah than those who are willing to sacrifice their necks (lives) for Allah. In this world our ultimate aim of '*sharia* or martyrdom' is now focused on the destruction of Pakistani rulers and army. The world knows that the military, intelligence agencies and the so called democratic players are the real hurdles in implementing *sharia* in Pakistan. We want to implement the *sharia* in place of the old Satanic system now in place. If you ever want to build a new home instead of the old one you have first demolish it. Destruction is a prerequisite for [re]construction. And that is why we first have to root out the old evil democratic system to realise the dream of implementing the *sharia*.[5]

The Taliban in Waziristan have not produced a large amount of literature. But what is available offers important clues about the ideology of its various factions, their vision of society and plans for action. In most tribal regions, fighting criminality has been a central plank of the Taliban strategy of winning support among local people. But this has sometimes been complicated by the criminal links of a sizeable number of Taliban cadres. In some cases, these factions had taken over entire criminal cartels.

In September 2006, Taliban groups in North Waziristan announced the formation of a joint security office in Miram Shah,[6] the administrative centre of the tribal district. The office was created in the wake of a surge of drive-by assassinations of tribal leaders by masked gunmen. 'We have completely banned the movement of masked people,' said a statement by the *amir* and *shura* of the North Waziristan Mujahedeen. 'If anybody sees a masked person, they should immediately contact our office. If you see that they are bothering people or trying to kill people, feel free to shoot them dead. We will be responsible.'[7] When TTP fighters were pushed into North Waziristan by the Pakistani military operation Rah-e Nijat, TTP leader Hakimullah Mehsud issued a warning to his followers against participating in criminal activities. 'I order all the mujahedeen of the Tehreek-e Taliban Pakistan to refrain from kidnappings, troublemaking, and interference in local affairs and other criminal activities in North Waziristan,' he wrote. 'Anybody not following these orders will be punished.'[8]

One important hallmark of the Taliban's rise in Waziristan was the keenness of factions to assume the functions of the state and tribe. This ambition was aided by the decline of the influence of Pakistani government administrators, known as political agents, and tribal elders. These administrators and elders had together arbitrated local disputes in *jirga* councils. Clans would often seek to counter crime waves through the declaration of a *teenga*, or binding decision, issued during a *jirga*.

The Taliban sought to assert their control over social life by issuing edicts. 'It is forbidden to display inappropriate pictures, watch movies [or listen to] music in the bazaars,' read a 2006 statement by the Mujahedeen Waziristan. 'We are directing all barbers to refrain from displaying pictures of actors and actresses in their shops. And they should also refrain from shaving or trimming beards. Giving locals a military style haircut is also forbidden. Violations will be punished in accordance with *sharia*.' The decree also included a stern warning for those considering joining Pakistani security institutions: 'Employment in Pakistani military, air force and related institutions is forbidden for everybody. Violators will be punished by death.'[9] In August, 2008, the Taliban in North Waziristan banned the selling of wheat flour to Afghan buyers. 'Vehicles violating this order will be seized and they will be punished with fines,' read a Taliban announcement.[10]

Regulating the arms trade was also a major Taliban priority. A major arms market was established in Miram Shah in the 1980s, during the anti-Soviet war, and it continued to thrive following the US-led intervention. 'We are informing all the residents of North Waziristan to stop trading in arms,' warned a 2007 Taliban announcement. 'They should stop selling weapons to [rival groups in neighbouring Kurram] in the name of [fighting the] Shias and [in support of the] Sunnis. [They should stop selling weapons to] Lashkar-e Islam and Ansarul Islam [in Khyber] and groups in Darra Adam Khel and Dera Bugti [in Balochistan]. Traders violating this policy will be severely punished through the confiscation of their vehicles and arms. Taking weapons to other regions weakens our strength and helps America.'[11] A decree banning the movement of heavy weapons out of Waziristan and encouraging their import was issued in September 2006.

Some Taliban groups used unique methods to raise revenue. The Mehsud Taliban required a 'donation' of 5,000 Pakistani rupees (about $90) from men who worked as drivers in Gulf nations when they returned to visit their families. Lower-paid overseas labourers who returned for visits were expected to pay 3,000 rupees ($50).[12]

While most Afghan Taliban literature is in Pashto prose, Pakistani Taliban literature is in Urdu. It is an unexpected choice, given that Urdu is primarily understood by those exposed to the Pakistani public school system. Most Taliban in Waziristan are local Pashtuns and few have ever been to schools. Their use of Urdu suggests the influence of Pakistani extremist groups.

Mullah Mohammad Omar enjoys the nominal status as leader of all Taliban in Pakistan. But the Afghan Taliban, particularly remnants of the Taliban regime from the Loy Kandahar region, have no tactical or strategic control over the Pakistani Taliban. In contrast to the Afghan Taliban's focus on Afghanistan, large segments of the Pakistani Taliban are devoted to Al-Qaeda's global jihad. Pride in ethnic affiliation, and being seen as part of a national struggle, are anathema to the Pakistanis. 'Remember, we are not fighting for the Pashtuns, the Punjabis, the Uzbeks or the Arabs,' the TTP said in a statement defending its spring 2011 killing of Colonel Imam, a former Pakistani intelligence agent. 'Praise be to Allah, we are purified from the contamination and filth of nationalism. We advocate the unity of the [Muslim] nation.'[13]

The Haqqanis

Pakistan's relationship with Mawlawi Jalaluddin Haqqani predates the communist coup and the Soviet invasion of Afghanistan. Haqqani was initially part of the 'contacts' Pakistani officials maintained among Pashtuns across the Durand Line. Haqqani was among a select number of Islamists that Islamabad encouraged to counter Afghan President Sardar Mohammad Daud Khan's secular Pashtun nationalism. He was educated in the Haqqania madrasa near Peshawar, which is thought to have provided him with insight into the life and politics of Pakistan. Haqqani emerged as one of the most effective mujahedeen commanders in the 1980s.

His base in Miram Shah made his ascendency possible. Despite his limited tribal ties to the region—few members of his Zadran tribe live in North Waziristan—Islamabad allowed the Haqqanis to build a formidable power base that influenced social, political and economic life there. Haqqani organised the Manba-ul Uloom madrasa near Miram Shah and patronised a network of madrasas across North Waziristan. These madrasas provided recruits for his training camps and gave him clout in local politics, in which mullahs played a prominent role. Miram Shah was relatively secluded, but easy road access to the town from major Pakistani cities made it a desirable base from which to launch covert operations in Afghanistan. In the 1980s, Miram Shah became a major hub for the arms trade, flush with weapons provided by Washington and Riyadh and distributed to the Afghan mujahedeen by the Pakistani Inter Services Intelligence Agency (ISI).

Haqqani, a fluent Arabic speaker, built lasting alliances with Arab volunteers. He made frequent trips to the Gulf to collect donations and married an Arab woman from the United Arab Emirates. Osama bin Laden became a friend and patron who built an extensive tunnel complex called the Massada al-Ansar, or Lion's Den, for him in Paktia Province's Jaji district in the mid-1980s. Bin Laden got his first exposure to combat under Haqqani's tutelage during a major Red Army offensive in south-eastern Afghanistan in 1987. Haqqani was a favourite of the ISI and was cheered on by Washington. He visited the Reagan White House and was called 'goodness personified' by Texas Congressman Charlie Wilson.[14] As Washington and Riyadh showered him with dollars, he acquired business interests in North Waziristan and expanded his local influence.

Haqqani maintained his Miram Shah base through the 1990s, when he served as justice minister in one of the mujahedeen cabinets. Miram Shah also hosted training camps for Pakistani militant groups fighting the insurgency in Kashmir. The training extended to sites controlled by Haqqani inside Afghanistan. His Zhawar Killi camp in south-eastern Khost Province was targeted by US cruise missiles in August 1998. The attacks were retaliation for Al-Qaeda's bombing of US embassies in Africa. But it was Kashmiri and Pakistani fighters who died in the American strikes.

After the Taliban seized control of Kabul, Haqqani's position as tribal affairs minister in the regime offered him access to potential recruits in the tribal areas. Many leaders of Taliban groups in Waziristan either fought under him or were acquainted with him. The region, unlike South Waziristan, is relatively easy to travel to from the major cities of Khyber

Pakhtunkhwa, and is a gateway to the Loya Paktia region composed of the Paktia, Paktika and Khost provinces of south-eastern Afghanistan. Its geographic features, which offer secure sanctuary and access to population centres in both Pakistan and Afghanistan, have ensured that North Waziristan remains a region from where militants launch attacks in south-eastern Afghanistan and even regions closer to Kabul.[15]

After 11 September 2001, Haqqani reportedly visited Islamabad, where he was introduced to Western officials as a 'moderate Taliban' by Pakistan's military government. But after the American bombing that toppled the Taliban began, Haqqani predicted a long fight. 'Even if the Americans or others manage to [capture Afghan cities] and a new government is installed there, we will not accept it,' he told a Pakistani newspaper.[16] 'We will retreat to the mountains and begin a long guerrilla war to reclaim our pure land from infidels and free our country again like we did against the Soviets.'

As the Taliban regime collapsed, Haqqani returned to Miram Shah. He was unsuccessful in overtures to reach an accommodation with the interim administration of Afghan President Hamid Karzai.[17] But the Haqqani Network was instrumental in providing shelter and escape routes to retreating Al-Qaeda fighters. American special forces attempted to target him, with Islamabad's help. But he was alerted and escaped well before he could have come under bombardment.[18]

After the initial rounds of fighting in South and North Waziristan, the Haqqanis appeared to be well positioned to play a central role in the revival of the Taliban in both Afghanistan and Pakistan. The network spearheaded the neo-Taliban insurgency in Afghanistan, and exerted a profound influence over the Taliban in Waziristan. The network issued a directive in 2006 that included the following decrees:

1. The Emirat-e Islami [Islamic Emirate of Afghanistan] has decided that the Wazir and Mehsud tribes of South Waziristan and the mujahedeen of North Waziristan should follow the orders of Mawlawi Jalaluddin Haqqani.
2. All mujahedeen fighters and commanders should follow the policies of the Islamic Emirate.
3. The policy of the Islamic Emirate is to avoid fighting with Pakistan. All *ansar* [locals] and *muhajireen* [foreigners] associated with the Islamic Emirate are directed not to fight against Pakistan because it only benefits the Americans.

4. The mujahedeen of South Waziristan should constitute an economic commission. They should collect revenues and deposit it in the finances of the Emirate. After consultation the Amir [leader] should order its distribution to deserving people.
5. A committee of pious *ulema* (religious leaders) and trustworthy people should be constituted to collect revenues from people without resorting to violence and force. These revenues should be deposited in the finances of the Emirate to ensure supplies to the mujahedeen.
6. The appointed *amirs* should perform their duties after mutual consultations.
7. All mujahedeen should follow the path of the Prophet [Muhammad]. They should encourage newcomers joining the mujahedeen ranks to do the same. This will help them in attracting Allah's help for achieving victory.
8. A consultative body comprised of *ulema* of the Wazirs and Mehsuds of South Waziristan and North Waziristan should be formed to avoid problems and to ensure co-operation when needed.
9. All *amirs* in Waziristan should maintain coordination and consult with their respective leaders [the Haqqanis] while performing their work.[19]

The document, whose intended audience was jihadist circles in Waziristan, suggests Haqqani was grooming his followers to be the leaders of a future Islamic emirate in Waziristan. These efforts were tantamount to a move to establish a parallel state in Pakistan. Yet Haqqani's influence continued to rise with Islamabad's quiet acquiescence. The document was issued before the ceasefire that ultimately led to a peace agreement between North Waziristan militants and Islamabad in September 2006.

Around this time, old age and ailments began to confine Jalaluddin Haqqani to bed. His son Sirajuddin Haqqani soon assumed the leadership role and begin running what Western coalition forces in Afghanistan termed the 'Haqqani Network', with the help of his father's senior aides.[20] Under the son's leadership, the Haqqani Network forged even deeper ties with Al-Qaeda extremists. Former Pakistani military dictator General Pervez Musharraf's closure of many Kashmiri training camps by 2006 forced jihadi veterans to relocate to the familiar territory of North Waziristan, where they further cemented the bond between Al-Qaeda and Pakistani extremists.

Sirajuddin Haqqani, born to Jalaluddin's Afghan wife and raised in North Waziristan, is called *Khalifa* in jihadist circles, signifying his status as his father's successor. He has regularly adjudicated disputes among the Taliban factions in Waziristan and elsewhere, and is part of the overall Taliban leadership council. As a mark of his influence, Sirajuddin Haqqani has even helped organise talks between the Pakistani military and the TTP. The Haqqanis run the jihadist market in Waziristan where locals, Arabs, Central Asians and the Punjabi extremists have set up shops. Perhaps, some say, the market is even leased to the Haqqanis by the Pakistani state.

Despite pressure from Washington, Islamabad has for years resisted taking serious action against the jihadist conglomerate in North Waziristan. Even as the Pakistani military carried out military operations targeting extremists in six other tribal agencies, North Waziristan stood as a known jihadist safe haven. In the case of South Waziristan, most TTP cadres fled the conflict to shelters in North Waziristan. To the surprise of local tribal leaders, the military did not pursue them into North Waziristan.

Islamabad resisted mounting a large-scale offensive, even after the Taliban issued repeated public statements declaring the 2006 peace accord to be dead. Leaked American diplomatic cables reveal that senior Pashtun politicians warned American diplomats that the Pakistani military was treating the Haqqanis 'separately' from other militants. 'The Haqqani family,' Pashtun politician Afrasiab Khattak told the American consul general in Peshawar, 'has already moved out of North Waziristan.' Khattak told Consul General Lynn Tracy in July 2009 that 'part of the Haqqani family lived in a rented house on the Kohat Road on the southern side of Peshawar. The other half is living in a house owned by the Haqqani family in the Rawalpindi cantonment.'[21]

It is important to note that Islamabad perceives the Haqqanis as a strategic asset to be deployed against the influence of arch-enemy India in Afghanistan. US and Afghan officials have blamed the Haqqani Network for attacks against Indian interests in Afghanistan. They point to the 7 July 2008 bombing of the Indian Embassy in Kabul as a sign of the Haqqani Network's leading role in targeting Indian government installations and construction projects in Afghanistan. The Kabul bombing killed fifty-four people, including the Indian military attaché.[22]

Pakistan also views the Haqqanis as a 'government in a box' for the all-important Loya Paktia region in south-eastern Afghanistan. Haqqani dominance in the region forestalls the re-emergence of an Afghan military officer corps there. Historically, the Loya Paktia tribes acted as surrogate armies for the Durrani Afghan kings, and later manned the officer corps of the royal and communist militaries.[23] In a rare interview, the usually media-shy former ISI chief Javed Ashraf Qazi summarised Islamabad's posture, saying on a popular Pakistani television show in 2011, 'The Haqqanis are fighting in Afghanistan. They are fighting to expel the foreign forces from Afghanistan. This is their right, because they are fighting their battle of independence. The Haqqani group has never taken any action inside Pakistan. They are not our enemies.'[24]

A New Abode for Al-Qaeda

It was Al-Qaeda, however, which radically transformed Waziristan. Al-Qaeda's retreat into Pakistan was not organised. Hundreds of foot soldiers who had hastily escaped the bombing in Tora Bora flooded into Shia villages around Parachinar. There, villagers arrested them and handed them over to the local administration. Many key Al-Qaeda leaders, however, escaped to Waziristan and soon began to regroup and plan attacks from Pakistani cities. Some of these figures were captured when President General Musharraf forced his intelligence service to co-operate with the Americans. Abu Zubaydah was the first major Al-Qaeda figure to be captured when he was arrested in the eastern city of Faisalabad in March 2002. His arrest was followed by the September 2002 arrest in Karachi of Ramzi Bin al-Shibh, a key conspirator in the organisation of the 11 September 2001 attacks.

The next big catch came in March 2003, when alleged 11 September mastermind Khalid Sheikh Muhammad was arrested in the garrison city of Rawalpindi. These arrests pushed Al-Qaeda to look to Waziristan as a preferred hideout because of its seclusion and impregnability to outsiders. The Arabs, in particular, found Taliban factions convenient to use as a local protection force. Abu Kasha, an Iraqi jihadist, had gone so far as to adopt a semi-native lifestyle that included an allied local force and his involvement in adjudicating local disputes around Mir Ali in North Waziristan.

Al-Qaeda's internal communications mentioned Waziristan as the group's headquarters in 2005. 'You send messengers from your end to Waziristan so that they meet with the brothers of the leadership, and the rational and experienced people and the sheikhs here,' Al-Qaeda leader

Atiyah Abd al-Rahman wrote to Abu Musab al-Zarqawi, the leader of its Iraqi branch, in a December 2005 letter.[25] In the years to come, Al-Qaeda would strengthen its influence in the region. The following passage gives an indication of how the radical outsiders envisioned transforming Waziristan:

The afterlife of the residents of the place chosen by Allah for jihad is blessed. And the doors of hallowed blessings in this world and the next (afterlife) are open up for them. Waziristan is a good example for us. Until recently this land was unknown to the world. But today 'Waziristan' dominates global radio, TV and newspaper headlines. This is not limited to Islamic world. Even the leaders of the infidel world pronounce 'Waziristan' in strange accents. The residents of this fortunate land are blessed with helping the jihad in this modern age. They challenged the mighty evils of the world to maintain a strong protective cover around the mujahedeen from around the world. They endangered their lives, families and properties to keep the flame of jihad alive.

It is the blessing of Jihad that this obscure land is now considered the strongest fort of Islam and a global bastion of jihad. It was once known for its ignorance, *bid'a*,[26] thievery, robberies, murder, pillage and drugs. *Alhamdullillah* (Praise be to Allah) the *muhajireen* (refugee)[27] mujahedeen and their families has been living in this land for the past eight years. During this time this tribal society has been able to closely observe these *muhajireen* men and women. This has enabled them to study their character and benefit from their knowledge and wisdom. It has enabled them to observe their dedication and benefit from their company.

The *muhajireen* too had been able to closely observe the *ansar* [local hosts].[28] Their seclusion from the evil civilisation of the cities has helped them to preserve the high qualities of generosity, courage, simplicity, straightforwardness, honour and dignity. The combination of the knowledge and piety of the *muhajireen* with the natural instincts of the *ansar* gave birth to a new Islamic society. Although this society is not completely devoid of human drawbacks, the blessed union of the *muhajireen* and the *ansar* has turned this land into a state of peace. This is marked contrast to the situation before the arrival of the [Al-Qaeda] mujahedeen, the region was known for insecurity, thievery and robberies.[29] Travelling after dark was considered dangerous and the tribal infighting was the norm. There is so much peace in Waziristan that that there are no incidents of theft or robbery even without the presence of the 'police' and 'sensitive (intelligence) agencies'. *Alhamdullillah*, we have many examples before us that drug peddlers, robber and rebellious characters of yesterday have turned into a mujahedeen in the path of Allah. It is the blessing of jihad that most of the *bid'a* and *shirk*[30] has ceased to exist in this region.[31]

Al-Qaeda's consolidation in the Tribal Areas gave it the opportunity to renew its plots to create mayhem in the West. A majority of the serious plots targeting Europe and North America since 2004 have been traced to Pakistan. Many of the perpetrators of these acts were either trained in the Tribal Areas or visited the region to receive Al-Qaeda's blessing. The most significant attack in the West since 11 September 2001, was the 7 July 2005 transport system bombings in London. Some of those bombers received training and direction from Al-Qaeda during visits to the FATA. In subsequent years, plots targeting Britain, continental Europe, Australia, the United States and Canada would be linked to the region.[32] Most of these plots were unsuccessful, but they showcased Al-Qaeda's ability to rebound from its losses in Afghanistan.

The apparent impunity enjoyed by the Haqqani Network in North Waziristan, and the control the TTP exerted over most of South Waziristan before 2010, effectively turned the zone into a global militant headquarters. The region also attracted new recruits from the West. The 2008 attempted attack on Barcelona's metro system was allegedly directed by the TTP, which trained one of its plotters.[33] In 2010, Najibullah Zazi, an Afghan citizen and permanent US legal resident, admitted to receiving bomb-making training from Al-Qaeda in Waziristan. He was planning to attack the New York subway system.[34] Faisal Shahzad, a US citizen of Pakistani origin, attempted to blow up a sport utility vehicle in New York's Times Square on May Day 2010. He, too, was trained by the TTP in Waziristan. The TTP sent him cash to orchestrate the attack.[35]

One example of the extent of TTP collaboration with Al-Qaeda is the case of Humam Khalil Abu Mulal al-Balawi. A Jordanian doctor and triple agent, al-Balawi smuggled a suicide bomb vest onto a remote US Central Intelligence Agency outpost in south-eastern Afghanistan's Khost Province. He detonated the bomb on 30 December 2009, killing his Jordanian handler, five US intelligence agents and two guards. Al-Balawi had been living with Al-Qaeda members in Miram Shah in the run-up to the attack. In a video appearance with TTP leader Hakimullah Mehsud recorded before the attack, Al-Balawi vowed to avenge the 2009 killing of Pakistani Taliban leader Baitullah Mehsud in a US drone strike.[36]

The Pakistani Taliban has not been alone among Pakistani groups signing on to the concept of global jihad. Evidence shows that Pakistani extremist groups active in Kashmir, such as the Harakatul Jihadul Islami, the anti-Shia Lashakr-e Jhangvi[37] and even the India-focused Lashkar-e Taiba have extensively networked with Al-Qaeda, relying on the Arabs for inspiration and, in some cases, resources.

Another significant development in Waziristan has been Al-Qaeda's close alliance with the Islamic Movement of Uzbekistan and the Islamic Jihad Union (IJU). This has raised the spectre of the birth of a pan-Turkic Al-Qaeda. The IMU has been transformed from a small band of militants focused on overthrowing Uzbekistan's dictatorship to a more ambitious organisation seeking to carry out operations in other former Soviet states and Europe. 'We are one with Sheikh Osama [bin Laden], Taliban, [and] Al-Qaeda,' IMU leader Tahir Yuldash told supporters in Waziristan in an undated video before his death in 2009. 'After taking over Afghanistan and Pakistan, one part of us will go to India and another part will go toward the CIS [Commonwealth of Independent States, an alliance of former Soviet states].'

IMU cadres were nearly wiped out in the American bombing of Afghanistan in the winter of 2001. Faced with bombardment, they sought refuge across the border in north-west Pakistan. Pakistani officials say the IMU and its splinter groups are deeply enmeshed with Al-Qaeda and constitute the majority of its foot soldiers in FATA. The May 2005 Andijon massacre, in which Uzbek troops opened fire on mass street protests against the government, provided a recruitment boost for the IMU and the jihadist movement in general. The deaths of hundreds, possibly thousands, of civilians in the largest city of the Ferghana Valley, which traverses Uzbekistan, Tajikistan and Kyrgyzstan, sent shockwaves across the region.

Afterwards, large numbers of Central Asian would-be militants came to Waziristan. But they were resented by locals, who accused them of engaging in kidnapping, targeted assassinations and other criminal enterprises.[38] In the spring of 2007, the IMU suffered a debilitating blow when Mullah Nazir Ahmad's Taliban faction in Wana opened an offensive against the group. Ahmad's forces were backed by Pakistan's military, which provided special forces in civilian garb. Nearly a month of skirmishes devastated the IMU. Remnants of the group went on to forge an alliance with Baithullah Mehsud, and have provided manpower for the TTP in subsequent years.

Before the 2009 death of Tahir Youldash, the IMU had also fostered a relationship with the Taliban in northern Afghanistan, helping the Taliban boost contacts with the ethnic Tajik, Uzbek and Turkmen communities. The IMU particularly appealed to Uzbeks who felt marginalised in the post-9/11 power-sharing in Afghanistan. In return, the

IMU was allowed small sanctuaries in remote regions along Afghanistan's northern border. This gave it the opportunity to train recruits, and put it in position to carry out strikes in neighbouring Uzbekistan, Turkmenistan and Tajikistan.[39]

Out of their Waziristan base, the IMU and IJU attracted recruits from Europe. It reportedly planned attacks in Germany that would be similar to the November 2008 attacks by Lashkar-e-Taiba in the Indian city of Mumbai. Rami Makanesi, a dual German-Syrian citizen, spent nearly a year in North Waziristan with the IMU and Al-Qaeda 2009 and 2010. His detailed account of the time he spent in North Waziristan provides insights into the IMU's ambition and its ties to Al-Qaeda.[40]

The Pakistani military may have failed to kill or capture significant Al-Qaeda figures in Waziristan, but it appears to have quietly condoned US drone strikes targeting these militants. It has even helped the US identify targets. The drone strikes began in 2004, but increased dramatically after January 2008. It is estimated that between 2,000 and 3,000 militants and civilians have been killed in more than 350 drone strikes conducted through early February 2013. Most of these strikes (225) targeted North and South Waziristan.[41] The strikes have killed prominent Arab Al-Qaeda figures, including: Abu Hamza Rabia and Haitham al-Yemeni (2005); Muhsin Musa Mutawali Atwah (2006); Abu Sulaiman Jazairi and Khalid Habib (2008); Abu Laith al-Libi and Abu Khabab al-Masri (2008); Abdullah Said al-Libi, Saleh Al-Somali, Osama al-Kini and Saad Bin Laden (2009); Mustafa Abu Yazid, Sheikh al-Fateh and Sheikh Mansoor (2010); Atiyah Abd al-Rahman and Abu Hafs al-Shari (2011); and Abu Yahya al-Libi and Abu Kasha (2012). Najmuddin Jalolov (also called Nizamuddin Zalalov), the leader of IJU, and IMU leader Tahir Yuldash were killed in drone attacks in Waziristan in 2009. Yuldash's successor Osman Odil was killed in 2012. Baitullah Mehsud, Ibn Amin, Qari Mohammad Zafar, Haji Omar and Qari Hussain Mehsud (2010), Ilyas Kashmiri (2011), Maulvi Nazir Ahmad, Wali-ur Rehman Mehsud and Hakimullah Mehsud (2013) were among prominent Pakistani militant leaders killed in drone strikes. Janbaz Zadran (2011), Badruddin Haqqani (2012) and Sangeen Zadran (2013) were notable Haqqani Network figures killed by drone strikes.

Pakistani authorities and media publicly oppose the strikes, but senior leaders privately praise them. It is inconceivable that targets for the strikes are identified without the help of the Pakistani intelligence agencies. Various public surveys show a mixed response from residents of the regions controlled by militants. Given the prevailing insecurity and uncertainty in the region, it is unlikely that such surveys can accurately gauge the true sentiment there.

Drones intensify the atmosphere of fear in Waziristan. But the extent of the civilian casualties is disputed, with some Pakistani sources reporting thousands of casualties and American officials portraying the strikes as highly accurate, with few civilian deaths. With no Pakistani or international observers allowed into Waziristan, the number of civilian casualties will remain disputed and a highly politicised issue.[42]

Islamabad's Stepchildren

Mir Zalam Khan was a tall, plump man. He was more commonly known as Haji for having performed the mandatory Muslim pilgrimage to Mecca. The light blue turban he wrapped around his head made him appear taller than he was. His grey beard and weather-beaten face gave him a singular appearance. A Waziristan legend suggests that his ancestor Karim Khon was responsible for capturing Wana from a rival Pashtun tribe.

It is said that Mir Zalam Khan, an elder of the Ahmadzai Wazir tribe in Wana, did his best to bring development to the region and to fight for the rights of his people. He inherited his status as *malak*, an honorary title given by the government to recognise him as a leader of his clan. The title came with preferential access to government contracts and other perks. The biggest privilege, perhaps, was easy access to officials of the regional political administration—the all-powerful and draconian governance arrangement that has turned FATA into a modern-day oligarchy.

In the years before Waziristan became home to Al-Qaeda extremists, Mir Zalam Khan spoke of his desire to build a cold-storage facility to store Wana's fruit and vegetables. He wanted a dam built on the Gomal River near Wana, and called for construction of a direct-access road to the plains of Dera Ismail Khan. Many Wazir tribesmen owned farms there, along the fertile banks of the Indus river, and such a road would bypass villages inhabited by the rival Mehsud tribe. However, once the obscure region hit the headlines because of Al-Qaeda's presence, Mir Zalam Khan had new worries.

When I interviewed him in 2003 and 2004, he deflected my questions, speaking in only a general way about the uninvited Arab and Central Asian guests. Perhaps his reticence was due to Islamabad's duplicitous attitude. Mir Zalam Khan regularly participated in official gatherings in Islamabad and Peshawar, where senior officials always emphasised their determination to rid the region of Al-Qaeda. Most such gatherings were dutifully covered by the Pakistani media, making sure the message reached Washington. But privately, the same leaders praised the Taliban for standing up to the only global superpower, and didn't shy away from striking deals with them.

In July 2005, Mir Zalam Khan was assassinated with his two brothers, a son and a nephew. There were hundreds more similar killings in Waziristan, depriving the tribes of crucial leaders at a time of great crisis. Not one of these murders has been solved.

Islamabad had always struggled to decide on a clear policy to fight extremism in Waziristan and other tribal regions. Military generals and senior politicians often spoke of the difficulty of fighting fellow citizens, but they have done little to change the circumstances under which Waziristan turned into Al-Qaeda's headquarters.

The root of this dilemma, of course, has been Islamabad's Afghan policy. Years before President Pervez Musharraf's 'double game' of distinguishing between 'good' Taliban—or those who fight in Afghanistan only—and 'bad' Taliban—or those who attack the Pakistani people and state—unravelled, senior Pashtun politician Mahmood Khan Achakzai had warned of the impending dangers. 'We should ask why a Chinese militant leader seeks shelter here,' he asked Pakistani lawmakers in late 2003. 'Why Uzbekistan's most-wanted person hides here. All fugitives from the Arab world are running towards you. What is so special about you [Pakistan]?' Predicting the course of events in Waziristan, he warned the generals that they would not 'reap any benefits by killing poor Waziris'. He urged Musharraf to finally determine if Pakistan was ready to live peacefully with its neighbours. 'The only way to save Pakistan is that we publically and honestly repent our past actions,' he said.

But few in Islamabad were willing to listen to such advice. With Washington busy in Iraq, Pakistani policymakers predicted an eventual American debacle in Afghanistan, which made keeping the Afghan Taliban alive a strategic imperative.[43] Afrasiab Khattak, another Pashtun politician, warned that the Pashtuns were being sacrificed at the altar of narrowly-defined state interests. 'In view of the past record of the present government, it is safer to assume that it is making an effort to hide behind the so-called inaccessibility of the tribal area for the failure of its security apparatus in nabbing the most wanted fugitives,' he wrote. 'The myth of "no man's land" and the "wild north-west" comes in quite handy as a spin and as a diversion when the government fails to muster the required political will for taking the bull of terrorism right by the horns.'[44]

In Islamabad, few paid attention to such warnings. After the initial rounds of fighting in Wana, the government paid four Taliban leaders $540,000 to pay off Al-Qaeda's debts.[45] Even more alarming were a series of 'peace accords' reached with Taliban factions in Waziristan between 2004 and 2006. Such agreements benefited the extremists, allowing them to reorganise and eventually exert greater control. After a series of agreements with the Taliban in South Waziristan, Islamabad struck a major deal in North Waziristan.

A 5 September 2006 agreement gave government recognition to the Taliban as a formal, legitimate party. Under the pact, the Taliban was expected to ensure that government and military installations were not attacked. It contained a clause saying the 'border with Afghanistan would not be crossed for any kind of militancy'. Another clause pledged that 'all foreigners present in North Waziristan will leave Pakistan'. But the pact contained no mechanisms to ensure Taliban compliance. The deal required the government to withdraw its forces from the region and return all weapons and vehicles that had been confiscated during past operations. The agreement officially recognised the elder of the Utmanzai Wazir tribe. But most residents are aware of the real power behind the pact.[46]

The agreement was widely criticised as a capitulation to the Taliban, but Islamabad, undeterred, declared it a success. The myopic approach adopted in Waziristan ultimately pushed Pakistan into a larger disaster. Remote and underdeveloped Waziristan remains a tinderbox, even after years of military operations, peace accords, mass migrations and waves of assassinations. Every second person in Waziristan, or nearly half a million people, has migrated since 2003. A majority of some 400,000 displaced Mehsuds living in the neighbouring Tank and Dera Ismail Khan districts since the autumn of 2009 are reluctant to return to their villages. The fire that began to burn in Waziristan took years to spread to other regions of Pakistan. But the government's blunders in the isolated region, particularly the callous attitude towards understanding and resolving its problems, have ultimately led to much bigger disasters.

5

VANISHING TRIBES

In the sweltering summer of 2007, Islamabad became a war zone. The extremist fire that had burned for years in the remote valleys of Waziristan finally reached Pakistan's capital. The 'strategic depth' the government had sought to create by cultivating Islamists in Afghanistan had come back to haunt Pakistan. In early July 2007, more than 100 people died in the eight-day siege of the Lal Masjid, or the Red Mosque.

The mosque's founding leader, Maulana Abdullah, had migrated from a village in Punjab Province in 1960. He soon began to build a power base as the government-appointed *khateeb* of one of the first and largest mosques in the newly-built capital.[1] In the 1980s, Abdullah's energetic anti-communist sermons endeared him to Pakistani military dictator Muhammad Zia-ul Haq, who encouraged Abdullah to nurture contacts with Arabs fighting in Afghanistan. Abdullah established a madrasa that attracted students from across Pakistan, and worked to ally himself with Pakistani Deobandi extremist organisations active in Afghanistan and Kashmir. During the Taliban ascendency in Kabul, Abdullah met Osama bin Laden.[2] After Abdullah was murdered in 1998, his sons Maulana Abdul Aziz and Abdul Rashid Ghazi assumed control of his organisation.

The leadership of the Red Mosque turned against its benefactors after the Pakistani military began operations in Waziristan. In 2004, mosque leaders issued a *fatwa* against the military.[3] The *fatwa* declared that the 'government operation in Wana is against *sharia*, therefore the participation of the military is not permissible'. What enraged then-President General Pervez Musharraf and the army was the assertion that soldiers participating in the offensive would be committing a cardinal sin. The *fatwa* stated, 'Nobody should participate in the funeral services of these soldiers and neither should anybody lead their prayers.'[4] Those killed by government soldiers, meanwhile, were to be considered 'martyrs'.

In the months leading to the violent summer 2007 climax, students at the Red Mosque attempted to organise what Pakistani officials called a 'parallel administration'. The students launched vigilante raids against alleged brothels, burned what they considered to be obscene DVDs and CDs, and called for the strict observance of *sharia*. The raids were carried out by female students of Jamia Hafsa, a seminary located next to the Red Mosque. They wielded long sticks and wrapped themselves in all-black burkas. In previous years, it would have been inconceivable that the authority of the Pakistani state would be challenged so brazenly—especially in a city, Islamabad, in which every third resident works for the government.[5]

After months of inaction, Pakistani security forces cordoned off the Red Mosque in late June. The government allowed thousands of students to leave the compound to surrender, but tensions continued to mount as days passed without a resolution. On 8 July, President Musharraf ordered an assault to flush out the remaining militants.

Abdul Rashid Ghazi, who led the resistance inside the Red Mosque, was frequently interviewed by Pakistani and international media. The son of the late Maulana Abdullah refused to compromise, categorically ruling out all government proposals for a peaceful end to the standoff. In one of his last telephone interviews, with a Pakistani television news station, Ghazi called for an Islamic revolution. 'My martyrdom is certain now,' he said, gunfire echoing in the background. 'Please change this system. This rotten [political] system forms the root of all our problems. There are enormous problems for the poor here. Just a few families are sucking the blood of everybody. So long as the Islamic *sharia* system is not implemented, there will be no solution to our problems.'[6]

In a nationally televised address on 12 July, Musharraf hailed the success of the operation. 'We vow that we won't let any mosque or madrasa be misused like the Red Mosque,' he declared. 'Wherever there is fundamentalism and extremism, we have to finish that, destroy that.'[7] The militants replied to the Red Mosque assault with a wave of suicide bombings and other attacks that killed more than 100 soldiers and police. Scores of civilians were killed and maimed. 'Muslims of Pakistan: your salvation is only through jihad,' Al-Qaeda's then-deputy leader Al-Zawahiri said in a video released on the internet in July. 'Rigged elections will not save you, politics will not save you, and bargaining, bootlicking, negotiations with the criminals, and political manoeuvres will not save you.'[8]

In September, Osama bin Laden issued an audio statement declaring war against Musharraf and urging the Pakistani people to rise up against their 'apostate ruler'.[9] One passage from the message illustrates how Al-Qaeda succeeded in turning the Pakistani military's investment in Sunni extremists against it:

> With Allah's grace, we fought with the Afghan mujahedeen against the Russians. Then the Afghan military, like a tool in the hands of the infidels, was used against us. Those Afghan soldiers offered prayers, they kept [Ramadan] fasts, but the important *ulema* of the Islamic world issued *fatwas* in favour of fighting them. Pakistani *ulema* were part of those efforts. After the Russians left Afghanistan, these Pakistani *ulema* backed the Taliban in its fight against the Northern Alliance. The Northern Alliance cadres, too, offered prayers and observed fasts. Is there any difference between Pervez, his army, Ahmed Shah Massoud, [Burhanuddin] Rabbani and [Abdul Rab Rasul] Sayyaf? Certainly there is no difference. Every one of them has accepted the duty of fighting against Islam in the service of the crusaders. Thus, the people who declare combat against Pervez and his military illegal [and immoral] defy clear injunctions. In reality, there is a disease in their hearts. They have preferred this world over the next.[10]

Every Valley Burns

The storming of the Red Mosque stoked the inferno raging in Pakistan's Tribal Areas. In the wake of the siege, the Taliban insurgency spread from Waziristan and began to engulf other valleys. Bajaur, the northernmost and smallest tribal agency, became a major battleground. The fertile valleys of Bajaur sit between Kunar in eastern Afghanistan, the mountainous Malakand region and the plains of the Peshawar Valley in Khyber Pakhtunkhwa. It is a natural crossroads of these three major Pashtun population centres.

Its strategic location had turned it into a base for the Afghan mujahedeen in the 1980s. A large, walled compound close to the district centre of Khar served as a base for Jamil ur-Rahman, one of the first Salafi

Afghan mujahedeen commanders in Kunar. His hard-line followers brought considerable Arab influence to the region. In the 1990s, the region had been under the sway of the Tehreek-e Nifaz-e Shahriat-e Muhammadi (TNSM), based in neighbouring Malakand. Jamil ur-Rahman and some TNSM leaders were educated at the madrasa of Maulana Muhammad Tahir, a twentieth-century Pashtun cleric who introduced Salafism to the eastern Pashtuns. He built a madrasa in his native village, Panjpir, and propagated a puritanical strand of Sunni Islam close to Salafism. Followers of the Panjpir movement are recognised as a distinct sect and are called Panjpiris.

In October 2001, clerics in Bajaur were at the forefront of protests against the US-led military operation against the Afghan Taliban. They contributed substantially to the formation of the 10,000-strong volunteer force the TNSM brought into Afghanistan, via Bajaur, to back the Taliban regime. Like Waziristan in the south, Pakistani and US-led forces failed to secure Bajaur, leaving it open for the retreat into Pakistan of the Taliban and Al-Qaeda.

A key figure who helped support the fleeing extremists was Maulvi Faqir Muhammad, a former deputy chief of the TNSM in Bajaur. He reportedly participated in the anti-Soviet jihad in Afghanistan in the 1980s and was a graduate of the Panjpir madrasa. Like many Taliban leaders in the Tribal Areas, Muhammad was an unknown figure before 11 September 2001. His name rose in prominence after Pakistani security forces raided his home in 2005 following the capture of Al-Qaeda leader Abu Faraj al-Libi in nearby Mardan. Muhammad was not at home during the raid and escaped capture. Al-Libi, Al-Qaeda's reputed operational chief, had reportedly visited a madrasa in Bajaur linked to Muhammad. Several other attempts were made to sideline Muhammad. In January 2006, a CIA drone targeted a mud house in Bajaur's Damadola district where Al-Qaeda's deputy head, Ayman al-Zawahiri, had been reportedly invited to a dinner hosted by Muhammad. A US drone strike in October 2006, killed Muhammad's deputy, Maulana Liaqat, and eighty students of his madrasa.

By early 2007, militants led by Muhammad controlled large portions of Bajaur.[11] In November of that year, Muhammad outlined a vision of war against the Pakistani establishment. 'The Taliban don't want power,' he insisted. 'Our only aim is to change the system. All the mujahedeen, be they Al-Qaeda, Sheikh Osama [bin Laden] or locals, they all do not want to destroy Pakistan. In fact, they are fighting against those who really want to damage Pakistan [by allying with the US].'[12] In December 2007, Muhammad took over as first deputy chief of the Tehreek-e Taliban Pakistan (TTP).

Islamabad responded to the rising threat in Bajaur as if it were a law-and-order issue. The government launched an operation led by the Frontier Corps, whose leaders are regular military officers but whose soldiers are recruited from Pashtun clans. The under-equipped and poorly trained force failed to deliver any significant blow against the TTP. In August 2008, Islamabad assigned General Tariq Khan, inspector-general of the Frontier Corps, to carry out a new offensive. Operation Sher Dil, or Lion Heart, was well planned and included the deployment of regular troops, tanks and attack helicopters. In what would prove to be a model for future operations in Swat, South Waziristan and Orakzai, General Khan forced much of the civilian population out of Bajaur. The militants were then decimated by long-range artillery, air strikes and ground force manoeuvres supported by attack helicopters. But the battlefield gains were quickly squandered when the government negotiated a peace agreement with the Taliban in March 2009.

The pact was poorly enforced and gave the militants a chance to recuperate. The militants used the opportunity to systematically target members of pro-government tribal vigilante groups known as 'peace *lashkars*' or peace committees.[13] Islamabad did little to protect the *lashkars* once the immediate military objectives had been achieved. Many Pashtuns subsequently accused government factions and institutions of secretly colluding with the extremists in order to continue the battle against NATO and Afghan forces across the border. Hundreds of thousands of displaced Bajauris filled the refugee camps around Peshawar. They received little assistance from the government.

After more operations in early 2010, Islamabad declared victory in Bajaur, saying the Taliban had been 'completely' defeated.[14] However, Pakistani forces never captured or killed Muhammad, who reportedly found shelter in neighbouring Kunar. In June 2011, Muhammad sought to crystallise the political thinking of the Pakistani Taliban. He ridiculed Islamabad's efforts to position itself as the key powerbroker. 'Everybody who thinks that such countries [Pakistan] can play a role in Afghanistan is mistaken,' he said in an interview. 'They cannot even bring peace to their own country.' Muhammad offered an explanation of the TTP's motives and its distinction from the Afghan Taliban:

> The TTP was formed as a result of the [Pakistani] double-dealing emanating from polices based on fear and dollars. Although many mujahedeen in the world consider Mullah Omar their leader, our movement is an independent movement in Pakistan. We don't need the Afghan Taliban for our struggle inside Pakistan; nor do they need us in their struggle in Afghanistan. Our battlefields are separate. Pakistan is our battleground, while Afghanistan is the arena for the Afghan Taliban.[15]

In March 2012, Muhammad became one of the most senior Taliban leaders to be forced out of the organisation. No reason was announced for his dismissal, but speculation centred on his public call for negotiations with the government.[16] The Taliban appointed Mullah Dadullah as the new amir, or leader, in Bajaur. Dadullah was killed in a US airstrike in August 2012, and replaced by Maulvi Abu Bakr. Muhammad reconciled with the TTP leadership in late 2012, but was not given a formal leadership position.[17] Afghan intelligence agents and special forces captured him in eastern Afghanistan in February 2013, after US drone strikes flushed him out of a more remote hideout.[18]

In early 2013, Islamabad proclaimed Bajaur one of the success stories in FATA. With the help of peace *lashkar*s and village defence committees, the government had been able to secure a tenuous peace and even lifted a night-time curfew. A large number of the region's displaced population returned—but the Taliban were far from defeated.[19]

The Red Mosque incident also contributed to the rise of the Taliban in the Mohmand tribal district bordering Bajaur. This region is named after the Mohmand Pashtun tribe, whose members constitute a majority of the district's population. Weeks after the conclusion of the Red Mosque siege, masked gunmen captured a shrine to the Pashtun freedom fighter Haji Sahib Turangzai. They named the mosque adjacent to the shrine Lal Masjid, in tribute to those who had died at the Red Mosque. The Mohmand militants were led by Abdul Wali (alias Omar Khalid).

The generally desolate Mohmand landscape is rich in marble and mineral resources, but offers little in terms of agriculture, which has led many of its inhabitants to migrate to the neighbouring Peshawar Valley. Like other FATA districts, Mohmand had hosted Afghan refugees and anti-Soviet mujahedeen fighters. The region served as a base for Jamil ur-Rahman in the 1980s, and was not immune from influences imported from the TNSM and the Panjpir madrasa.

Emulating techniques employed by the Taliban elsewhere, Abdul Wali's organisation targeted the power of local criminal cartels. In the autumn of 2007, it staged public beheadings. By December, Wali's group had joined forces with the TTP. In 2008, it succeeded in neutering local Salafi jihadist rivals, giving Wali dominance across the region. The group's seizure of the region's marble trade provided a constant stream of funding. By mid-2008, the Taliban were actively settling local disputes, imposing taxes, controlling the drug trade and operating their own courts and prisons.[20] Some members of the group were also linked to crimes including the kidnapping of wealthy individuals from regions bordering Mohmand.

As in Bajaur, the Taliban in Mohmand hunted their opponents with impunity. Two suicide attacks, in July and December of 2010, targeted anti-Taliban tribal figures and killed hundreds. The group also regularly attacked members of peace *lashkars*. A May 2008 agreement with the government only strengthened the militants. Under the pact, the government agreed to ban the activities of nongovernmental organisations in the region. In return, the Taliban pledged to refrain from attacking government personnel and installations.[21] But the deal soon collapsed, and in late 2008 the military expanded its operations from Bajaur into Mohmand.

'The good news is that the Army/Frontier Corps are engaged in combat in Bajaur and Mohmand,' the US Ambassador to Pakistan, Ann Patterson, wrote in a diplomatic cable in February 2009, ahead of a visit to Washington by General Ashfaq Parvez Kayani, Pakistan's military chief. '[President] Zardari is committed to the fight, he knows that Osama bin Laden has publicly targeted Pakistan and admits "the militants are after me and my job". The bad news is that the militants increasingly are setting the agenda.'

By the summer of 2011, Islamabad claimed to have re-established complete control in Mohmand. However, security in the region remained tenuous. A large population of displaced Mohmand residents continued to shelter around Peshawar, hesitant to return home. They rightly continued to fear the Taliban, whose ranks had largely remained intact even after years of military operations. In November 2011, a NATO air strike in Mohmand killed twenty-four Pakistani soldiers. In response, Islamabad banned the transport of NATO supplies through Pakistani territory for the next eight months. It also shut down a US drone base in south-western Balochistan Province. Over the years the Taliban faction in Mohmand has proved resilient and a major nuisance to security in the Peshawar Valley.

The Khyber tribal district, named after the historic strategic pass connecting South and Central Asia, became an important economic hub in the 1960s and 1970s, due largely to its role as a transit route for goods bound for Afghanistan. As in neighbouring Mohmand, members of the Shinwari and Afridi tribes are ubiquitous traders in Peshawar, which abuts Khyber. In the 1980s, when the region's role was magnified during the anti-Soviet war, religious leaders from Afridi lineages rose to prominence in local politics. But these leaders subscribed to different strains of Islam, stirring up sectarian strife. Arab militants attempted to enforce their version of Islam in Khyber in the 1990s, but they were eventually forced out by Afridis in the Tirah Valley. Haji Namdar, a local Afridi who had lived in Saudi Arabia for years, later fashioned a model for jihadists in Khyber. In 2003, he began FM broadcasts and formed a vigilante group to regulate local life.[22]

Competition between Deobandis and Barelvis in Khyber intensified in 2005, when two rival clerics founded illegal FM radio stations. Both were outsiders, but attracted considerable local followings.[23] Mufti Munir Shakir, a radical Deobandi preacher from Hangu, and Pir Saifur Rehman, an Afghan Barelvi cleric, became notorious for using their broadcasts to spread intolerance. They traded insults frequently, declaring each other *kafir*, or infidel.[24] Each eventually founded his own private militia. Shakir found an ally in Mangal Bagh and founded Lashkar-e Islam in 2005. The next year, Rehman joined forces with Qazi Mahboobul Haq to form Ansar-ul Islam.

After Shakir was expelled from the region in late 2005, Mangal Bagh, a previously unknown figure in Khyber, took command of Lashkar-e Islam. Prolonged spells of fighting between Lashkar-e Islam and Ansar-ul Islam led to hundreds of deaths. Khyber was split in two, with each group controlling separate parts of the territory. Mangal Bagh even imposed the *jizya* tax on a small Sikh community in the town of Bara.[25] Pakistani military operations did little to counter the influence of Lashkar-e Islam. Bagh, however, was challenged in April 2011, when the Zakha Khel clan of the Afridis revolted. His organisation split into factions, and Bagh faded from the scene.[26]

The TTP secured a bridgehead in the region in 2008, after the death of Haji Namdar. Namdar had fallen out with the TTP after initially allowing the group to set up a safe haven to attack NATO's main supply line from Pakistan to Afghanistan. Disrupting NATO supply lines through Pakistan has been a key militant strategy since 2008. 'According to Pakistani and American officials, 80 to 90 per cent of coalition supplies reach Afghanistan through Pakistan,' a prominent jihadi magazine in Pakistan claimed in 2010.[27]

Local observers suggested that Lashkar-e Islam directly competed with the TTP for control of criminal cartels, particularly gangs involved in drug smuggling and kidnapping for ransom. Mangal Bagh's opposition to the TTP won him supporters among local officials and perhaps explains why he survived as long as he did. However, he reportedly made peace with the TTP before his rupture with the Zakha Khels and the collapse of his organisation.[28]

By 2013, meanwhile, Ansar-ul Islam had earned a reputation for being the last defence against the TTP and Lashkar-e Islam. The group made itself acceptable to local civilian officials in the remote Tirah region by refraining from suicide bombings and criminality, and helping to provide residents with health care and education. Ansar-ul Islam was instrumental in blocking a TTP attempt to seize control of the strategic Maidan region in January 2013. The previous summer, the TTP had established a foothold by capturing a few villages close to Maidan. Its aim was to create a new sanctuary for Al-Qaeda fighters, who were coming under relentless US drone attacks in North Waziristan, 300 kilometres south of Khyber. The TTP eventually launched an assault on Ansar-ul Islam. More than 100 people were killed in days of fighting, but Ansar-ul Islam prevailed in the clash.[29]

The Afridi clans of Khyber extend into Darra Adam Khel (simply called Darra), a sliver of territory between Peshawar and the southern Kohat district. The Taliban wrested control of Darra by using its tried-and-tested formula of first mobilising local extremists to confront local criminals, then asserting absolute control by eliminating local leaders. The Taliban faction in the region was headed by Tariq Afridi. It was a constant threat to Peshawar and the highway connecting the provincial capital to southern districts. The group claimed responsibility for the February 2009 murder of Polish engineer Piotr Stanczak, who was kidnapped in Punjab Province in September 2008. Sporadic Pakistani military operations in Darra had mixed results, but the instability was devastating to the livelihood of ordinary residents. The Pakistani military claimed to have killed Tariq Afridi in an airstrike in May 2011, after chasing him out of Darra. He was again reported killed in August 2012. In February 2013, the Taliban finally confirmed his death, saying he died from wounds suffered in an attack the previous summer.[30]

Hatred Under White Mountain

A river flows the length of the nearly 70-kilometre-long Kurram Valley. Safed Koh, or White Mountain, named after its snow-capped peak, lends Kurram's main city of Parachinar an aura of alpine beauty. In 2007, clashes broke out between Shia and Sunnis in Parachinar, plunging it into sectarian war and clearing the way for Taliban intervention.

Most residents of Parachinar hail from the Turi tribe. With an estimated 500,000 members, Turis are unique among Pashtuns for their adherence to Shia Islam. They occupy a chunk of borderland known as Peiwar Kotal, or Parrot's Beak, which juts westward into Afghanistan. The Afghan capital Kabul is just 100 kilometres from Parachinar. For the most part, the Turis and Bangash Shia clans lived in harmony with neighbouring Sunni tribes for centuries. But in the 1980s, tensions began to rise. Hundreds of people from both sides were killed in unprecedented sectarian violence in Kurram in 1987. Islamabad backed predominantly Sunni Afghan guerillas during the 1980s fight to repel the Red Army. But resistance from the Turis frustrated Islamist attempts to seize the strategically important region.

The conflict in Kurram is often painted as local and sectarian in nature. But the Taliban attempt to overrun Parachinar in 2008 was evidence of a broader extremist strategy to control the Parrot's Beak. The conflict put great pressure on the Shia majority. In the early stages, the Shia became trapped inside Parachinar, hemmed in by fleeing Sunnis who blocked exit roads. Subsequent Taliban attacks led to a renewal of sectarian violence. Each side accused the other of serving as proxies for outside powers. Shia complained that their Sunni neighbours had invited in the Taliban to persecute them. Some Sunnis blamed Iran for supporting and radicalising the Shia. The extremists took advantage of Parachinar's isolation to implement a siege that lasted nearly four years. With road links severed, Shia were forced to detour across eastern Afghan provinces to visit Peshawar, the region's main economic hub.

More than 3,000 people died and thousands were injured in the fighting. The fighting raged, even as the two sides understood that the real benefactor of the conflict was the TTP, which was seeking to exploit the chaos to expand its control. The warring parties signed a government-sponsored peace agreement in October 2008. Islamabad, however, failed to support the agreement by deploying security forces. The TTP thus had a free hand to harass local factions and target individuals opposed to its presence.

In early 2011, hopes of a peace deal were renewed. A ceasefire in February received Islamabad's backing. The government promised aid to thousands of displaced families and the deployment of troops to protect key routes. The pact was met with rejoicing by both Shia and Sunnis. Businessman and politician Munir Khan Orakzai told me both sects realised they had fought a useless war that had killed many innocent people. 'There can be no logical end to this [sectarian violence],' said Orakzai, who represented Kurram's Sunnis in parliament. 'That's why people concluded this agreement.'[31]

Critics claimed the deal was less about forging a lasting peace than about facilitating the infiltration of insurgents from Kurram into Afghanistan. Pundits suggested the Haqqani Network, which was seeking a sanctuary from which to target Afghan and NATO forces, was the hidden beneficiary. They argued that the Haqqanis and their followers wanted to leave their sanctuary in adjacent North Waziristan, where they had come under frequent attack by CIA drones.[32]

The fragile peace in Kurram was shattered on 26 March 2011, when TTP fighters attacked a convoy travelling from Peshawar to Parachinar and kidnapped twenty-two Shia passengers. TTP leader Hakimullah Mehsud sought to ransom the hostages for badly needed funds, but the tactic caused a rift between Mehsud and his associates Noor Muhammad and Fazal Saeed Haqqani. Noor Muhammad even killed some hostages to prevent them from being ransomed. An infuriated Hakimullah Mehsud killed Noor Muhammad. Fazal Saeed Haqqani was replaced by a previously unknown figure.

Fazal Saeed Haqqani responded by announcing the formation of a new group called the Tehreek-e Taliban Islami. 'I repeatedly told the leadership council of Tehreek-i-Taliban Pakistan that they should stop suicide attacks against mosques, markets and other civilian targets,' he claimed. 'Islam does not allow killings of innocent civilians in suicide attacks.' Haqqani, however, failed to muster significant support among armed militants. In the summer of 2011, the Pakistani military launched operation Koh-e Sufaid in a bid to again free Kurram from the TTP's grip.[33]

Orakzai, which abuts Kurram to the south and Khyber to the west, is the only tribal district or agency without a border with Afghanistan. This precluded it from becoming a major base for the Afghan mujahedeen during the 1980s. But Orakzai has not been spared the consequences of war. One effect was the aggravation of conflict among Orakzai Shia and Sunnis over the shrine of a local saint. These local differences would become entangled with the sectarian conflict in neighbouring Kurram and the larger conflict in the Pakistani heartland.

The TTP began using Orakzai as a sanctuary after the first Pakistani military operations in Waziristan in 2004. The TTP methodically crushed all opposition as it transformed the mountainous region into a base by early 2008. In a few cases, it sent suicide bombers to target tribal councils that had convened to discuss ways to counter the militants. In October 2008, a suicide car bomb attack on a *jirga* of the region's large Alikhel clan killed nearly 200 tribesmen, including significant local anti-Taliban figures. Such attacks and targeted assassinations strengthened Taliban control over the predominately Sunni-populated regions of Upper Orakzai. The Shia clans of Lower Orakzai, however, followed the example of Parachinar's Turis and successfully resisted Taliban incursions into their regions. The Taliban were never able to enter the picturesque Kalaya area inhabited by the Shias.[34]

Maulvi Noor Jamal, a militant commander best known by his *nom de guerre*, Mullah Tofan, was selected in 2009 to head the TTP in Orakzai. In 2010, he was even considered a possible replacement for overall TTP leader Hakimullah Mehsud. Noor Jamal was a prayer leader who taught at a madrasa in Orakzai. His native roots gave him an edge in an organisation led by many outsiders. Noor Jamal helped enforce the blockade of Parachinar for years.

After an offensive in the spring and summer of 2010, the Pakistani military claimed to have practically eliminated extremists from Orakzai. Locals disagree, saying the region remains a sanctuary for TTP leaders who fled South Waziristan in late 2009. Like much of the Pashtun tribal arc in western Pakistan, stability in Orakzai remains tenuous at best. In 2013, Noor Jamal was reported active in fighting in the neighbouring Khyber district.

Collective Punishment

The violence in Pakistan's FATA is generally perceived by the global audience through the narrow and simplistic prism of the War on Terror, as defined by Washington in the wake of the 11 September 2001 attacks. FATA is a holdover from the British Raj in South Asia. In many ways, it is an administrative, political and economic anomaly within Pakistan.

FATA has an area of some 27,000 square kilometres and shares a 600-kilometre border with Afghanistan. It is slightly smaller than Belgium and around the size of Massachusetts. FATA is divided into seven agencies, or administrative units, which from north to south include: Bajaur, Mohmand, Khyber, Orakzai, Kurram, and North and South Waziristan. It also includes a few frontier regions adjacent to the settled districts of Peshawar, Kohat, Dera Ismail Khan, Bannu, Lakki Marwat and Tank. The area had a population of some 3.1 million people at the time of the 1998 census. Current unofficial estimates suggest it could now be home to seven million people. Ninety-nine per cent of the region's population is ethnic Pashtun. Most tribes in FATA straddle the Durand Line.

The region has always been difficult for independent journalists and scholars to visit, but it has become even more inaccessible since 2004. Much of the current international understanding of the region derives from British colonial literature and its narrative of fanatical 'wild tribes'. Analysts across the decades have often resorted to superlatives to describe how 'dangerous' or 'threatening' FATA is to regional and global security. This view became especially prominent after 11 September 2001. But analysts have generally paid little attention to the region's history of contorted governance that continues to exacerbate conflict.[35]

Effective governance in FATA has long been stymied by labyrinthine diarchal arrangements, keeping the region isolated and marginalised. Under Pakistan's 1973 constitution, the president, using his executive authority, can implement any policy he chooses in FATA. In practice, the governor of Khyber Pakhtunkhwa Province exercises this enormous authority as the president's representative. The residents of FATA have representation in both houses of the national legislature, but parliament has virtually no role in shaping laws for the region. Crucially, FATA is denied representation in the legislature of Khyber Pakhtunkhwa, which surrounds the region from three sides. The elected provincial government thus has no role in running FATA.[36]

Over the decades, this administrative arrangement has deprived tribes of political participation and economic development. Additionally, due to a range of restrictions, political parties, aid agencies and civil society organisations have found it nearly impossible to function in FATA. Radical extremist clerics of all stripes, however, have remained free to campaign. They consequently won most elections after adult franchise was introduced in 1996.[37]

In 2006, Islamabad upgraded the office tasked with dealing with the region, giving it the name Civil Secretariat FATA. The office is home to the bureaucrats charged with overseeing the delivery of services such as health care, education, agriculture and communication. These bureaucrats coordinate their policies with the governor of Khyber Pakhtunkhwa and the federal Ministry of States and Frontier Regions. Also in 2006, a presidential order established a separate FATA Development Authority, tasked with promoting infrastructure development. The creation of these institutions succeeded in expanding the Pakistani bureaucracy, but the essence of governance in FATA remained the same.

On the micro level, a 'political agent' or government-appointed bureaucrat, is supposed to be the ultimate authority in a tribal district. Under the current governing structure, the political agent combines legislative, law enforcement and economic management functions. The political agent is empowered to serve as judge, jury, prosecutor, police chief and prison administrator. The political agent can oversee development projects and direct public services such as health care, education and agriculture. The political agent can raise revenues by taxing transportation and trade, and there is little oversight on how such funds might be spent. The political agent's authority also extends to the regulation of tribal affairs. They can handpick their own *jirgas*, or tribal councils, to handle civil and criminal cases. They can manipulate local politics by providing allowances and other economic incentives to tribal leaders in exchange for loyalty. Before the onset of militancy in FATA, a political agent's job was considered regal and lucrative. Many senior bureaucrats bribed politicians to get such a posting.

The political agent operates under a legal regime called the Frontier Crimes Regulations, or FCR. Since British colonialists finalised the current form of the FCR in 1901, it has been used as a whip to control Pashtun tribes. The British, and their Pakistani successors, say the FCR is rooted in tribal customs and traditions. But it contradicts the egalitarian Pashtun ethos, where all members of society are considered equal. In Pashtun society, the notion of being ruled by a bureaucrat, who may often be an outsider, is alien. The archaic law also contradicts many provisions of the Pakistani constitution, which enshrines fundamental citizen rights.

Under FCR powers, a political agent can impose an economic blockade of a whole region. Under the concept of 'collective punishment', the political agent can impose fines on entire communities where alleged crimes took place. This can result in a whole tribe being held responsible for the crimes of a single individual, or any crime that has occurred on its territory. The political agent can prohibit the construction of houses, and order the razing of houses of tribesmen for not meeting the political agent's demands. The FCR empowers the political agent, or tribal area administrator, to deliver multi-year jail sentences without due process. Such verdicts can now be challenged in a tribunal composed of former bureaucrats, but this mechanism hardly guarantees justice.[38]

FCR clauses have been repeatedly invoked across FATA since the onset of militancy, but the use of collective punishment has produced few positive results. In 2010, Amnesty International called FATA a 'human-rights-free zone'. The report observed that an estimated four million Pashtuns in the region were trapped under Taliban rule and had been effectively abandoned by Pakistan's central government.[39] In December 2012, Amnesty International said the Pakistani justice system was ineffective in dealing with human rights abuses committed by both the Pakistani security forces and militants. The report said that after a decade of violence, the Tribal Areas were mired in crisis, with courts unable to extend fundamental rights protections to residents. 'State and non-state perpetrators of human rights violations and abuses continue to act with total impunity in the Tribal Areas,' the report observed.[40]

Indeed, the large-scale deployment of the Pakistani military to FATA has altered the region's governance for the worse. After operations were launched against militants in South Waziristan in 2004, the Musharraf regime effectively sidelined political agents and empowered army generals. The arrangement gave the military's Peshawar command control over development funding in the tribal regions. In many areas, military leaders and Taliban commanders set up what amounted to power-sharing, or cohabitation, arrangements. Many residents began to look towards the generals as the *de facto* representatives of the Pakistani state.[41] However, the Taliban's assassinations of hundreds of *malaks*, or clan representatives, deprived the government of important links to the communities. Islamabad's failure to investigate the murders or provide protection to those threatened further alienated the population, making them more vulnerable to the influence of militants. Numerous tribal leaders told me they feared the government, particularly its intelligence agencies, as much as the Taliban.

Too Little, Too Late

Successive Pakistani governments pledged reforms in FATA, but took little action. Most Pakistani political parties also advocated reforms. But the bureaucracy dealing with FATA, fearing a loss of its fiefdom, has consistently frustrated moves for change. Bureaucrats seeking to maintain the *status quo* have mobilised *malaks*, FATA lawmakers and former bureaucrats to campaign against reforms. In some cases, officials even pushed tribal leaders or their former colleagues to call press conferences to condemn reform efforts, arguing that such moves could undermine the security of Pakistan's western borders.

Repealing the FCR was high on the agenda of the ruling Pakistan People's Party, which campaigned on promises of reform in the 2008 elections. During his inaugural speech, Prime Minister Yusuf Raza Gilani pledged his government would abolish the 'obsolete' FCR. He also vowed to bring 'economic, social, and political reforms' to the Tribal Areas. His administration announced the formation of a four-member parliamentary committee to examine FCR reforms. Many FATA locals considered the initiative a last-ditch opportunity to liberate the region from the abuses of militants and the army.

During Pakistani Independence Day celebrations in August 2009, President Asif Ali Zardari announced a FATA reform package. The reforms curtailed some powers of the political agents, introduced a degree of accountability and repealed some of the harshest clauses of the FCR. But the military prevailed on the civilian administration to suspend implementation of the reforms. The army wanted to keep the region isolated as it continued operations against extremists. Civilian supporters of the changes were infuriated. 'The reforms package will not undermine FATA. These reforms will enhance its security,' octogenarian politician Farhatullah Babar, who served as a spokesman for the Pakistani president, told me in late 2010. He rejected the notion that the abolition of the FCR would hinder the fight against militants. 'In Swat we successfully fought the militancy, but there was no FCR,' he noted.[42]

It was announced with great fanfare in August 2011, that the reforms had come into force. Broadcasts were flush with government-sponsored advertisements highlighting the two executive orders President Zardari signed on 12 August. The Urdu-language adverts congratulated Zardari for curtailing the powers of Tribal Area administrators, who were portrayed as now facing greater legal and financial scrutiny. For the first time in a century, political parties would now be able to freely campaign in FATA. The law in the region was coming more in line with modern human rights standards. FCR clauses permitting collective punishments were being diluted. It would no longer be permissible for authorities to imprison children younger than sixteen and women older than sixty-five. FATA residents would be able to challenge official decisions in a government-appointed tribunal.[43]

But the proclamation of progress turned out to be a misdirection. The military had again moved behind the scenes to secure its interests. In July, President Zardari signed into law an exception granting sweeping powers to the military in FATA and some districts of Khyber Pakhtunkhwa. The measure, entitled 'Actions in Aid of Civil Power', again permitted security forces to detain suspected militants for prolonged periods. It also empowered military and civilian officials to hand down severe punishments. Many of the FCR reforms were thus rendered irrelevant.

Full implementation of the reforms seems a distant prospect. Pakistani leaders remain preoccupied with a dizzying array of intrigues and challenges, and the country itself continues to teeter dangerously close to complete chaos. FATA seems certain to remain a sanctuary for extremists for the foreseeable future, and Islamabad's policy of using force against them offers little prospect of an early resolution. Pakistani generals continue to view FATA's fate as inextricably tied to events in Afghanistan. Like other regional players, the generals are biding their time and planning for the aftermath of the withdrawal of Western forces from Afghanistan at the end of 2014.

The war in Afghanistan has fundamentally altered the tribal economy of the Pashtun borderlands. Over the past four decades, the region has seen a nearly complete transition from subsistence agriculture and nomadic livelihoods, to dependence on unregulated cross-border trade, including in contraband such as drugs and arms. In 2010, Afghanistan and Pakistan agreed to a transit trade agreement giving the two countries access to India and Central Asia across each other's territories. But implementation of the agreement has been hampered by bureaucratic obstacles. Military operations have also contributed to the decline of cross-border trade. The lack of an alternative economic model in FATA has pushed many to destitution and swelled the ranks of militant groups.

Warfare has worsened the key human development indicators in the region. Poverty levels are as high as 60 per cent, or twice those in the rest of Pakistan. Official statistics released nearly a decade ago showed a literacy rate in the tribal territories of just 17.4 per cent—29.5 per cent for men and less than 3 per cent for women. The primary school enrollment rate for boys was 68 per cent and a mere 19 per cent for girls. There were only 102 colleges (equivalent to Western high schools) in the Tribal Areas, with no more than three of them reserved for women. The number of madrasas, or Islamic seminaries, has mushroomed, with up to 300 in the region. In the mid-2000s, there were only 524 doctors for FATA—or one doctor for every 6,307 people—and some remote regions don't have a single health care facility. Only two or three hospitals in all of FATA have facilities for life-saving surgery.[44] Hundreds of schools, bridges and other infrastructure have been destroyed by militants since 2004.[45] Girls' schools, in particular, have been forced to close because of fears of extremist attack. The military and the FATA Development Authority list many completed projects, but it is difficult to see their impact.

About 2.4 per cent of Pakistan's population lives in FATA, but it receives only about 1 per cent of national resources. The per capita development allocation is one-third of the national average. Few aid agencies are permitted to work in the tribal belt, but they are allowed to operate substantial development projects in other regions. The per capita income in FATA is half that of the national average of about $2,500. The region had the highest out-migration ratio even before the advent of Islamist militancy. Since the start of fighting, nearly half the population has left. The official unemployment rate has sometimes hit 80 per cent.[46]

1. A village in Lower Dir, Khyber Pakhtunkhwa Province, © Majeed Babar

2. Some Loya Paktia delegates in the Loya Jirga, Kabul, January 2004, © Author

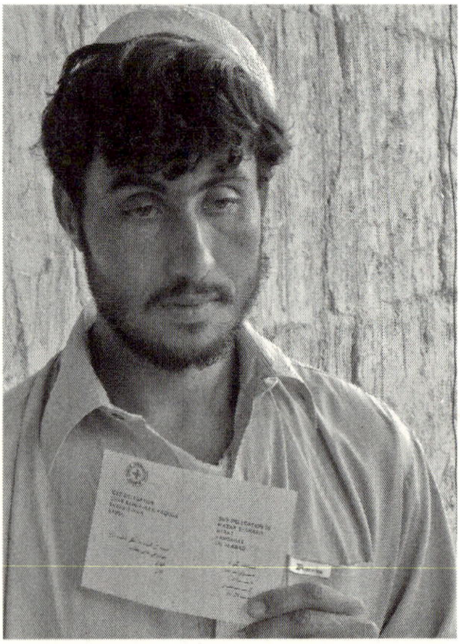

3. Noor Habibullah, a former detainee of the Guantanamo Bay prison in Jalalabad, summer 2004, © Author

4. Former Taliban diplomat Mullah Abdul Salam Zaeef, Kabul 2010, © Author

5. Afrasiab Khattak, October 2010, © Author

6. Folk musicians in Swat, © Shaheen Buneri

7. Maulana Noor Muhammad, a pro-Taliban JUI leader in Balochistan, © Abdul Hai Kakar

8. A distraught Pashtun mother showing the picture of her disappeared son, Jalalabad, 2004, © Author

9. A British-era hilltop security post in Landikotal, Khyber Pass, © Majeed Babar

10. Malam Jabba in Swat, © Majeed Babar

11. The ruined Darul Aman Palace in Kabul, 2003, © Author

12. Afghan National Army recruits being trained, Kabul, 2004, © Author

13. Rusting tanks leftover from the Soviet Occupation in 1980s, Kabul, 2004, © Author

14. The road to Gardez, capital of Paktia Province, © Author

15. Remains of the ancient Bala Hissar fort in Kabul, © Author

16. The mausoleum of Afghan Emperor Ahmad Shah Durrani in Kandahar, © Author

17. The Shaheedano Chowk (Martyrs Square) in Kandahar, © Author

18. A paramilitary check post in Swat, © Shaheen Buneri

19. A Pashtun nomad woman near Kandahar, February 2002, © Author

6

TERROR IN PAKHTUNKHWA

The blast shattered the jubilation of the February evening. Pashtun politician Afrasiab Khattak instinctively brought his arms over his head to protect himself from the rain of falling debris. Shards of red brick tile plunged from the high verandah and exploded against the pavement. Through the smoke, Qasim Ali Khan, a friend and fellow politician, shouted at Khattak, 'Are you okay?'

Khattak survived the bomb, as did everyone who sat with him that evening on the verandah of the *hujra*, the traditional male quarters that double as a community centre in northern Pakistan's Pashtun regions. But the crowd on the lawn facing them, boisterous and celebratory just seconds before, was now a chorus of voices crying for help. Pieces of charred bodies were scattered about. The stench of burning flesh hung in the air.

Khattak recalled the evening of 9 February 2008 with stoic calm. The suicide bomber had claimed twenty-five lives and left scores of injured, most of them Pashtun villagers who had gathered to hear leaders of the Awami National Party (ANP). Khattak headed the moderate political party in what was then called the North West Frontier Province.[1] Earlier that evening, he had canvassed in a small agricultural village near Peshawar to mobilise his party's traditional support base in rural areas of the Peshawar Valley. The party had promised peace if residents would vote them into power.

Revolutionary Politics

At nearly six feet tall, Khattak cuts a distinguished figure. His neatly combed hair, pencil-thin moustache, bright eyes and serious yet genial demeanour lend him the air of an academic from a bygone era. During the fifteen years I have known him, he has never failed to impress with his wide knowledge and precise speaking style.

Khattak has led the adventurous life of a nonconformist politician. Unlike most of the privileged, feudal politicians in Pakistan, Khattak was born to a poor rural Pashtun family. He experienced tribal life in Waziristan as a young boy in the 1960s, when an uncle serving in the Frontier Corps sponsored his schooling there. During the next decade, he emerged as a student leader who aspired to modernise Pashtun society by renewing its politics. In line with the trend of postcolonial societies of the time, many Pashtun leaders, including Khattak, looked toward the Soviet Union as a revolutionary model that could propel their tribal and agrarian polity into the modern age. Such thinking ran counter to the ruling elite in Islamabad, which was highly suspicious of Moscow.

In the decades before Khattak's emergence as a young leader in the 1970s, Pashtun politicians played a major role in the pro-democracy currents of Pakistani politics. Their role was enhanced by the formation of the National Awami Party (NAP) in 1957. Under the leadership of a Bengali socialist cleric, Maulana Abdul Hamid Khan Bhashani, the NAP emerged as a coalition of leftist and ethno-nationalist factions. Pashtun stalwarts Abdul Ghaffar Khan and Abdul Samad Khan Achackzai were key leaders of the NAP. These Pashtun leaders united with Sindhi, Baloch and Bengali nationalists against the new country's centralising policies. Such policies included the adoption of Islam as Pakistan's unifying identity, and the adoption of the Urdu language and other cultural symbols of Muslim migrants from India. NAP leaders viewed these efforts as alienating and discriminatory, an attempt to dismiss their centuries-old identities, histories and cultures.

The NAP regarded the marginalisation of their peoples as part of an effort by civil and military bureaucrats and politicians from the eastern Punjab Province to establish dominance in the new state.[2] The NAP consistently resisted military dictatorship and pushed for democracy and secularism. It sought to address Pakistan's nationalities question by advocating equality and regional autonomy for all ethnic groups. It also stood against the growing economic and political hegemony exercised by the Punjabis. The NAP's international outlook was anti-imperialist and opposed Islamabad's alliance with Washington.

In 1967, the party suffered a major split as China and the Soviet Union moved to divide the communist world into separate spheres of interest. Bhashani retained the leadership of a pro-Chinese faction in the former East Pakistan, while Abdul Ghaffar Khan's son, Abdul Wali Khan, emerged as the leader of the pro-Soviet faction in West Pakistan. After the separation of East Pakistan as independent Bangladesh in 1971, Wali Khan's party rose to become the main opposition to Zulfiqar Ali Bhutto's government of the new Pakistan. The NAP, strengthened by victories in the Pashtun and Baloch regions in the 1970 elections, allied with the Deobandi Jamiat Ulema-e Islam and formed coalition provincial administrations in Balochistan and the former North West Frontier Province (NWFP) in April 1972. But the Balochistan government was sacked in February 1973, prompting the government in the NWFP to resign in protest.

This was a huge setback for the moderate Pashtun nationalist movement, which by now had become the longest lasting leftist movement in the country. The NAP's political vision for the country had been vindicated by the separation of East Pakistan. But the party was banned in 1975, accused by authorities of promoting Pashtun and Baloch secessionism. As a student leader in the early 1970s, Khattak had fallen out with elements of the then-ruling Pakistan People's Party. On several occasions, he was forced to flee to Afghanistan to avoid arrest. The police finally caught up with Khattak in the late 1970s, when he was arrested and charged, along with other secular Pashtun and Baloch leaders, with conspiring to challenge Pakistan's territorial sovereignty by advocating independence for minority ethnic groups.

At the time, it was as an unprecedented move by the government against its critics. But Khattak recalls his nearly two years in prison as one of the best episodes of his political career. He fondly talks about the days of incarceration as a time of great learning. His fellow inmates included some leading Pashtun and Baloch political leaders and prominent leftist writers, and the discussions would often last for hours.[3] Khattak won a brief reprieve when the special tribunal tasked with prosecuting the case was disbanded after a military coup in 1977. Khattak, however, was soon rearrested and sentenced to a year of hard labour by a military court in 1979.

It was a time of great turmoil. The April 1978 communist coup in neighbouring Afghanistan, and the Soviet invasion of Afghanistan the next year, sent Pakistan's military rulers into action. Khattak became a target of a regime bent on eliminating all political opposition. One evening in 1980, a bureaucrat friend in Peshawar advised Khattak to go into exile if he wanted to avoid assassination.

Khattak turned to his friend Mohammad Najibullah, the intelligence chief of the Afghan communist regime, whose revolution was now backed by 100,000 Red Army troops. Khattak, known in Kabul as Akbar Khan, was the guest of the communist government for eight years. Exile in Kabul gave him insight into Afghan politics and society. He also used the opportunity to travel extensively within the Soviet bloc. He soon realised that the utopia the Soviets were constantly promising would be difficult to make reality.

Khattak returned to Pakistan in 1989 after the death of military dictator General Muhammad Zia-ul Haq. Prime Minister Benazir Bhutto declared a general amnesty for all opponents of the military regime. Back in Peshawar, Khattak took on the role of diplomat, serving as a personal envoy of Mohammad Najibullah, who was now the Afghan president, in talks with Peshawar-based Afghan mujahedeen leaders. Khattak's career in Pakistani politics, however, was slow to ignite. Lacking money for his campaigns, he lost several elections in the early 1990s after the ANP had expelled him, along with other progressive intellectuals, on charges of being communists. Unbowed, Khattak joined the Pakistani human rights movement.

Khattak exemplified two major currents of Pashtun politics in the twentieth century. First, he was inspired by the ideals of a peaceful Pashtun society, as envisioned by the Khudai Khitmatgars, or the Servants of God movement of Abdul Ghaffar Khan. Second, he sought to achieve these ideals through progressive-minded development, of the kind promoted by international socialist movements. The strategy had mixed results. During the Cold War, socialist movements in the developing world were often cleverly exploited by the Soviet Union. They tended to be marginalised in Western capitals, where the focus was on countering Soviet influence.

I met Khattak for the first time in 1997, at a seminar in Peshawar marking the first anniversary of the death of President Najibullah. The Taliban had swept through most of Afghanistan in 1996, punctuating their conquest of Kabul by hanging Najibullah from a lamp post near the presidential palace. Khattak was critical of Islamabad's support for the extremists, but lacked a clear political plan to counter it. The Taliban's victory had energised Pakistani Islamist political parties. They had never before won an election, but now dreamed of establishing a puritanical Islamic polity in Pakistan, Afghanistan and beyond.

Khattak worried these movements would radically alter Pashtun society and politics. He often spoke of how the Pashtuns had been left behind as the world moved towards increased globalism. He pointed out that while Pashtuns had made great sacrifices in the Cold War, they had been deprived of any meaningful benefits arising from the end of the ideological clash between Washington and Moscow. He foresaw the Pashtun lands, already vulnerable, becoming a laboratory for extremism and violence. 'We are a low-pressure zone in terms of socioeconomic development,' he told me. 'I am afraid it will attract storms.'

At the start of the twenty-first century, Islamist groups, both violent and non-violent, had become a force that could no longer be ignored. In early April 2001, a month after the Taliban destroyed the historic Bamiyan Buddhist statues in central Afghanistan, JUI, a leading Pakistani Islamist party, held a three-day gathering called the 'International Deoband Conference' in Peshawar. The event was intended as a show of power. Islamist hard-liners saw themselves as on their way to dominating society and politics in Afghanistan and Pakistan. Resolutions adopted by the gathering called for the end of United Nations sanctions against the Taliban, Iraq and Libya. Participants also demanded the immediate departure of Western troops from Saudi Arabia and the Gulf states. JUI leader Maulana Fazlur Rahman vowed that if the United States 'continues to speak in the language of force', Muslims were ready 'to fight back and defend themselves'.

Taliban leader Mullah Mohammad Omar also delivered a statement to the gathering. 'The infidels consider Islam a threat to their worldwide interests, so every effort is made to weaken Muslims,' Omar said in an audio message. 'In Afghanistan, we control 95 per cent of the country, but we are referred to as one of the factions and denied recognition.' Al-Qaeda leader Osama bin Laden used the occasion to urge support for the Taliban. He called Afghanistan a real Islamic country and urged Muslim youth to flock to it for military training. 'The people [of Afghanistan] are waiting for your decisions. Do not be afraid. Speak loudly and implement the Islamic system,' bin Laden said.[4]

Khattak saw such events as an omen. He became increasingly worried that moderate Pashtuns would be devoured by Islamic extremism. Khattak believed the October 1999 military coup by Pakistani General Pervez Musharraf had only helped to boost the appeal of extremists. He was suspicious of Pakistani military intelligence and suggested it may have played a role in organising the Deobandi gathering in Peshawar. Khattak was not persuaded that Musharraf was sincere about secularism, viewing the general as closely tied to the military's political and economic interests. Khattak was also disappointed by the West's failure to devote resources to bringing about a lasting political solution in Afghanistan. He was concerned that Washington and its allies were minimising the threat posed by Al-Qaeda.

Khattak's fears were reinforced by the Western response to the 11 September 2001 attacks on New York and Washington. He supported Washington's effort to prop up an anti-Taliban alliance as an interim arrangement in Afghanistan after the fall of the Taliban regime in late 2001. But he was pessimistic about the West's reliance on Musharraf on the front line of what the Bush administration had begun to call the Global War On Terrorism.

'He is a military dictator [and] usurper, an unconstitutional ruler, a fellow whose rule is not supported based on the constitution and law,' Khattak said of Musharraf in an appearance on a US news programme. 'But unfortunately, because of the events after September 11 and his joining the coalition, he has become a good guy. He is getting good press in the West, and unfortunately the restoration of democracy in Pakistan has gone to the back burner.'[5]

Khattak was among the first to publically warn about the Pakistani military playing a 'double game'. He viewed the October 2002 election victory of an alliance of religious political parties in Pakistan's Pashtun regions as part of a new campaign to empower Islamists. The Islamists swept the elections in the NWFP, the FATA and northern Balochistan. The big losers included secular parties such as the ANP, which failed to win a single seat in the national parliament. International observers declared the polls deeply flawed, while secular politicians and independent observers accused the military-controlled intelligence agencies of working to enlarge the Islamist victory. They argued the military wanted the Islamists to win in order to scare Washington and push it into giving the Musharraf regime more resources to fight an extremist takeover.[6]

Khattak understood the intricacies of the game. He didn't see it resulting in long-term benefits for Pashtuns. He believed Pashtuns had to embrace an alternative vision to save themselves from obliteration.

Khattak rejoined the ANP in 2003. He is credited with providing the party, whose leaders include landed gentry and urban businessmen, with a new sense of direction, informed by his work as a human rights campaigner.[7] He soon became a trusted confidant of ANP leader Asfandiyar Wali Khan. As violence flared in the FATA, the ANP campaigned for peace, advocating a union of the mosque and the *hujra* to save the Pashtuns from impending disaster. The party also reached out to media and international diplomats to challenge the narrative of Pashtuns being war-like and prone to violence.

Musharraf and his lieutenants, meanwhile, sought to characterise the Taliban insurgency as a burgeoning Pashtun national-liberation movement. Such attacks angered many Pashtun leaders. 'The Taliban are not the creation of Pashtun society, but the creation of the Pakistan army,' ANP chief Khan declared in late 2006.[8] The ANP's rising profile as a secular and democratic alternative to the Taliban endeared it to Washington. This eventually forced Musharraf to reach out to the party. With Khattak's help, Khan put forward the party's demands. Michael Spangler, the US consul in Peshawar, reported after meeting the ANP head:

> Asfandiyar Wali Khan would actively support President Musharraf's government if the GOP [Government of Pakistan] embraced three key ANP initiatives: (1) provincial autonomy in health, local government, education, and agriculture; (2) changing the name of the Northwest Frontier Province (NWFP) to Pakhtunkhwa; and (3) comprehensive political development in the FATA. Senator Asfandiyar claims a GOP-ANP alliance would demonstrate Musharraf's genuine commitment to 'enlightened moderation' and give the ANP a fair chance to challenge anti-American religious parties that currently fill the political vacuum here created by the exclusion of mainstream parties in the 2002 general elections. Asfandiyar was not sanguine about receiving his chance.[9]

The December 2007 assassination of former Pakistani Prime Minister Benazir Bhutto derailed Musharraf's plans to cling to power on the back of a secular alliance—something he had proposed to Washington as an antidote to extremism. In the preceding months, Musharraf had lost much of his domestic political legitimacy after failing to stave off a protest movement spearheaded by lawyers. The November 2007 handover of the military command to his deputy, Ashfaq Parvez Kayani, deprived Musharraf of his powers as army chief. The February 2008 parliamentary elections would seal his fate and clear the way for his exit.

The ANP, campaigning on promises to deliver 'peace, democracy and development', emerged as the single largest party in Khyber Pakhtunkhwa, winning nearly half the provincial assembly seats. The ANP soon formed a coalition government with the Pakistan People's Party in Islamabad and Peshawar. However, the real test awaited in the mountainous Malakand region, north of Peshawar.

From Paradise to Hell

Swat is one of seven districts in Malakand. The ANP swept the election in Swat, winning seven of its eight provincial assembly seats. 'The verdict of Pakhtunkhwa is that we prefer school uniforms rather than suicide jackets,' ANP leader Khan said after the victory. Afrasiab Khattak, however, had a more considered response. He was concerned the new provincial government was not equipped to handle the momentous security challenge posed by the extremists. 'Terrorism in NWFP is only a manifestation of the militarised state of Pakistan,' he said after being voted into office. 'Being the main source of instability, if this anomaly is corrected at Islamabad HQ [Pakistani military's General Headquarters], normality will naturally return to the entire nation.'[10]

As the new provincial government took charge in April 2008, Swat was almost completely under Taliban control. The militant group had recovered from the Pakistani military's initial push into the region in late 2007. Most of the police stations in rural areas of the district were seized by Taliban fighters after police officers deserted, and most government agencies were barely functioning. The Taliban did not spare anyone who opposed their aim of implementing Islamic *sharia* law. 'We tried to remove every obstacle, whether small or big, loyal to the government or its opponent,' Ustad Fateh, the military commander of the Swat Taliban, told Al-Qaeda's media arm Al-Sahab.[11] 'What were those obstacles? They were the government institutions and security personnel, including police officers, Frontier Corps, spies and political leaders.'[12]

ANP leaders knew the situation was grim. Hundreds had already died in the conflict and thousands more were affected. In May 2008, the ANP saw no choice but to sign a military-brokered agreement with the

Taliban. But the agreement, which promised that the Taliban would accept government authority in return for the implementation of *sharia* in Swat, failed within months. Most analysts believe the Taliban were simply reluctant to give up the control they could exercise thanks to their thousands of fighters. Swat soon turned into a battle zone in which hundreds more people were killed in targeted assassinations, suicide bombings and military raids.

It was a disturbing fate for the scenic resort territory, which once had been praised by Britain's Queen Elizabeth as the 'Switzerland of Asia' during a visit in the 1960s. The region, predominantly populated by Yousafzai Pashtuns, became a suzerain state within the Raj in the early twentieth century. Local scholars describe the formation of the princely state as an attempt by Swatis to break free from tribal life. Swat retained its preferential status after the departure of the British, and under its autocratic but progressive ruler Miangul Jehanzeb, it developed at a faster rate compared to surrounding districts. The region blossomed with schools, colleges and road networks. Development, however, stalled after the Swat's 1969 merger with Pakistan. Some Swatis remain nostalgic for the old system as they struggle with Pakistan's hopelessly inefficient bureaucracy.

Politics in Swat and the surrounding region were shaken by the arrival of TNSM.[13] Maulana Sufi Muhammad, a Deobandi cleric and former local leader of the Jammat-e Islami, founded the organisation in 1989. It debuted as a potent force in 1994, when it blocked roads to Malakand. Scores died in Swat, Dir, Buner and other regions of Malakand as TNSM activists pursued implementation of *sharia*. The group's motto, '*sharia* or *shahada*', or *sharia* or martyrdom, left no doubt about the movement's commitment. Scores more people died when the Frontier Corps were sent in to retake areas seized by the TNSM.

'Western democracy is opposed to Muhammad's *sharia*. That system stands on [political] parties, which are prone to dissent,' Sufi Muhammad said in an interview in 1995. 'The Koran, however, counts unity as an important precondition [for social well-being]. So this system of opposition and discord can never be in line with *sharia*. We can never have *sharia* as long as the political parties exist here. We are against this democracy and its elections.'[14]

The government offered concessions to the TNSM, but the movement had lost political influence in the wake of the 1994 bloodshed.

That began to change, however, after the October 2001 US-led attacks against the Taliban regime in Afghanistan. Sufi Muhammad's zealous speeches persuaded thousands of militant volunteers to follow him into Afghanistan. Many never returned. I interviewed a few who managed to survive in the spring of 2002. They were disillusioned over the suffering they had experienced and were bitter about being abandoned by Sufi Muhammad, who safely returned to Pakistan in late 2001. He was later convicted over his alleged role in recruiting volunteers and was sentenced to seven years in prison. The TNSM was officially banned in 2002, but it remained a force to be reckoned with.[15]

As Sufi Muhammad languished in a prison cell, his son-in-law began to rise in prominence. Maulana Fazlullah had worked as a chairlift operator in the village of Mam Dheri before becoming a preacher. He never completed formal religious training at a madrasa, but claimed to have been inspired by his father-in-law.[16] The illegal FM radio station he opened in 2004 amplified his message across Swat. His following eventually grew to include some key powerbrokers. He bankrolled his organisation and a sprawling madrasa complex with donations from locals. Women, converted by his broadcasts, were his major donors. Some even donated their jewellery. Maulana Fazlullah also developed links with Taliban groups in the Tribal Areas. Locals spoke of the presence of militants from outside Swat long before the July 2007, military operation against the Red Mosque militants.

Maulana Fazlullah, who had close ties to the Red Mosque clerics, was among those who had clamoured for revenge. Maulana Abdul Aziz and Abdul Rashid Ghazi had gained stature through sermons to Swat locals broadcast over Fazlullah's FM station.[17] Maulana Fazlullah was formally declared the *amir* of the Swat Taliban when the Tehreek-e Taliban Pakistan emerged in December 2007. By then, Fazlullah had established control over large Swat population centres. In a broadcast around that time, he warned, 'I have an announcement for the police officers. If you are Muslims and were born to a Muslim mother, please don't waste your lives for a few thousand rupees. Please don't light this fire. I am warning you: No one will be able to put it out.'[18]

The rise of the Swat Taliban was aided by a coalition of six Islamist political parties known as the Muttahida Majlis-e Ammal (MMA). During its five-year rule in Khyber Pakhtunkhwa Province, from 2002 to late 2007, the MMA turned a blind eye to the rise of Taliban militancy in Swat. Some MMA leaders even encouraged and supported the Taliban. To strengthen their local control, one of the Taliban's first acts was to crack down on Swat's dancing girls. They closed the Banr neighbourhood in Mingora, where the dancing girls lived and performed. The Taliban terrified artists by publically executing one of Swat's most famous dancers, Shabana, in 2009. They even tried to vandalise Swat's rich Buddhist archeological heritage by attempting to blow-up a 1,500-year-old stone carving of Buddha in 2007.[19]

Taliban influence peaked in Swat after the first peace agreement with the ANP failed in the summer of 2008. The militants created a parallel administration and sought to regulate public life through night letters, or leaflets, and FM radio broadcasts. Terrified locals were forced to listen regularly to keep themselves informed about Taliban directives. Some prominent Swatis told me they listened to the broadcasts so they could either escape or prepare to defend themselves in the event they were accused of violating Taliban diktats. Sayed Muhammad Javed, the most senior civilian bureaucrat in Swat at the time, boosted Taliban ambitions by publically engaging them and relying on a Taliban security detail. Locals dubbed him the 'Taliban commissioner'.[20]

Schools, girls' schools in particular, were blown up frequently. 'We request all women refrain from going out shopping unnecessarily,' declared a Taliban leaflet distributed in the city of Mingora. Militants also dumped bodies in Green Square, which locals dubbed 'Khoni Chowk' or Bloody Square, in reference to the headless or mutilated bodies that would regularly be found there in the morning. 'The Tehreek-e Taliban Swat is presenting this gift to the NWFP Chief Minister [Amir] Haider [Khan] Hoti and Asfandiyar Wali Khan in return for the [government's] new military operation in Swat,' said a note taped to the mutilated corpse of a policeman in Khoni Chowk in the summer of 2008.

To establish complete control over Swat's 1.3 million residents, the Taliban targeted the *khans* or local landed gentry and elected officials, placing their names on 'most-wanted' lists. The militants also seized control of the region's timber business and emerald mines.[21] Sirajul Haq, a senior leader of Jammat-e Islami, viewed the class struggle between rich and poor—the *khans* and the peasants—as the historic backdrop to the rise of the Taliban. 'Some of the rank-and-file among the Taliban in the region had suffered because of some feudal lords,' Haq said. 'Thus, the Taliban provided them a platform and means to avenge what they saw as the wrongs done to them. This explains why they insulted the khans, forced them out of the region and [in some cases] sold their household items in an apparent bid to repeat what these khans had done to their families.'[22]

The Taliban also went after rival centres of religious authority. The TNSM had imbibed strong influences of Panjpiri puritanism. It had opposed rival sects and Sufism. The killing and hanging of the corpse of Pir Samiullah, a Sufi spiritual leader, and the public beheadings of some of his followers in December 2008, was a signal to Swati religious leaders to either fall in line or prepare for a similar fate.[23] The next year, the Taliban captured the shrine of Pir Baba in the neighbouring Buner district and banned all Sufi religious observances in the sanctuary, which is considered by Pashtuns to be one of the most revered Sufi shrines.

One elderly ANP politician, however, decided to stay and fight. Afzal Khan, eighty-four, topped the Taliban hit list, but refused to either appear before a Taliban court or leave Swat. 'If the Taliban had their own state, and they had a president or a prime minister or a king, and it functioned like a [legitimate state] system—then they would have a judicial system and courts that would follow Islamic law, *sharia*. But if they don't have a state or a political system, then whose court should I go to and why?' he asked. Khan, whom locals called Lala, or elder brother, lost two of his young grandsons in a Taliban ambush. He was attacked in 2007 and sustained gunshot injuries. 'When I was being treated in the hospital, I told journalists that if I ever met our attackers, I would ask them, "What was our crime? I have never even slapped anybody. Why then are you trying to kill us?"'[24]

By January 2009, government authority in Swat had completely collapsed—something that was privately acknowledged by senior Pakistani officials. '[General] Kayani was clear that the GOP [Government of Pakistan] had lost control of the Swat Valley,' US Ambassador Ann Patterson wrote in a diplomatic cable after a January 2009 meeting between Pakistani military chief Ashfaq Parvez Kayani and US Central Command head General David Petraeus. 'He said the police had no ability to come in after the army to hold territory. He recounted that half of the 600 police officers, supposedly from the NWFP's elite police units, destined for Swat had deserted, largely because there was no command structure.'

Faced with bad choices, ANP leaders decided to negotiate a new peace deal with the Taliban. Their priority was to use Sufi Muhammad's influence to rein in his renegade son-in-law. Afrasiab Khattak told me suicide bombers were present in the room as he and other party representatives negotiated with Sufi Muhammad. He said the Taliban delegation began to include more radical Islamists, whose aims were never limited to Swat. 'Enforcing *sharia* was not their main aim,' said Khattak. 'They were bent on seizing power by force.'

The negotiations resulted in a peace agreement in February 2009. Despite international and domestic pressures, the ANP agreed to establish new *sharia* courts to meet the demands of the TNSM. But the strength of the agreement was soon in doubt. The ANP, with the backing of Islamabad and the military, wanted to use the agreement to pressure Fazlullah's estimated 6,000 supporters to disarm. The TNSM and the Taliban declined to talk about disarmament. They also accused the government of harassing their cadres. 'After the peace arrangement, Swat does not really appear as part of the Pakistani state,' Pakistani intellectual Tariq Rahman concluded. 'It has passed into the hands of the Taliban. It is, to all intents and purposes, a Taliban state, and this hard reality should sink into the minds of our ruling elite.'[25]

The agreement generated intense debate in Pakistan. Unlike FATA, Swat was accessible to the media and dominated headlines. Higher literacy levels and associations with political parties meant that Swatis were comfortable telling their story to the outside world—something the Pashtuns of FATA had failed to do.

The ANP pushed for implementation of the accord, and the agreed legal changes were endorsed by Pakistan's national parliament and signed into law by President Asif Ali Zardari in April 2009. The ANP privately pushed Sufi Muhammad to hold a public gathering in Swat to call on the Taliban to lay down their arms. Wajid Ali Khan, an ANP provincial minister from Swat, was among those who spoke to the elderly leader. 'He used to tell us that if the government implements *sharia*, I will issue a decree and declare all those who will not follow it infidels,' Wajid Ali Khan recalled.[26]

On 19 April 2009, Sufi Muhammad did an abrupt about-face. Instead of calling on the Taliban to give up their arms, he declared the Pakistani political system and constitution un-Islamic. Many politicians knew immediately that the peace agreement was finished.

'In Swat, Maulana Sufi Muhammad was not the main player,' former Interior Minister Aftab Sherpao recalled. 'He had even lost the influence that he had back in 1994 and 1995. The real player there was Maulana Fazlullah. They concluded this agreement with Maulana Sufi Muhammad because they thought he would influence his son-in-law. But he didn't have that kind of influence and the agreement was bound to fail.'[27]

The Taliban went on to extend its control into the Buner and Dir districts east and west of Swat. Amir Haider Khan Hoti, the chief minister of Khyber Pakhtunkhwa, expressed the view of many when he alleged that the Taliban used peace accords to expand their reach. 'A large part of their leadership used the dialogue to buy time,' he recalled. 'They used it to fan the fire they had lit in Swat.'[28]

By May 2009, the Taliban had committed so many flagrant abuses that most residents had lost all trust in the militants and turned against them. The ANP's controversial peace agreement had exposed the extremists' true intentions. But the point was mostly lost on the Pakistani media and public, whose information about the region generally came from reporters who followed the government's line or relayed a misleading picture of what was happening.

Some incidents of Taliban atrocities in Swat triggered public protests against the Taliban and forced the government to change course. President Asif Ali Zardari ordered an official inquiry into the public flogging of a young girl. A grainy cell-phone video of the incident received many views on *YouTube* and was broadcast on Pakistani television news stations. It showed a young girl dressed in the all-enveloping *burka* veil being flogged while pinned down by unidentified men. Her cries of pain can be plainly heard. Islamabad faced a fresh international backlash in the wake of the video. 'I think that the Pakistani government is basically abdicating to the Taliban and to the extremists,' US Secretary of State Hillary Clinton told the House Foreign Affairs Committee in late April 2009. She warned that Pakistan's instability to counter Taliban expansion posed a 'mortal threat' to world peace.[29]

The Pakistani military moved into Swat in late April 2009. Over the next two months, some 2.5 million people were displaced. The military had decimated the Taliban network by early August. It killed and captured some of the key Swati Taliban leaders, and forces were left behind to maintain stability after major combat operations had ended. The operation enjoyed broad public support, but was not without controversy. In early July 2009, Afrasiab Khattak told Lynn Tracy, the US consul in Peshawar, that the provincial administration had defied ISI pressure to release Sufi Muhammad from custody and accept the brokered surrender of Swat Taliban leaders. 'Khattak declared flatly that the provincial government wanted nothing to do with this plan,' Tracy wrote in a July 2009, diplomatic cable to Washington released by WikiLeaks. 'Operations in Swat,' he said, 'should come to a "logical conclusion"—killing or capturing militant leadership.'

The military, however, failed to deal with Maulana Fazlullah, who re-emerged in the eastern Afghan province of Nuristan in the summer of 2010. His survival kept alive hopes of a Taliban revival in Swat. The Pakistani military's continued presence in Swat and Malakand is seen as preventing the extremists from mounting a full-scale comeback—though they were able to mount a series of devastating attacks. In October 2012, a militant shot and seriously wounded peace icon Malala Yousafzai. The fifteen-year-old girl had become known for campaigning for peace and girls' education. She had written a blog for the BBC's Urdu Service, chronicling Taliban atrocities in Swat in 2009. Her shooting proved a huge public relations disaster for the Taliban. It galvanised support for anti-Taliban Pashtuns and united most Pakistanis in condemnation of Taliban brutalities. Fazlullah returned to the limelight after he assumed the leadership of the TTP following the killing of Hakimullah Mehsud in a U.S. drone strike in November 2013.

The Military's Pashtun Wars

In September 2011, on the tenth anniversary of the 11 September attacks, an entity calling itself the 'Government of Pakistan' placed a prominent half-page advertisement in *The Wall Street Journal*. 'Which country can do more for your peace?' the advert's headline asked. 'Since 2001 a nation of 180 million has been fighting for the future of the world's 7 billion!' was the answer. 'Can any other country do so? Only Pakistan—promising peace to the world.' The advertisement listed Islamabad's sacrifices: 2,795 soldiers killed and 8,671 wounded in 3,486 bomb blasts and 283 major suicide bombings, which also killed and injured 21,672 civilians. Some 3.5 million people displaced from their homes. National economic losses of $68 billion.

The advert featured a photograph of the assassinated former Prime Minister Benazir Bhutto, and claimed authorities had foiled more than a dozen assassination plots against her widower, President Asif Ali Zardari, and Prime Minister Sayed Yusuf Raza Gilani. A blog in *The Wall Street Journal* claimed that *The New York Times* refused to carry the advert because the paper had asked for 'more clarity in the ad about who was placing it', and this information was not provided. Café Pyala, a popular Pakistani blog, cited unnamed sources claiming that the advert might have been placed by the country's premier military-controlled intelligence agency, the Directorate of Inter-Services Intelligence (ISI).[30]

Irrespective of who placed the advert, it reflected the Pakistani military's standard narrative to counter Western suspicions over its alleged links to militants. The military frequently offers the kind of statistics showcased in the advert in briefings to journalists and diplomats. To understand the Pakistani military's paradoxical role in the struggle against extremism in the western Pashtun regions, one needs to examine its past role in domestic politics and its internal culture.

I have heard many Pakistani intellectuals characterise the military in stark terms. But perhaps a popular joke describes it best: 'All countries have armies—but here, an army has a country.' The nation's history reveals the essential truth of the joke. Since Pakistani independence in 1947, four generals have ruled the nation for a total of thirty-four years: Ayub Khan (1958–1969), Yahya Khan (1969–1971), Muhammad Zia-ul Haq (1977–1988) and Pervez Musharraf (1999–2008). It has long been the case that the military dominates national decision-making and defines what Pakistan's national interests are. Pakistan is thus a 'security state', where the military actively shapes the lives of the citizenry.

During the Cold War, political support and financial aid from the United States and the West served as a crucial enabler of the military's dominance. But the relationship between the military and Washington has often been tumultuous, with the US treating Pakistan as an ally when its interests required it, or punishing Islamabad over, for example, its nuclear programme. Relations hewed to this pattern after 11 September 2001. Within days of the attacks on New York and Washington, General Musharraf declared allegiance to US war aims. But Pakistan's intelligence services were quietly backing plans for a Taliban return to power in Kabul.[31] As the Afghan insurgency intensified, Islamabad and Washington engaged in a sort of proxy war. The US and its allies sent more forces to Afghanistan to prop up Karzai's government. They encouraged anti-Taliban factions inside Pakistan. Islamabad, meanwhile, continued to shelter the Afghan Taliban leadership and tolerated their cross-border operations.[32]

The Pakistani military's power is not limited to the security and political spheres. During its decades of dominance, the military has also built a corporate and real-estate empire, turning its generals into a privileged class armed with wealth, power and advantages. According to Pakistani security analyst Ayesha Siddiqa, this empire is estimated to have more than $10 billion in assets, including nearly 5 million hectares of land. She says the military's economic tentacles extend to all major sectors of the economy—agriculture, manufacturing and services. 'They are one of the major stakeholders in the country's economy,' she told me. 'From an institutional perspective, I think, they would be the largest.' The military also takes the lion's share of foreign aid. Most of the $20 billion Pakistan received from Washington after 11 September 2001 ended up in the military's coffers. Controversy over the military's considerable perks and privileges has never led to significant reforms. None of Pakistan's military dictators has ever been held accountable. The military receives at least 25 per cent of national budgets, and these are not open to civilian scrutiny.[33]

A fundamental, if nuanced, internal transformation of Pakistan's military took place after Islamabad became the West's frontline ally in the 1980s jihadist war against the Soviet invaders of Afghanistan. At their founding, the army and other forces had inherited the secular traditions of their predecessor, the British imperial military. Strong checks and balances in this internal culture were intended to maintain discipline. But this began to change when military dictator General Zia-ul Haq introduced numerous 'Islamic' laws regulating public life. He also encouraged Islamists from around the world to join the Afghan jihad.

The military's internal culture did not escape this process of 'Islamization'. The military's motto was changed to 'Islamic faith, Piety and Jihad in the Path of Allah'. The task of promoting religious observance within the military was handed to the bureaucracy. Grand mosques soon sprouted inside military garrisons and a cadre of mullahs was enlisted to serve as chaplains. The military's heritage strongly discouraged officers and soldiers from joining political parties, but loyalty to conservative proselytising Islamic organisations was tolerated.[34]

This internal transformation was a reflection of the military's strategic policies. The military formed the core of what Pakistanis call the 'establishment'—an elite group composed of pro-military politicians, bureaucrats, judges and generals. The establishment adopted the strategy of supporting Islamist extremist proxies during the 1971 war that resulted in Pakistan's eastern wing becoming Bangladesh. The apparent success of the Afghan mujahedeen in the 1980s encouraged the establishment to test the model against arch-rival India in the disputed Kashmir region in the 1990s. The establishment also permitted a larger role for religious political parties in national politics. Pashtun regions in Afghanistan and Pakistan served as sanctuaries and recruiting grounds for jihadis. One result of this policy was an increase in attacks by Sunni extremists on minority Shia. The extremists claimed to be fearful of a repeat in Pakistan of Iran's Shia-led 1979 Islamic revolution.[35]

After 11 September 2001, the Pakistani military was suddenly expected to fight against an extremist entity it helped create. In what was billed as a landmark speech in January 2002, General Musharraf formally banned many of the organisations his intelligence services had fostered during the 1990s. However, the reversal he promised never materialised, and the banned organisations continued to flourish after changing their names and putting up new signboards. Pakistan was thus both hosting the Afghan Taliban and failing to check the rise of the Pakistani Taliban. At the same time, the Pakistani military helped Washington by arresting and killing some Al-Qaeda figures.

The military was pleasing no one, and creating new enemies in the process. The story of a Taliban commander in Swat is a telling example:

> Pakistan's ISI intelligence agency arrested me at my home on August 29, 2004. I had to spend the next two years and three months in their prison. Jihad was the only reason for my arrest. Every evil thing is allowed in this county. There is freedom for debauchery and obscenity, but only true jihad is banned. While in prison, I got an insight into what the government was doing to the mujahedeen. I came to know what was happening to Pakistani mujahedeen who were working under the [intelligence] agency. While waging jihad in Kashmir and Afghanistan, they were unable to stray from their orders even one step. So when I and my friends came out of prison, we quit waging the jihad under the directions of the [intelligence] agency and began waging the jihad for Allah alone.[36]

Pashtun leaders privately urged Islamabad to change course. At the height of Taliban influence in Swat, in January 2009, elderly Pashtun politician Afzal Khan advised Pakistani military chief Kayani to protect the military's good standing by launching a decisive offensive against the Taliban. 'The people of Swat believe that the army and the Taliban are one and you need to do something decisively to wash away such perceptions from public minds,' Khan said he had told Kayani.[37]

Islamabad's duplicity was no secret to Western policymakers. The Afghan government had repeatedly cited Pakistani interference as a major problem. But Washington hoped that carrots, in the form of aid and alliances, would help Pakistan's military overcome its security paranoia. Robust behind-the-scenes diplomatic efforts by Washington eased potentially devastating confrontations between India and Pakistan after major Islamic militant attacks in New Delhi in 2001 and Mumbai in 2008. Senior American officials showered praise on Islamabad and expressed sympathy for its positions.

When I asked US Vice President Joe Biden in October 2009 whether he saw progress against extremism in Pakistan, given that insecurity increased after every military operation, his answer seemed to favour Islamabad. 'The [Pakistani] military is reacting appropriately, and they face a very difficult problem, but I would argue the opposite,' said Biden. 'It is not the action of the military that has produced the reaction of the jihadis and the radical Islamists there. It has been that the military has had to react to the overreaching on the part of the TTP and others, the Haqqani Network, and others in the region. And so we look at their actions as being appropriate.'[38] Washington, however, eventually came to see the Pakistani military as an impediment to its efforts in Afghanistan because of its influence over insurgents who planned attacks in Afghanistan from bases in Pakistan.

For many observers, the Pakistani 'double game' was glaringly exposed when elite US Navy SEALs infiltrated deep into Pakistan on 2 May 2011 and shot dead Al-Qaeda leader Osama bin Laden at a compound in Abbottabad, located close to a premier Pakistani military training academy. The ISI was forced to acknowledge 'embarrassment' over its failure to detect the presence of the world's most-hunted man on its front lawn. Pakistan's civilian government, on the other hand, took the opportunity to reiterate its commitment to the global fight against extremism. President Asif Ali Zardari expressed his 'satisfaction' over the US killing of bin Laden. 'We have not yet won this war, but we now clearly can see the beginning of the end, and the kind of South and Central Asia that lies in our future,' he wrote in an op-ed published in *The Washington Post* a day after bin Laden was killed.[39]

In the wake of the bin Laden raid, General Talat Massoud, a septuagenarian former army general and influential analyst, said Pakistani generals were losing their room for manoeuvre. 'There is no other choice left except to face very squarely all the militant organisations and be as transparent as possible and take the people in confidence, or alienate the rest of the world,' he told me. 'So I think there is no choice whatsoever.'[40] The military, however, rejected that option.

The military also came under criticism from politicians in the eastern Punjab Province. Most Pakistani soldiers and officers come from among Punjab's estimated 80 million people. Former Prime Minister Nawaz Sharif, who lost his government in the 1999 military coup, broke with the tradition of Punjabi politicians toeing the military's line. 'What is happening here? Who is taking Pakistan in this direction of [anarchy and destruction]?' he asked in a June 2011 speech. 'We created Pakistan for the rule of law and the supremacy of the constitution, not for these [despicable] scenes that our 180 million people watch on their televisions every day.'

After losing key backers in the US establishment, the military's main challenge became navigating a collision course with Washington. 'In choosing to use violent extremism as an instrument of policy, the government of Pakistan—and most especially the Pakistani Army and ISI—jeopardises not only the prospect of our strategic partnership but Pakistan's opportunity to be a respected nation with legitimate regional influence,' America's top military commander, Admiral Michael Mullen, told senators in September 2011, as he prepared to leave the post.

Mullen, the chairman of the Joint Chiefs of Staff, had cultivated a personal friendship with army chief General Kayani in hopes of securing Pakistani military co-operation. But he was withering in his condemnation of Pakistani activities, saying they had not been successful. '[The government of Pakistan] may believe that, by using these proxies, they are hedging their bets or redressing what they feel is an imbalance in regional power, but in reality they have already lost that bet,' Mullen said, echoing what Pakistani politicians and intellectuals had been saying for years. He concluded, 'By exporting violence, they have eroded their internal security and their position in the region. They have undermined their international credibility and threatened their economic well-being. Only a decision to break with this policy can pave the road to a positive future for Pakistan.'[41]

Mullen clearly insinuated that the ISI was in direct confrontation with US forces in Afghanistan. He told lawmakers on the Senate Armed

Services Committee that the Haqqani Network 'acts as a veritable arm' of Pakistan's ISI [Inter-Services Intelligence] agency. He alleged that 'with ISI support', Haqqani Network fighters attacked the US Embassy in Kabul on 13 September 2011, and carried out a 10 September truck-bomb attack on a NATO outpost in central Wardak Province. The two attacks killed at least twenty-one Afghan police officers and civilians and injured seventy-seven coalition troops—one of the worst single-day casualties of the 10-year war.[42]

Even before Mullen's testimony, all US military aid to Pakistan had been suspended. But Mullen's criticism prompted analysts to devise new ways of dealing with the Pakistani military. 'It is time to move to a policy of containment, which would mean a more hostile relationship. But it should be a focused hostility, aimed not at hurting Pakistan's people but at holding its army and intelligence branches accountable,' former CIA Officer Bruce Riedel wrote in an op-ed article in *The New York Times*. 'When we learn that an officer from Pakistan's Inter-Services Intelligence, or ISI, is aiding terrorism, whether in Afghanistan or India, we should put him on wanted lists, sanction him at the United Nations and, if he is dangerous enough, track him down.'[43]

Mansoor Ijaz, an American investor of Pakistani ancestry, advocated targeted actions against the military. 'ISI embodies the scourge of radicalism that has become a cornerstone of Pakistan's foreign policy,' he wrote. 'The time has come for America to take the lead in shutting down the political and financial support that sustains an organ of the Pakistani state that undermines global anti-terrorism efforts at every turn. More precise policies are needed to remove the cancer that ISI and its rogue wings have become on the Pakistani state.' He added, 'The time has come for the State Department to declare the S-Wing [of the ISI] a sponsor of terrorism under the designation of "foreign governmental organisations".'[44]

Washington never went that far. Indeed, it apologised to Islamabad in July 2012, after twenty-four Pakistani troops were killed by a US air strike near the Afghan border in November 2011. Islamabad had demanded the apology in exchange for reopening NATO supply routes to Afghanistan through Pakistan. The US did, however, signal its unhappiness over the continued presence of militant networks in Pakistan and continued drone strikes in the Tribal Areas.[45]

In January 2012 I met again with Afrasiab Khattak. He was a very busy man. His duties as provincial head of the ANP in Khyber Pakhtunkhwa, and as a Pakistani senator, required him to divide his time between Peshawar and Islamabad. He was also now forced to rely on a sophisticated array of security measures in order to avoid Taliban assassins. I had the opportunity to travel with him by car to Peshawar.[46]

Khattak told me his years in the government had convinced him that the extremism in Afghanistan and Pakistan was aimed at stamping out Pashtun identity and replacing it with pan-Islamism. He, however, remained committed to pursuing peace. He told me the ANP's sacrifices after assuming power in 2008 had not been in vain.[47] Khattak pointed to the sea change in Pakistani public opinion, which had swung solidly against the extremists since their botched attempt to rule Swat. He was optimistic the Pashtuns would ultimately survive Islamic extremists, just as they had survived conquerors and superpowers before. He told me that forces seeking to capture strategic advantage by stoking instability in the Pashtun heartland would eventually be forced to reconsider. 'We are like the ozone layer for this country,' he said. 'We protect it from many dangers and bad influences. Our destruction will expose it to unthinkable hazards.'

7

SIMMERING BALOCHISTAN

A TALIBAN HAVEN

It was not difficult to find Afghan Taliban fighters in Quetta, the capital of Pakistan's south-western Balochistan Province. There were hundreds of them, perhaps thousands, living amid the dusty roads, narrow allies and mud huts of the city's Pashtunabad neighbourhood. In the fall of 2003, I visited Balochistan with my friend Ahmed Rashid. I had agreed to assist Rashid with an investigation into the rise of the 'neo-Taliban'—militants who had regrouped in Pakistan and were making waves with a new campaign of violence.

To outsiders, the residents of Pashtunabad may have seemed largely indistinguishable. But their white turbans, long tunics and baggy trousers made the Afghan Taliban fighters easy to spot. To expert local eyes, the way they fastened their turbans, the slight variations of their Pashto dialect, their unkempt long beards and hair, and the way they walked around in packs, distinguished the Afghan Taliban from ordinary residents.

Within our first hour, we encountered many Taliban. They poured into the streets after offering afternoon prayers. There were so many of them that some had been forced to live in shop space. There simply wasn't any further room in the private homes, mosques and madrasas of the neighbourhood. We saw Taliban drinking tea at roadside stalls, eating meals in the small restaurants that lined the filthy streets, or eating ice cream and chewing sugarcane. Locals had even renamed a park 'Al-

Qaeda Park' because of all the young Taliban fighters who gathered there to engage in traditional Kandahari sports such as *khusai* and *ghaizha*, both forms of wrestling.

This Taliban sanctuary in Balochistan had been established with the active support of the JUI, the party which dominated the provincial administration. Support had also been provided through the active, but invisible, support of the Pakistani military through its intelligence agencies, the ISI in particular.

The fighters we spoke to complained of having been harassed by the new Afghan authorities and their American backers. They were intent on overthrowing the government, ousting the Americans and restoring Taliban rule. '[Afghan President Hamid] Karzai's time is finished,' said Hafiz Hussain Sharodi, who was then Balochistan's information minister and a senior JUI leader. 'Only the Taliban can constitute the real government in Afghanistan.'[1]

Taliban Redux

That autumn, Quetta was the stage for the launch of an elaborate 'double game' by Pakistan's military establishment. The strategy relied on exploiting Western ignorance of Pashtun dynamics. President Pervez Musharraf had skillfully manipulated Western policymakers by persuading them that his co-operation was central to winning what Washington called the 'Global War on Terrorism'. At the same time, Islamabad was permitting and, according to many accounts, facilitating the recuperation of the Taliban in Pakistan's Pashtun borderlands. This kept alive the possibility of a Taliban return to power in Afghanistan.

When Washington launched the invasion of Iraq in March 2003, Quetta was home to the most important remnants of the Taliban regime, including—probably—Mullah Mohammad Omar. With US attention focused on Saddam Hussein, the pressure on Islamabad eased. Pakistan again began to view Afghanistan as a mere tool to be used in its broader conflict with India. Pakistani support again flowed to hard-line Afghan networks.

In the summer of 2003, Taliban attacks in southern Afghanistan claimed the lives of some 400 Afghan civilians, soldiers and aid workers. As Western leaders heaped praise on Musharraf, President Karzai warned of Islamabad's duplicity. 'For us to be truly satisfied, we need all such terrorist acts to stop in Afghanistan,' Karzai said after meeting US Deputy Secretary of State Richard Armitage in early October 2003. Perhaps worried about US criticism, Pakistan launched a commando raid in South Waziristan during Armitage's visit. Officials announced that the raid killed Ahmed Said Khadr, a key Al-Qaeda financier. Such high-profile raids, arrests and killings became a signature Pakistani tactic to fend off Western criticism.[2]

Close social links between the residents of Balochistan and southern Afghanistan aided the Taliban comeback. Even a century after they were separated into different state systems, southern Afghanistan and much of northern Balochistan's Pashtun-populated regions possess many of the same traits. The major Pashtun tribes in Balochistan—the Kakar, Tareen, and various clans of the Ghilzai and Durrani—share links with communities in the southern Afghan provinces of Kandahar, Helmand, Zabul, Uruzgan and Farah. These connections were strengthened by the arrival of Afghan refugees during the Soviet occupation of Afghanistan in the 1980s.

To protect against the potential political mobilisation of Pashtuns, Islamabad sought to use Islamist Pashtuns, the JUI in particular, to disrupt nationalist ambitions. In the 1970s and 1980s, Islamabad warily eyed the sanctuary that Pashtun and Baloch ethno-nationalists enjoyed in Afghanistan. Some of these nationalists even supported the Afghan socialist regime's war effort against the mujahedeen guerillas.[3]

The eventual victory of the anti-communist mujahedeen compounded the complexity of cross-border relations. Divisions among the mujahedeen soon turned into active rivalries and vendettas. For most mujahedeen commanders, their commitment to Islamist causes receded. Their local prestige and access to funds raised from the region's trade and drug production weakened their dependence on their erstwhile Pakistani military benefactors. Many among the southern mujahedeen had also maintained links to the Afghan royalist elite. Their commitment to Afghan nationalism made the mujahedeen unreliable allies for Islamabad. While the mujahedeen fought among themselves, Pakistan in the 1990s was plagued by its own instability, including ineffective civilian governments, conflicts between civilian and military leaders, simmering ethnic and sectarian conflicts, and growing international isolation because of its nuclear weapons programme.

The birth of the Taliban in the mid-1990s proved a boon for the JUI. The Taliban partly originated in JUI madrasas in the Pashtun districts of northern Balochistan. The JUI counted some key Taliban leaders among its alumni, and its cadres and madrasas provided fighters for the militia. Many JUI leaders frequented Kandahar and openly declared solidarity with the Taliban. Veteran JUI provincial minister Maulana Abdul Bari Agha, Maulana Noor Muhammad and Maulvi Asmatullah were key pro-Taliban ideologues. Maulana Abdul Ghani, a JUI lawmaker and rector of a large madrasa in the border town of Chaman, was revered by Taliban leaders and cadres. His October 2011 death in a traffic accident was publically mourned by the Taliban. The movement declared him a 'martyr for the cause of jihad' and said he would be difficult to replace. In what appeared to be the first formal acknowledgement of their links with the JUI, a Taliban spokesman praised Ghani for showing great courage in supporting the movement after the US-led invasion of Afghanistan.[4]

Washington declared the Taliban defeated after the regime was smashed by US air strikes and special forces units working with anti-Taliban Afghan factions in late 2001. The movement's rule in Kabul may have been toppled, but the militants were far from finished. As the Americans set to work installing a new government in Afghanistan, Taliban fighters melted away into Pakistan's FATA and Balochistan's northern Pashtun districts.[5] They reorganised in the Quetta Shura, led by Mullah Mohammad Omar, and began planning for an eventual return to power. In 2003, the militants orchestrated a campaign of violence across southern Afghanistan. Many former Taliban members, feeling oppressed by the new authorities, enthusiastically joined the insurgency. The Afghan presidential elections in 2004, seen as a success by the international community, alarmed the Taliban and prompted the group to unleash even greater violence. The 2005 parliamentary elections were targeted with more insurgent attacks than the presidential vote.

Quetta's status as the base of the Taliban insurgency had become well known. 'Quetta had become a kind of free zone where strategies could be formed, funds picked up, interviews given and victories relished,' wrote American journalist Elizabeth Rubin. She was among the few Western journalists to report from Quetta. To veteran observers, the activity in Quetta resembled Peshawar in the 1980s, when the Pakistani military was providing wide support for the mujahedeen. 'A suspicious place of spies and counterspies and double agents,' Rubin wrote of Quetta. JUI support for the Taliban was frequently transparent. Its provincial ministers attended funerals and eulogised locals who had died in Afghan battles. The party openly engaged in fundraising. An estimated 10,000 Taliban fighters were active at the time.[6]

Among those operating from Quetta was Mullah Dadullah. The forty-year-old former student of Noor Muhammad had shown himself to be the most effective field commander in southern Afghanistan. His reputation as a ruthless commander won him praise from his former teacher. 'I am proud of him,' Noor Muhammad told the German news magazine *Der Spiegel*. While Mullah Dadullah hid in plain sight in Balochistan, Islamabad was continuing to cling to its policy of denial. David Richards, the British commander of NATO forces in Afghanistan, confronted Musharraf with videos, satellite images and testimonies from captured insurgents documenting Pakistani aid to the Taliban. But Islamabad refused to alter its policy.[7]

By 2007, Western diplomats in Pakistan and Afghanistan concluded that Pakistan's military intelligence was helping to restore the Taliban. Islamabad remained committed to its strategy of preventing India from establishing a foothold in Afghanistan. Potential encirclement by India has always been seen as a catastrophic scenario by Pakistani generals. Islamic extremism, cultivated in the Pashtun regions, was seen by Islamabad as an easy—and relatively cheap—weapon that could be used to counter Indian encirclement.

Taliban who attempted to reach out to the government in Kabul could be in great danger. Carlotta Gall, a long-time Pakistan and Afghanistan correspondent for *The New York Times*, interviewed many former Taliban members and Pashtun tribal elders in Balochistan. They told her that Taliban cadres reluctant to fight in Afghanistan were periodically rounded up and paraded 'as part of Pakistan's crackdown on the Taliban in Pakistan'.[8] A Pakistani operation in 2010 resulted in the arrest of Taliban military chief Mullah Abdul Ghani Baradar in the southern seaport of Karachi.

The Taliban surge in Afghanistan was made possible by Pakistani volunteers, particularly Pashtuns from Balochistan. Pishin, an agricultural district south-west of Quetta, provided many volunteers. The recruitment was supported by the JUI, with the Pakistani military's acquiescence. Azizullah Agha, for example, emerged from the village of Karbala to become a key Taliban figure. When he was killed in a US air strike in May 2006, he was replaced by his brother Naseebullah Agha.

Azizullah Agha had been only twenty-five, and his funeral attracted thousands of mourners, including senior JUI provincial ministers. Naseebullah Agha continued aiding the Taliban's recruitment efforts. The recruits were often forced into fighting. Their parents were often unable to find them before their dead bodies were delivered home. Sometimes, news of their whereabouts came via Taliban propaganda DVDs containing videos of statements by the young men before they went out on suicide bombing missions. Balochistan newspapers frequently carried funeral announcements for those killed in Afghanistan.[9]

Taliban sanctuaries were spread throughout the Pashtun belt in Balochistan. Chagai, a large and predominantly Baloch-district south of Quetta, provided a link to the southern Afghan province of Helmand. The district also borders Iran, thus forming a triangular borderland between Pakistan, Afghanistan and Iran. This region is home to a major smuggling route. Baramcha, a small border town between Helmand and Chagai inside Afghanistan, remained under Taliban control for years. There, the militants operated improvised explosive device factories and training camps and planned military activities across southern Afghanistan.

The Taliban in Baramcha were controlled by the Quetta Shura. Taliban fighters treated their injured in Dalbandin, the major town in Chagai, but the main Afghan Taliban concentration remained in Quetta. New neighbourhoods, often named after Pashtun clans, sprung up in the dusty suburbs of the provincial metropolis. These neighbourhoods, such as Ishaqzai Colony and Alizai Colony, housed commanders and senior officials of the Taliban shadow government. They were occasionally observed attending wedding parties and other social functions. Injured Taliban were treated in Balochistan's hospitals. A large number of Taliban lived in Kuchlack, a small Pashtun town north of Quetta.[10] They used the mountains of Toba Achakzai to slip into Kandahar, where even the 2010 US troop surge failed to reverse Taliban momentum. Qilla Saifullah, a Pashtun town some 200 kilometres north of Quetta, served as another infiltration route into Afghanistan through the Toba Kakar range.[11]

It is difficult to determine the full extent of Pakistani control over the Taliban. But Taliban foot soldiers and officials interviewed in Balochistan paint a picture of the Pakistani secret services exerting near absolute control. These extremists maintain that, in addition to offering a sanctuary, Islamabad also provided the bulk of funding for the insurgents. The

Taliban well understood that their survival depended on keeping their Pakistani patrons happy. 'I wouldn't be surprised if the ISI arrested us all in one day,' a former Talban cabinet minister told *Newsweek*. 'We are like sheep the Pakistanis can round up whenever they want.'[12]

The Taliban suspected the Pakistanis of betraying two key leaders, Mullah Akhter Muhammad Usmani and Mullah Dadullah, to NATO. Both were killed in southern Afghanistan, in 2006 and 2007. Usmani had fled his Quetta hideout after a Pakistani raid. Taliban leaders are frequently rounded up and released after 'indoctrination' sessions, where their absolute loyalty to Pakistan was reinforced. In one such major sweep, Taliban military chief Abdul Qayum Zakir and other senior commanders were picked up. This occurred after Pakistan's February 2010 arrest of the former Taliban military leader Abdul Ghani Baradar. Zakir and the others were released a few days later after offering assurances that they remained loyal to Islamabad's objectives in Afghanistan.[13]

In return for Taliban loyalty, Islamabad ensured that Quetta remained off-limits for US drone strikes and spies. Balochistan was still considered safe for Taliban, even as the CIA carried out dozens of drone strikes targeting suspected militants in the Tribal Areas. Abdul Qayum Zakir oversaw the largest Taliban surge, in 2010 and 2011, from Quetta. He was reportedly replaced by Akhtar Mohammad Mansour toward the end of 2012. Their sanctuary was never directly threatened by NATO or Pakistani actions. The sanctuary in Balochistan remained unaffected even after the May 2011 killing of Osama bin Laden in the Pakistani north-western garrison town of Abbottabad.[14]

Divided Deobandis

Islamabad's support for the Afghan Taliban ended up bitterly dividing JUI leaders, making Pakistan's biggest Deobandi party a victim of the rehabilitation of the Taliban.[15] With the Taliban gaining strength and influence in Pakistan, Islamist leaders found themselves marginalised. Maulana Hassan Jan, a senior JUI leader, was assassinated in Peshawar in 2007 after voicing opposition to suicide bombings. The residence of Maulana Fazalur Rahman was attacked. Many senior Deobandi clerics not affiliated with the JUI were assassinated, paving the way for new radical leaders. Divisions over the Taliban were particularly bitter in Balochistan, and led to a split of the JUI into two factions.

Maulana Muhammad Khan Sherani, a tall man with a flowing white beard and locks, has been the *amir*, or leader, of JUI in Balochistan for years.[16] He distinguished himself by publically opposing the Taliban, and ranks among the handful of Deobandi clerics in Pakistan who never endorsed the Taliban insurgencies as jihad. This has made him a target for Taliban assassins. During the past decade, he has been attacked three times, including a suicide bombing in 2009 that left eight people dead. Sherani, both privately and publically, has criticised the Pakistani military for supporting the Taliban.

Sherani said at the end of 2010, 'I once asked [former Pakistani military dictator General Pervez] Musharraf, "Why are you sending people [militants] to Afghanistan?" He replied, "We are not sending anybody [to Afghanistan]." I told him, "Let me take you to the border in Chaman to show you if you are sending somebody or not." He told me, "Maulana sahib, we have not passed any such order." I told him, "You are stealing [doing covert action] and nobody gives orders for such actions."'[17]

The JUI split led to the party's *nazaryati*, or ideological, branch emerging as a radical splinter group in 2008. This faction openly supported the Afghan Taliban and opposed Pakistani military operations in Swat and the Tribal Areas. Maulvi Asmatullah, the leader of JUI *nazaryati*, defeated Maulana Mohammad Khan Sherani in the February 2008 parliamentary elections. In a December 2010 interview, Maulvi Asmatullah outlined his reasons for the split, 'Our main difference is that Maulana [Mohammad Khan Sherani] says this [fighting in Afghanistan] is not a jihad, but is a *fasad* (corruption or fraud)… Secondly, the JUI engaged in large-scale corruption, which saddened religious people. And thirdly, they supported Musharraf.'[18]

Maulvi Asmatullah, however, opposes armed struggle inside Pakistan. 'We are not convinced that Islam can be forced on Pakistan with weapons and violence because we have a parliamentary culture here,' he said. 'All Islamist political parties have participated in the elections here. The [political] atmosphere in Afghanistan is very different from the one in Pakistan. The key blunder of the Pakistani Taliban is that they are trying to imitate the actions needed inside Afghanistan.'

Maulvi Asmatullah, who maintains close contacts with Afghan Taliban leaders, said the Afghan Taliban are opposed to the Pakistani Taliban because they need Pakistani government support for sanctuary. 'They are also concerned about earning a bad name in Pakistani society [because of violence],' he said. 'I have heard that Mullah Omar is against military resistance in Pakistan,' he added about the reclusive Taliban leader. This analysis is key to understanding the Pakistani military strategy of trying to engage the mullahs, instead of marginalising them and pushing them towards militancy. 'We are leading the emotional religious people,' Maulvi Asmatullah said. 'And we are not allowing them to begin an armed struggle inside Pakistan. It will only lead to further destruction.'[19]

Sherani maintains that Islamabad wanted to create an indigenous jihadist movement among Pashtuns in Balochistan, with the aim of eventually using it to fight secular-minded Baloch nationalists who have launched a separatist insurgency. 'It would have pitted the Pashtuns against the Baloch and *sharia* against nationalism,' he said. Abdul Rahim Mandokhel, leader of the nationalist Pashtunkhwa Milli Awami Party, claims that secular and religious Pashtun leaders foiled plans by Islamabad to foment an insurgency. 'Our people saw how they were misused and the kind of destruction these [extremist militants] inevitably brought,' he said, explaining why the region was spared a Taliban insurgency. 'Our people looked at Afghanistan, Khyber Pakhtunkhwa and Central Pakhtunkhwa (FATA), and learned a lesson.'[20]

Balochistan: Crossroads of Conflict

Pakistan's military has for decades sought to dominate Balochistan, a resource-abundant and strategically-located region. But, quite separately from the activities of Islamist militants, Islamabad's rule there has been challenged by a series of ethnic Baloch insurrections.

The vast region borders Iran and Afghanistan and is hemmed in by FATA and the Khyber Pakhtunkhwa, Punjab and Sindh provinces. While Balochistan makes up nearly half of Pakistan's 800,000-square-kilometre territory, its population—nearly half of whom are Pashtuns—makes up less than 5 per cent of Pakistan's 180 million people. Rich in hydrocarbon resources and minerals, including one of the world's largest gold mines, the region has a long shoreline on the Arabian Sea, one of the world's busiest shipping routes. In 2013, Pakistan awarded China the right to operate Balochistan's increasingly important port of Gwadar, located not far from the mouth of the Persian Gulf. In Iran, ethnic Baloch make up around 2 per cent of the country's population of 80 million.

Balochistan's location at the crossroads of Central Asia, South Asia, the Middle East and west Asia has raised the stakes of the regional rivalries and insurgent movements being played out there. Islamabad succeeded in crushing Baloch insurgencies in 1948, 1958, 1962, and from 1973 to 1977, but the separatist movement has refused to die.[21] Thousands of separatist fighters, government soldiers, political leaders and civilians have been killed since the 2004 onset of the fifth Baloch insurgency. Nearly 200,000 people have been displaced, many of them ethnic Punjabis. The Baloch in Iran, meanwhile, live under severe political and cultural oppression, a Sunni Muslim minority under the nation's Shi'ite clerical regime.

So-called 'kill-and-dump' operations have become a hallmark of the latest Baloch insurgency. According to human rights watchdogs, hundreds of suspected militants and activists have become victims of 'enforced' disappearances carried out by Pakistan's military and intelligence agencies and the paramilitary Frontier Corps. Some have been found dead after torture. There are indications Islamabad has followed the 'Sri Lankan model' to target suspected Baloch separatists. Activists have been kidnapped and their decomposing corpses found weeks later, dumped by the side of the road. Baloch nationalists accuse the Pakistani security forces of orchestrating such killings.

Pakistan, for its part, has accused separatist insurgents of killing ethnic Punjabi migrants and politicians loyal to Islamabad. The conflict has been radicalised to the extent that now even moderate nationalists fear that hard-line militants are pushing them to completely abandon electoral politics and relations with Islamabad. The murders of ethnic Hazaras—a tiny Shi'ite minority—by suspected Sunni extremists has added to the complexity of the conflict. Attacks against Hazaras escalated in early 2013, when two large truck bombs targeting the minority killed more than 200. Most attacks against the Hazaras have been claimed by Lashkar-e Jhangvi, a radical Sunni group rooted in Punjab.

Balochistan is also a battleground for competing regional interests. Pakistan has publicly accused India of supporting Baloch separatists and is suspicious of an Indian-financed road network linking south-western Afghanistan to the south-eastern Iranian port of Chabahar, a predominantly ethnic Baloch city. Tehran has invested in an Arabian Sea Port project, hoping to attract business from across Central Asia. Over the past decade, China has invested more than 80 per cent of some $300 million in the development of the Gwadar Port. In February 2013 Beijing took over the management of the port.[22] Many observers believe the project showcases a Sino-Pakistani alliance and may signal their co-operation in Afghanistan—co-operation eyed with suspicion by New Delhi.

Islamabad has funded its battle against the Baloch insurgency by occasionally diverting resources it received from the West to fight the Taliban and Al-Qaeda. Washington and its allies have considered ending the Balochistan sanctuary of Mullah Omar and the Afghan Taliban in a bid to force the Taliban to the negotiating table. This has created further friction in relations between Islamabad and Washington. Some Baloch activists said they believe one reason for the increased effort to crush their insurgency is to ensure the protection of the Afghan Taliban's sanctuaries.

Despite differences over Afghanistan, Tehran and Islamabad appear to be largely in accord on how to deal with their respective Baloch populations. In the summer of 2010, Iran and Pakistan signed a deal on a multi-billion-dollar gas-pipeline project envisioned as meeting energy-hungry South Asia's needs for decades. In March 2013 Pakistani President Asif Ali Zardari and his Iranian counterpart Mahmoud Ahmadinejad inaugurated the construction of the pipeline, parts of which Tehran had already built. Islamabad still needs $1.5 billion of investment to build its part of the pipeline. Pakistan could also face US sanctions over its dealings with Tehran, which Washington is seeking to punish over its refusal to curb the Islamic republic's nuclear programme.[23] The Turkmenistan-Afghanistan-Pakistan-India gas route, meanwhile, has support from the Asian Development Bank. But its viability will remain in question as long as Baloch insurgents continue to blow up pipelines. Guaranteeing the security of the project has been seen as a factor influencing harsh policies on both sides of the Iran-Pakistan border.

But all has not been well between Pakistan and Iran. Some officials in Islamabad are privately suspicious that Tehran may be providing assistance to Baloch separatists, or allowing New Delhi to use its territory to do so. Iran has meanwhile publically accused Pakistan of sheltering members of the militant group Jundallah, which is mostly composed of Sunni Baloch. The Baloch insurgency has also further frayed Afghan-Pakistan ties. Islamabad has accused Kabul of sheltering Baloch rebel leader Brahamdagh Khan Bugti for years. In the 1970s, Afghanistan supported a Baloch insurrection and later sheltered insurgents.

But unlike in the past, when insurgents followed the directives of tribal leaders, the latest generation of Baloch separatists is loyal to middle-class leaders. If Islamabad wants to satisfy them, it will take more than offering cabinet slots and amnesty. As the situation in Balochistan attests, Islamabad's obsession with shaping the destiny of Afghanistan has actively contributed to destabilisation in its own backyard. Like Afghanistan, Balochistan will require regional co-operation to spur development and a permanent settlement to its ongoing conflicts. The military's push to crush 'treacherous' Baloch leaders and their followers will only prolong bloodshed and inequality.

PART THREE

AFGHANISTAN

8

OLD AND NEW ISLAMISTS IN LOY NANGARHAR

In March 1989, Abdul Rashid Waziri received an unexpected telephone call from Afghan President Dr. Mohammad Najibullah. Rafiq Najib, or Comrade Najib, as the president was known within the cadres of the PDPA, exchanged pleasantries with Waziri and quickly got down to business. The president wanted Waziri to brief Manokai Mangal about the situation in eastern Afghanistan.

As a member of the politburo of the PDPA and a deputy minister for tribal affairs, Waziri knew Afghanistan's border region with Pakistan like the back of his hand. That evening, Waziri met the chain-smoking Mangal in downtown Kabul. Their talk concerned the possible mujahedeen offensive in eastern Nangarhar Province. They agreed that defending the city of Jalalabad was the government's only option. Waziri spoke of threats from across the border in Pakistan. He noted that the Pakistani intelligence service was pushing Afghan mujahedeen leaders to mount a decisive military push in the wake of the Soviet withdrawal.

Mangal, forty and a physician by training, had a double role. He was both head of the eastern region's defence council and governor of Nangarhar. At the end of their meeting, he took with him a few pages from the intelligence files Waziri had shown him. Waziri knew Mangal was going to face one of the most difficult military challenges that the then ten-year-old war with Islamic rebels had presented the socialist regime.[1]

Two weeks before the meeting, most Soviet troops had departed Afghanistan. On 15 February 1989, the Red Army's last combat troops crossed the Friendship Bridge over the Amu Darya and entered the neighbouring Uzbek Soviet Socialist Republic. President Najibullah declared 15 February a day of 'national salvation'. But there were no celebrations among the PDPA leadership. Instead, the mood was sombre and determined. Many believed a major jihadist attack on Jalalabad was imminent.

On 16 February, Najibullah delivered a rousing speech to party cadres, soldiers and ordinary people on a public square outside the Arg-e Shahi palace in Kabul. 'Today, after the last Soviet combat troops have left, we are not on the last gasp, but independently defending our homeland with valour. Look where the enemies of the revolution are. They have training camps and offices in Pakistan. They play in the hands of foreign intelligence services, particularly the Pakistani military intelligence service. From there they send weapons and fire to destroy your homeland.

'Yesterday, they claimed our homeland was occupied by the Soviet Union. But they [the Red Army] have left. Now, others have fixed their dirty eyes on our country. And they want to invade it. They need to remember that the people of Afghanistan, members of the PDPA, our allies and our armed forces are waiting to teach them an exemplary and unforgettable lesson.' In the climax of his speech, Najibullah sought to rally his supporters with the battle cry of Jalalabad: 'We will sacrifice our lives, but we will not surrender our trenches.'[2]

Waziri remembers an electrified mood in Kabul in the wake of the address, and the party's headquarters being inundated with volunteers offering to be deployed to Jalalabad. Najibullah's aggressive stance and nationalist rhetoric also had another impact: it succeeded in unnerving the Afghan jihad's powerful sponsors in the Pakistani military.

Najibullah had put 20,000 Afghan mullahs on his payroll to counter the religious appeal of his enemies.[3] He had reached out to India and the West to break free from his party's reliance on the Soviet Union. More significantly, perhaps, he had unveiled an ambitious national reconciliation programme and moved away from the Marxist ideology guiding the Soviet system. He renamed his party 'Watan' or Homeland, and encouraged the participation of non-partisans in the government. He talked of attracting foreign investment. Even his Afghan opponents privately admitted that he was moving to address the mistakes of his predecessors.[4]

Across the Khyber Pass in Peshawar and Islamabad, Najibullah's moves were being watched with alarm. In February 1989 the ISI, using

$25 million in Saudi funding, cobbled together an interim Afghan government in Rawalpindi. The ISI pitched plans to the Americans and Pakistani civilian leaders for an all-out offensive to capture Jalalabad. Their plan called for the city, Afghanistan's third largest, to be used by the interim mujahedeen government as its headquarters—thus positioning the movement for an eventual takeover of Kabul.

Hamid Gul, the ISI chief, told Benazir Bhutto that Jalalabad would fall within weeks—so long as the Pakistani prime minister was 'prepared to allow for certain bloodshed'. In characteristic bravado, Gul invoked Islamic symbolism. 'War must go on until Darul Harb [house of war] is cleansed and becomes Darul Amn [house of peace]!' he reportedly told Bhutto.[5]

The battle began with the mujahedeen overrunning the front line east of Jalalabad on 6 March 1989. The militants captured the Afghan army's 11th Corps headquarters at Samar Khel, a few kilometres outside the city, but failed to overrun the nearby airport. In the following days and weeks, mujahedeen lines became easy targets for government soldiers. Despite Hamid Gul's repeated assurances to Bhutto, Jalalabad did not fall.

By May, mujahedeen casualties had run into the thousands, with Peshawar's hospitals filled with injured young fighters. The best the rebels were able to do was lay siege to Jalalabad by controlling its surrounding mountain peaks. However, they were unable to completely cut it off from Kabul. Mostly, they fired rockets almost at random, sometimes hitting civilians. By early July, an Afghan military counteroffensive had retaken all lost ground and pushed the front line closer to the Pakistani border. In September, the government flew Western journalists to Jalalabad to witness the suffering that the mujahedeen siege of the city had brought to beleaguered residents.

More than 10,000 combatants were estimated to have been killed during the four-month-long battle. It was one of the bloodiest episodes of the more than decade-long conflict between the Soviet-backed communists and the US-backed mujahedeen. In a telling warning to Islamabad and Washington, Mangal later said that the Battle of Jalalabad should have convinced people that 'the problems of Afghanistan cannot be solved by fighting'.[6]

But Mangal was wrong—the battle of Jalalabad only seemed to whet the appetite of Islamabad and Washington for more fighting. The

Geneva Accords, signed in 1988, had achieved the Soviet withdrawal. Contrary to their obligations under the agreement, however, both Washington and Moscow continued to provide more weapons to their Afghan allies, fuelling further violence.

The battle for Jalalabad marked the high point of fighting by international jihadists in the war. During most of the 1980s, Arabs had mostly played a supporting role by bankrolling the Afghan mujahedeen. Osama bin Laden established camps and bunker complexes in the Safed Koh, or White Mountain range. One of the camps, Al-Masada (Lion's Den in Arabic), in the Tora Bora region, played a significant role in the fighting for Jalalabad in 1989.

Bin Laden himself led some Arab units during fighting east of Jalalabad, around the village of Chaprihar. Most accounts suggest he led the fighters without concern for his own safety. But bin Laden's lack of military experience led them into a virtual bloodbath. Some fighters were apparently so zealous that they wept upon realising they had survived combat and had not become martyrs for their vision of Islam. 'I must have committed some sin, for Allah has not chosen us to go to heaven,' some of them reportedly said. Bin Laden encouraged this thinking, saying the battlefield trenches were the 'gate to heaven' for the scores of Saudis, Yemenis and Kuwaitis killed in the fighting. Some 187 Arabs from bin Laden's units died, and overall, more Arabs were killed in Jalalabad than in the rest of the Afghan war.[7] Some of them were remembered for paying Afghan mujahedeen commanders in exchange for communist prisoners, whom they publicly slaughtered. Engineer Mahmud, a key mujahedeen commander in Jalalabad, even reportedly sold regime defectors or captured soldiers to Arabs for $10,000. The sold men were then duly executed.[8]

The Battle of Jalalabad offered a glimpse of things to come. It highlighted Pakistan's obsessive ambition to shape the future of its neighbour. It highlighted the ascendency of the Arab jihadist. And, significantly, it showcased disunity among Afghans. What had begun as nascent leftist and Islamist movements in the 1960s would result in unprecedented death and destruction in Afghanistan over the next three decades.

The growing political and social fissures in Afghanistan reflected the international ideological polarisation of the time. Large numbers of Afghan students, intellectuals and military officers were drawn to the communist movement. A smaller number of intellectuals and *ulema* formed an Islamist movement in opposition. The rivalry peaked during Daud's presidency in the 1970s, when communists in the government orchestrated a campaign to repress the Islamists. Pakistan was quick to exploit the rift, hosting Afghan Islamist leaders and training some 5,000 Afghans in guerilla combat by the mid-1970s—long before the communist coup and Soviet occupation.[9]

The communist coup of April 1978 was resisted by many Afghans. Before the takeover, some communist-inspired radical land and social reforms had already provoked uprisings in rural regions. After the Soviet invasion, resistance to the occupation solidified along Islamist lines. Sunni factions that spearheaded the struggle from Pakistan were rooted in four distinct social networks, which sometimes overlapped.

The most visible network was based around Kabul University. Pan-Islamist in outlook, it found inspiration in the Egyptian Muslim Brotherhood and Jammat-e Islami in Pakistan. The Hizb-e Islami (Islamic Party), of Gulbuddin Hekmatyar and Jamiat-e Islami (Islamic Society), led by former Kabul University professor Burhannuddin Rabbani, were two offshoots of this network.[10]

Another network was that of the *mawlawis*, or mullahs, who ran madrasas and led mosque congregations in Pashtun regions. Prominent in this group were Mawlawi Younas Khalis and his deputy Jalaluddin Haqqani, in Nangarhar and Paktia provinces, and Mawlawi Mohammad Nabi Mohammadi and Nasrullah Mansur in the south-eastern provinces of Logar and Paktia. Jabha-yi Tulaba, or fronts of religious students, emerged in the south-western Pashtun heartland under the umbrella of these two parties.[11] None of these networks had as their chief interest the international Islamism of Hizb-e Islami. They were not animated by finding answers to the questions of modernity, nor were they much concerned with creating a contemporary Islamic political model. They were the precursors to the Taliban.

A third network, of Sufis, was found in the parties of Pir Sayed Ahmed Gilani and Sibghatullah Mujadidi. Their Mahaz-e Milli Islami Afghanistan (National Islamic Front of Afghanistan) and Jabha-e Nijat-e Milli Afghanistan (National Liberation Front) organisations were the preferred outlets for many Pashtun royalists, modernising intelligentsia and tribal leaders. These parties followed the Naqshbandia and Qadiria *silsala* or Sufi orders.

The fourth network was organised around Pashtun tribal leaders of the royalist elite. The exiled leaders of the tribal networks were detested by Islamabad because of their nationalism and loyalty to the Afghan monarchy, which prompted them to join the parties of Gilani and Mujadidi. Prominent members included the Durrani, Karlani and Ghilzai Pashtun tribal chiefs, as well as intellectuals and former officials. In many Pashtun regions, these old elites were in direct competition with the growing influence of the *mawlawi* and Islamist networks.[12]

An early battleground in the war was Loy Nangarhar, or Mashriqi, a region that serves as a gateway from Pakistan to Afghanistan through the Khyber Pass. The region—in the provinces of Nangarhar, Kunar, Laghman and Nuristan—has been for at least a century a leading trade artery to Afghanistan. Jalalabad had been the winter capital of Afghan kings after Peshawar was lost to the Sikhs in the early nineteenth century. The region's proximity to Kabul and the Indian subcontinent also meant that Loy Nangarhar remained a centre of learning and intellect. As the Afghan state developed, the region provided many bureaucrats, politicians, intellectuals and religious scholars.

For generations, Jalalabad also served as a base for Islamist movements and *ulema* networks. The region's tribes had long posed a critical strategic threat to rulers in Kabul. The Shinwari Rebellion of 1929 brought down the reformist King Amanullah Khan, while the Safi rebellion in the late 1940s severely tested the authority of the Musahiban dynasty. This prompted Kabul to attempt to control the region through development. The construction of major dams and agricultural projects in 1960 brought considerable growth to the region.

Olivier Roy observes that the *ulema* of Mashriqi had a 'well established tradition of fundamentalism and anti-imperialism'. Figures such as the Mullah of Hadda (Mullah Najmuddin) attracted support during struggles against the British and opposition to the Afghan monarchs. Other mullahs in the region led tribal uprisings against the 'infidels'. 'The fundamentalism of the Mashriqi *ulema* had always been more radical and anti-traditionalist than in other regions,' Roy wrote.[13] It should come as little surprise that some of the most prominent Afghan Islamist leaders in modern times have come from this region.

Archetype Mullah

Mawlawi Younas Khalis was among the founders of the modern Afghan Islamist movement.[14] His rise to prominence established a role model for the following generations of madrasa-educated Pashtun Islamist leaders. Following in his footsteps, they sought both worldly power and divine deliverance in jihad. Like many Pashtun clerics, suffering was an integral part of Mawlawi Younas Khalis's long and eventful life. He lost his father at a young age. Poverty in his native Nangarhar pushed him and his two brothers to seek free madrasa educations in the Peshawar Valley and Swat. He graduated from the Haqqania Madrasa in Akora Khattak, where he was one of the favoured students of its charismatic founder Maulana Abdul Haq. His early exposure to the power and influence of Haqqania undoubtedly left an imprint on him. Maulana Abdul Haq's work as a Pashtun cleric and political leader in Pakistan attracted followers for decades. His madrasa was a bastion of the conservative Deobandi movement and inspired generations of Pashtun clerics to strive to impose an Islamic order.

Mawlawi Younas Khalis became an imam at a rural mosque in Nangarhar in early 1950. Soon, he took a government job as a school teacher and moved to Kabul. In the 1960s, he became a mid-ranking government bureaucrat, but also continued teaching at madrasas in Nangarhar. In Kabul, he was among the founding members of Afghanistan's burgeoning Islamist movement. He published the first Afghan translations of the works of the influential Muslim Brotherhood theorist Sayyid Qutb, including 'Islam Wa Adalat-e Ijtemaee' (Islam and Social Justice).[15]

The 1973 republican coup empowered the communists at the expense of the Islamists. Some Islamists went underground, while others went into exile in Pakistan. Khalis went to the Khyber tribal district after his friend Minhajuddin Gahez was assassinated and his elder son sent to prison by the communists.[16] In Pakistan, Khalis initially tried to distance himself from the feuds of Peshawar-based Islamist leaders, choosing to live off the proceeds of a shop he operated in the small border town of Landi Kotal. Khalis did not play a prominent role in the 1976–1977 conflict between Burhannuddin Rabbani and Gulbuddin Hekmatyar, whose split resulted in Rabbani setting up the Jamiat-e Islami and Hekmatyar establishing the Hizb-e Islami. He also kept a distance when the two factions later merged into the Harakat-e Inqilab-e Islami Afghanistan under the leadership of Mawlawi Mohammad Nabi Mohammadi.

In 1979, Khalis established his own Hizb-e Islami, which adopted his name (Hizb-e Islami Khalis) to distinguish it from Hekmatyar's organisation. Although the party's name suggested a link to the politically-active Muslim Brotherhood of Egypt, it initially remained an association of conservative clerics. The split between Khalis and Hekmatyar represented a broader division between older conservative *ulema* and a younger generation of modernist Islamists obsessed with adopting Islam as a political system. The upstarts accused the *ulema* of confining Islam to rituals. The *ulema*, in turn, mocked the radicals' lack of genuine Islamic credentials. Khalis even referred to them as *maktabian*—Pashto for 'school boys'.[17]

After the Soviet occupation, Hizb-e Islami Khalis became increasingly potent. Khalis successfully utilised the methods of modern political organisation to optimise the party's influence in traditional society. Khalis, who was firmly rooted in his native Khugiani tribe in Nangarhar, followed the model of Pashtun religious leaders who mobilised particular tribes for localised wars. Together with his leading commanders, Abdul Haq and Jalaluddin Haqqani, Khalis' Hizb-e Islami was instrumental in leading the uprising of the Pashtun tribes of eastern and south-eastern Afghanistan. He established his headquarters in the mountains of Tora Bora, in his native Khugyani district, and ran an organised military campaign. His base was regularly bombed. One of the first Soviet pilots captured in the war was detained at his headquarters and later handed over to the Soviet Embassy in Pakistan.[18]

Khalis represented the decline of the traditional *khan* and the rise of the *mawlawi* in rural Pashtun regions. His alliance with the aristocratic Arsala family granted him access to their Jabbar Khel Ghilzai clan, which had been a strong regional ally of the Durrani kings in eastern Afghanistan. He mentored the three Arsala brothers—Haji Abdul Qadeer, Deen Muhammad and Abdul Haq. Accentuating his status as a role model was his prowess in combat. He was the only senior mujahedeen leader who preferred to fight in the trenches of Tora Bora rather than enrich himself in the comfort of Peshawar. Both Abdul Haq and Jalaluddin Haqqani, his main commanders, were considered among the most successful during the decade-long war.[19]

Khalis was adept at meshing his Pashtun identity with religious fervour. Unlike the Islamists, he was not opposed to flaunting his Pashtun identity and projecting his own kind of Pashtun nationalism. His Pashto poetry is well regarded by critics, and he even wrote a book about Pashtun nationalism, something that was anathema to most *ulema* because of its association with modernity and secularism. Khalis never recognised the Durand Line, saying any borders should be decided by local people rather than a few leaders.

These qualities were on display when he visited Ronald Reagan's White House in 1987. Reagan praised the mujahedeen for their internal unity and battlefield advances. In response, Khalis called for increased Western political support.[20] He also invited Reagan to convert to Islam. 'He handed Reagan the Quran, asking the president to accept Islam so that the two could enter paradise together. The president politely declined,' former American diplomat Peter Tomsen wrote about the encounter.[21]

The Soviet withdrawal in 1989 presented Khalis with the problem of dealing with the fragmented and frequently vicious world of politics. He perhaps represented the most anti-Shia Deobandi streak of the mujahedeen. He was thus in opposition to United Nations-brokered peace efforts, such as the concept of a broad-based multi-ethnic Afghan government. He rejected elections and advocated a government of the mujahedeen. 'The mujahedeen have given their blood, they have liberated their country, and if they are not treated the right way, the problem will not be solved,' he wrote to the leadership council of the anti-Soviet guerillas. 'Secondly, the current problems are the result of [Soviet] intellectual imperialism, so we need to look for its causes and give the government to people who will prevent the rise of similar circumstances. Thirdly, we need to think about why the nation revolted. We need to strengthen that feeling and organise our nation around that principle.'[22]

Khalis was the only senior mujahedeen leader who effectively dissolved his organisation and distanced himself from the mujahedeen civil war after the collapse of Najibullah's regime in April 1992. Many of his commanders, however, took part in the internecine fighting. He was disheartened by the bloodshed and Afghanistan's eventual abandonment by the international community. 'We are like orphans. Anybody who is kind, uses us for their benefits,' he said ruefully.

The veteran jihadi leader continued to prefer a simple life in Jalalabad over life in exile in Pakistan. After the Taliban captured Jalalabad in 1996, he went to Kandahar to speak to the movement's leaders, advising them to be 'flexible enough to be acceptable to the Afghans and the world'. The Taliban, however, accused him of being their opponent.

Khalis was perhaps the only public figure who dared oppose the Taliban while living in the regions they controlled. Some Taliban leaders had been former commanders in his organisation, and few in the Taliban leadership could question his clerical and jihadi credentials. He was outspoken in his opposition to the Taliban ban on music and television. 'Today, a government that cannot even establish a television station cannot be considered a proper government,' he told an Afghan journalist. Unlike most jihadis and the Taliban, Khalis supported holding a *loya jirga* and even backed the return of former King Mohammad Zahir Shah to help unite Afghans.[23]

Khalis was bedridden during the late 1990s and remained confined to his home after the demise of the Taliban regime in late 2001. The Arsala clan, with whom he had formed an alliance, backed the new internationally-supported government led by Hamid Karzai. The Taliban killed Abdul Haq in October 2001. Haji Qadeer became a vice president in the transitional administration, while Din Mohammad became the governor of Nangarhar. In October 2003, Khalis disappeared from public life, possibly moving to Pakistan, after expressing his support for Taliban insurgents. Many in Nangarhar believe that his sons moved him to a secret location against his will. After suffering a stroke, Khalis was not even capable of communicating with his family, let alone helping to run a guerilla campaign.[24]

His son Anwarul Haq Mujahid announced his father's death in July 2006. Both the Afghan government and the Taliban declared him a hero and celebrated him separately. As the Taliban insurgency gathered momentum, Mujahid announced the Tora Bora Military Front in early 2007. Mujahid was reportedly detained in Pakistan in May 2009. His group had merged with the mainstream Taliban and he was considered the Taliban's shadow governor in Tora Bora at the time of his arrest.[25] Khalis' family, together with the Haqqanis, Mansurs, and Mohammadis, are among a handful of former mujahedeen leaders who allied themselves with the Taliban.

Salafism in Kunar

In late 1979, Afghanistan's eastern Kunar Province became one of the first centres of resistance against the communist regime. Early uprisings were organised along tribal lines, with individual clans mounting attacks against government forces. But the war gradually imposed a new social order, forged through the rise of radical Islamist leaders and cadres who often lived in exile in Pakistan. There, they found unprecedented access to training and support because of their adherence to Salafism—the official religion of Saudi Arabia and other oil-rich Gulf states.

The Salafis bankrolled religious education for Afghan refugees in Pakistan. The madrasa of Mawlawi Shamsuddin in Peshawar, in particular, served as a catalyst in spreading Salafism among the Pashtuns of Kunar. Mawlawi Shamsuddin was a native of Swat, but had lived in Kunar's Pech Valley before the Soviet invasion. He married into an influential local family and migrated to Peshawar after the war intensified in the early 1980s. Mawlawi Shamsuddin's large Salafi madrasa in Peshawar appealed to the exiles of Kunar because of its promise to train students in a 'pure' form of Islam. A new generation of Salafi zealots, backed in part by Gulf petro-dollars, thus eventually arose in Kunar.[26] The region, which includes the Nuristan highlands, hosted two small Salafi states, or emirates, in the 1980s and 1990s. Both were set up by alumni of the Panjpir madrasa, a bastion of Salafi Islam.

After Kabul lost direct control of Nuristan in 1978, Mawlawi Afzal, a native of the Barg-e Matal district, established in northern Nuristan a mini-state called Dawlat-e Inqilabi Islami Nuristan. The region was largely peaceful in the 1980s, and the Dawlat entity even enriched itself by levying taxes on supplies to mujahedeen groups in other regions. Throughout the 1980s, the mini-state was directly supported by Salafi donors in Saudi Arabia and Kuwait. Saudi Arabia even formally recognised Dawlat in the late 1980s and helped it establish consulates in Saudi Arabia and Pakistan.[27]

This state of affairs gradually led to the elimination of most of the traditional leadership in the region. As Mawlawi Afzal strengthened his grip, however, Nuristan remained one of Afghanistan's most underdeveloped regions, with very low literacy levels. Mawlawi Afzal went to Kabul after the mujahedeen seized the capital, but returned to Nuristan after the Taliban takeover in 1996. But his rule was soon beset by problems. Parts of the population, inspired by Hizb-e Islami, revolted against taxes he imposed. The Taliban resolved the dispute by sending him into exile in Pakistan, where he found a refuge with the Salafi Lashkar-e Taiba. During the 1980s, he developed links with the Pakistani Salafi movement called Ahl-e Hadith, which later transformed into Lashkar-e Taiba.[28]

While Mawlawi Afzal established a model of local Salafi rule in Nuristan, his influence among the Pashtuns of Kunar was limited. In the

1980s, his Arab backers launched a search for a new leader among the region's Pashtuns. These Arabs mostly worked for charities supporting the Afghan mujahedeen and refugees in Pakistan. They chose another alumnus of the Panjpir madrasa, Mawlawi Jamil ur-Rahman, to establish a Salafist emirate in Kunar.[29]

Early on, Jamil ur-Rahman attracted a large following from his Safi tribe. He had gained notice as a commander of the Hizb-e Islami, but his organisation, established in 1985, was independent. The Jamaat al-Dawa al-Quran wa-Sunah established control over most of the province by the late 1980s, expelling other jihadi parties.[30] It was a successful effort, in part because of strong financial support from patrons in Saudi Arabia and Kuwait. Arab volunteers swelled the ranks of ur-Rahman's followers.

After the Soviet withdrawal in 1989, ur-Rahman emerged firmly in control. He established a Salafi emirate in 1991, with a government and cabinet. His zealous followers soon began forcing their ultra-orthodox views on the local Pashtun population. Their campaign included targeting the mausoleums of holy men. They insisted that graveyard visits and flying flags over the graves of martyrs was un-Islamic. Jamil ur-Rahman's past in Hizb-e Islami also caught up with him. He was soon engaged in an intense rivalry with Gulbuddin Hekmatyar. Their supporters took part in armed clashes, and both sides committed atrocities against civilians. The conflict ended with the still-unexplained August 1991 assassination of ur-Rahman by one of his Egyptian guards.[31]

Jamil ur-Rahman's family remained relevant in Kunar's politics after his death. His nephews Haji Rohullah Wakil (commonly known as Haji Rohullah) and Haji Hayatullah kept a distance from the Taliban regime. They lived in exile in Peshawar and even claimed to oppose Taliban rule.[32] They flirted with some of the peace processes championed by Afghan exiles. Haji Rohullah Wakil travelled to Cyprus to participate in a fledgling peace forum organised by former mujahedeen and supported by Iran. He also made contact with the so-called Rome Process, which involved a group of Afghan aristocrats who advocated the return of former King Zahir Shah to convene a *loya jirga* to promote national unity and reconciliation.[33]

In late 2001, Haji Rohullah Wakil and his Jamaat al-Dawa al-Quran wa-Sunah returned to Kunar to claim their share in the post-Taliban transitional administration. Haji Rohullah became one of the key powerbrokers in Kunar and represented the province in the emergency *loya jirga* of June 2002. But he was arrested in August of that year and transferred to the American-run Guantanamo Bay prison. One of his deputies, Sabr Lal Melma, was also detained and sent to Guantanamo Bay. His detainee assessment file claims he received money and cellular phones from a British government representative. In March 2002, he reportedly received $12,000 from the ISI 'to finance military operations' against the interim Afghan administration. He was also accused of providing safe passage to Al-Qaeda-linked Arabs, allegedly aiding them as they moved in and out of Afghanistan and Pakistan.[34]

Ironically, most Arab prisoners in Guantanamo are reported to have despised him. Although a June 2005 assessment report recommended he be kept in continued detention, Haji Rohullah was transferred to Afghan custody in the summer of 2008. He was freed soon after. He assumed a lower profile, resuming his role as a community leader among his Safi tribesman. His deputy, and presumably his younger brother, Haji Hayatullah, continued the group's activities from Pakistan.[35]

But the lack of a prominent leader did not stop an anti-US insurgency from developing in Kunar. After a lull of nearly two years, the Kunar insurgency began to gather momentum in 2003. The neo-Taliban—as the new insurgency was dubbed—began to organise in the Bajaur tribal district, where Kunar's Salafis were headquartered in the 1980s. Kunar and Nuristan eventually became a battleground for an assortment of militant groups, including Al-Qaeda, Emarat-e Islami Afghanistan (remnants of the Taliban regime and fighters loyal to Mullah Mohammad Omar), Hizb-e Islami, Tehreek-e Taliban Pakistan and affiliated Pakistan-centric Deobandi groups, and Lashkar-e Taiba.[36] Qari Zia Ur Rehman, a commander associated with the Emarat-e Islami Afghanistan, was a key figure. He was partly based in Pakistan. At times, he led battles from Bajaur, where he also fought against the Pakistani military.[37]

The network of Salafi fighters in Kunar, however, remained the largest and most potent. Jamaat al-Dawa al-Quran wa-Sunah and other Salafi networks gradually developed closer ties to the Taliban and were even dubbed Salafi Taliban. In early 2010, the group formally joined the Taliban by merging their organisation with the Emarat-e Islami Afghanistan.[38]

Since 2005, Salafi fighters—including Pashtuns, Nuristanis, Punjabis, Arabs and Central Asians—have played a key role in the conflict in Kunar and Nuristan. The Pech and Korengal valleys in Kunar and the Waygal

Valley in Nuristan have seen some of the most intense fighting between militants and US troops. Pech is considered the main valley, while Korengal and Waygal are smaller valleys flanking Pech. The US established outposts in the nearly ten-kilometre-long Korengal Valley in a bid to prevent the infiltration of fighters into Pech and other regions. The deployment proved disastrous. Some forty-two US service members were killed and hundreds were injured by the time the deployment in Korengal ended in 2010. US troops nicknamed the region 'the valley of death'.[39]

US forces suffered one of their worst battlefield losses in Wanat, a village in the Waygal Valley. In July 2008, forty-five American troops came to the village to establish an outpost. At least nine of them were killed and twenty-seven wounded in a battle that was later characterised as the 'Black Hawk Down' of Afghanistan.[40] The Americans withdrew from the Pech Valley in early 2011, but returned six months later. More than 100 US service members have been killed there since 2003.[41]

Pakistan's predominantly Punjabi Salafi organisation, Lashkar-e Taiba, also left its mark on the fighting in Kunar and Nuristan. Its ties to the Salafi Jamaat al-Dawa al-Quran wa-Sunah date back to the 1980s. As the insurgency gained pace in Kunar, Lashkar-e Taiba established training camps for Kunar residents in Afghan refugee villages around Peshawar. The group's fighters were considered more skilled and capable than ordinary Afghan insurgents and were involved in the Pech Valley fighting.[42]

The Pakistani Taliban carved out a sanctuary in Nuristan after being driven from Swat in 2009. In 2010, its fighters briefly captured the Afghan border district of Barg-e Matal. In 2011, 2012 and 2013, the group continued to claim cross-border attacks that targeted Pakistani security forces in the mountainous Upper Dir district of Khyber Pakhtunkhwa Province.[43]

Hizb-e Islami also ran its militant campaign from sanctuaries in Pakistan, and was one of the most active organisations in Kunar and Nuristan. Hizb-e Islami was in the beneficial position of being in the government and the opposition at the same time. Many former members of Hizb-e Islami have served as lawmakers, governors and cabinet members in Karzai administrations since 2001. Kashmir Khan, the group's commander in Kunar, has become something of a legend for remaining on the battlefield for more than three decades. He has fought against the Red Army, the Salafis and other mujahedeen factions, the Taliban and US-led international forces. His reputation as a dedicated fighter is perhaps only exceeded by Jalaluddin Haqqani in south-eastern Afghanistan.

OLD AND NEW ISLAMISTS IN LOY NANGARHAR

Loy Nangarhar, or Mashriqi, has many of the same problems as other Pashtun regions of Afghanistan. In scores of interviews, Pashtun leaders and lawmakers have lamented the shrinking authority of government in the region. In addition to being challenged by an insurgency based in Pakistan, Loy Nangarhar's governance was hobbled by persistent corruption and mismanagement, as well as the inefficient or ineffectual efforts of international officials and foreigners who ostensibly came to Afghanistan to help. Many leaders said the weakening of Pashtun institutions has intensified instability and marred the government's ability to implement, or even attempt to implement, important policies.

9

TRIBES, COMMUNISTS AND GENERATIONAL JIHADISTS IN LOYA PAKTIA

On 14 September 1980, Faiz Mohammad, Afghanistan's communist minister of border and tribal affairs, was killed in an ambush in the remote south-eastern Wazi Zadran region.[1] Several mujahedeen factions claimed responsibility for the assassination, but it was widely understood that the responsibility lay with Mawlavi Jalaluddin Haqqani.[2]

In the days leading to his assassination, Faiz Mohammad had stayed in the regional capital of Gardez, meeting with the leaders of the region's tribes. His mission had been to prevent the powerful Zadran tribe from joining the new Pakistan-based insurgency. In line with regional traditions, he invoked Islamic principles and the values of *Pashtunwali* to convince Zadran elders that opposing the Soviet-backed communist regime was not in their interests. He accepted their invitation to travel to remote Zadran villages in the mountains, without any extra security, to demonstrate his trust in their hospitality.

Faiz Mohammad's killing proved to be a watershed moment in Loya Paktia. It marked the failure of traditional approaches to persuade the region's tribes to embrace policies backed by the central government. More significantly, Faiz Mohammad's life and death illuminated the clash between communist radicalism and Islamic extremism—a clash that would decimate tribal solidarity and social cohesion and fuel the conflagration that would consume the region over the next three decades.

Through a combination of luck, hard work and his own personal charisma, Faiz Muhammad achieved unusual success. He was born in the early 1940s to an impoverished Mehsud family in South Waziristan. Most adult males in his tribe had, at one time or another, fought the British. At the time of Faiz Mohammad's birth, few in the region had any exposure to modern education.

In 1949, he became among the first youngsters from Waziristan to be sent to Kabul. He was just seven years old when he joined the first batch of Pashtun students from the Tribal Areas to study at Khushal Khan high school. The Afghan royal court had built the school for the eastern Pashtun tribes who had helped the Durrani Musahiban dynasty gain the throne in 1929. Faiz Mohammad excelled at school and was selected to join the Afghan military's officer training academy in 1960. He graduated with distinction three years later, and was appointed a junior officer in a commando battalion. Like many young Afghan officers, Faiz Mohammad was sent for professional training in the Soviet Union in 1968. There, his year in a Soviet special forces academy exposed him to communism. After returning home, he secretly joined the Parcham faction of the socialist PDPA, and was promoted to become the second-in-command of the Afghan commando force.[3]

In 1972, Faiz Mohammad became a confidant of Mohammad Daud Khan, the former prime minister and mercurial first cousin of King Zahir Shah. At the time, the elderly prince, who had been out of government for nearly a decade, was quietly plotting a palace coup against his cousin. In July 1973, Faiz Mohammad became one of the key players in Daud Khan's coup. According to one participant, he distributed weapons to the units that were dispatched to arrest ministers.[4] The coup was launched by communist officers who had benefited from the close relationships Daud Khan had established with Soviet leaders in the 1950s. After Zahir Shah surrendered power without a fight, Faiz Mohammad was appointed Daud's interior minister. This was one of the most coveted posts because of the ministry's control over police forces and provincial administrations.

By 1975, Daud had begun to purge his cabinet of members of the Parcham faction, and Faiz Mohammad was relegated to head the less powerful Ministry of Border and Tribal Affairs. In 1976, Faiz Mohammad was appointed to the even less influential post of ambassador to Indonesia. Such appointments were part of an Afghan tradition of sidelining opponents by effectively sending them into political exile.

The April 1978 killing of Daud Khan in a military coup, staged by officers loyal to the Khalq, or pro-communist 'Masses' faction of the PDPA, heralded the full-bore arrival of communist rule in Afghanistan. The Parcham and Khalq factions united after the coup, but the alliance did not last long. As a result, Faiz Mohammad was again sent away—this time as the Afghan envoy to Iraq. But he would soon return to Kabul. In late 1978, he was again appointed minister of border and tribal affairs, tasked with dealing with a series of tribal uprisings against the new regime.

Faiz Mohammad's Pashtun ethnicity and connections to the major Loya Paktia tribes seem to have made his appointment acceptable to Khalq leaders Nur Mohammad Taraki and Hafizullah Amin. He was also appointed a full member of the powerful Central Committee of the PDPA. He networked extensively among the border tribes to win their backing for the new regime. Loya Paktia, which he considered his homeland, was the focus of his attention.[5] In part because of the region's proximity to Kabul, the inhabitants of Loya Paktia have played a crucial role in shaping modern Afghan history.

Loya Paktia—or 'Greater Paktia' in Pashto—formally includes the south-eastern Afghan provinces of Paktia, Paktika and Khost, but tribal links and history can be said to extend it into parts of Logar, Wardak and Ghazni provinces. The region's Pashtun tribes are derived from the Karlani Confederacy, whose descendants also live in neighbouring Pakistan, in the FATA and Khyber Pakhtunkhwa. The major Karlani tribes of Loya Paktia include the Zadran, Mangal, Zazi or Jaji, Tani, Samkani, Sabari, Muqbil, Khostwal (used as an umbrella identity for many small tribes), Gurbuz, Wazir and Mehsud (Maseed). The Ahmadzai, Sulaiman Khels, Totakhel, Andar, Kharotis and the smaller Kochi, or nomadic clans, are the region's Ghilzai tribes. The Mangal and Zadran are the two largest tribes of the region, their population spanning the provinces of Paktia, Paktika and Khost.

Loya Paktia proved its strategic significance when its tribes fought the Third-Anglo Afghan War, also known as Afghanistan's war of independence, in 1919. In 1929, the tribes helped restore the Durrani dynasty by helping Nadir Khan defeat Habibullah Kalakani (or Bach-e Saqao). In the wake of that struggle, Loya Paktia emerged as a distinct administrative unit and adopted its own identity, which was retained even after it was divided into three provinces in the 1970s and 1980s. Loya Paktia's tribes were exempt from taxes and conscription. They were largely autonomous and could bear arms. This mostly worked to the advantage of Kabul, which continued to occasionally call on the services of their warriors.[6] Until the 1950s, when Afghanistan's professional military became firmly established, the region's tribes acted as Afghanistan's surrogate military. Loya Paktia has provided many men who would go on to earn distinction in the modern Afghan military's officer corps.[7]

Since the early twentieth century, Loya Paktia's tribes have divided themselves into two *gwands*, or blocs: the *towr*, or black, and *spin*, or white, after their corresponding flags. These blocs provided platforms for larger alliance-building, beyond the tribes and clans defined along bloodlines. The tribes of each bloc have customarily relied on each other to settle disputes and regulate public life. The two blocs would come together to resolve larger questions that involved the whole of Loya Paktia, particularly when members of the two blocs were in opposition.[8] All the major tribes of Paktia still practise their own *narkhs*, or local legal codes, to interpret the values of *Pashtunwali*. Tribal solidarity was also invoked in case of the need for collective action to defend territory.[9]

The region has experienced some of the worst violence of the country's recent history. The instability has led to large-scale displacement, in some cases emptying entire valleys of their populations. Loya Paktia's natural forests have also been severely damaged.[10] Some rebuilding assistance has been provided by remittances from labourers and traders from the region who work in the Gulf countries. But the tumultuous changes have devastated tribal solidarity. The rise of communist partisans and extremist mullahs since the early 1980s has damaged the authority of tribal leaders, whose leadership appeal traditionally relied on personal charisma, family lineage and negotiation skills. The communists and the mullahs who sought to subvert the authority of tribal leaders share a large responsibility for what has become of Loya Paktia.

Marx Among the Tribes

Faiz Mohammad was from a generation of prominent Loya Paktia communist generals, intellectuals and ideologues. Many of these men had been sent to the Soviet Union in the 1950s, 1960s and 1970s, charged with gaining insight and training to be used to bring development and modernity to Afghanistan. They came back indoctrinated, and instead of serving in professional roles, became prominent leaders of Afghan communist factions. Loya Paktia thus had an outsized share in the leadership of the Khalq and Parcham factions of the PDPA, who captured power by infiltrating the officer corps of the Afghan military and through Soviet patronage.

Afghanistan's last socialist president, Najibullah, came from the region. Defence and interior ministers, including Sayyed Mohammad Gulabzoi, Mohammad Aslam Watanjar and Shahnawaz Tanai, were from Loya Paktia. Nazar Mohammad, Sulemain Layeq, Raz Mohammad Pakteen, Pacha Gul Wafadar, Khial Mohammad Katawazi, Mahmud Suma, Abdul Rashid Waziri, Mir Sahib Karwal, Shahzar Lewal, Engineer Guldad, Habib Mangal and Manokai Mangal were other prominent PDPA leaders from the region.[11]

The communists proved even more divisive than the intensely competitive clans of Paktia. The quarrel between the Khalq and Parcham factions had started long before the military coup known as the Saur Revolution. But personal rivalries would soon escalate into feuds and vendettas after the Khalq faction ascended to power in April 1978.[12] The internal bickering, combined with the revolutionary zeal of the young communist leadership, alienated the regime from the tribes. The communists' antipathy towards religion and tradition also played a key role in pushing away the tribal leadership. Most significantly, the behaviour of the communists confused and disturbed ordinary people, and the regime failed to secure strong popular backing.

Islamabad, long weary of the region's links with Pakistan's domestic Pashtun nationalist movement, seized the opportunity to turn the region into a theatre for war against communist rule and Soviet occupation. Arms markets and training camps sprouted in Pakistan's Kurram and Waziristan tribal regions across the border from Loya Paktia. Some of the largest battles of the nearly nine-year Soviet occupation were fought in Loya Paktia.

In late 1987, Loya Paktia saw the biggest set-piece battle of the Soviet occupation. Under the leadership of Lt. General Boris Gromov, the Red Army launched Operation Magistral to open the highway connecting the Loya Paktia towns of Gardez and Khost. The border town of Khost, sometimes referred to as 'Little Moscow', was under siege by the mujahedeen for years. The Red Army was forced to rely on its air superiority and artillery. After more than a month of fighting, Soviet and Afghan forces finally succeeded in occupying the strategic peaks of the Satukandov Pass and breaking the siege of Khost.

The victory won Gromov his country's highest military honour. He was awarded the Hero of the Soviet Union, as were Col. Valery Vostrotin and other soldiers of the Red Army's 9th Company, who had repelled a mujahedeen attack on a peak simply called 3234—its height in metres.[13] But the costly campaign did not deter the mujahedeen after the Red Army left in late 1988.

Amir Shah Kargar, a former communist official, was a witness to those dark days. Under instructions from President Najibullah in the late 1980s, he returned to Khost to oversee their regime's policy of reconciliation. Back in his native town, he was in position to observe the impact of diminished Soviet aid following the Red Army's withdrawal in the aftermath of the 1988 Geneva Accords. The morale of Afghan government forces continued to plunge as their capacity to fight the mujahedeen declined.

Washington and Islamabad continued to arm and support the mujahedeen. Kargar saw how thousands of Afghan troops endured enormous suffering during the siege of Khost. Most of the fighting in the region was carried out by military officers from the region and tribal militias. Kargar remembers the agony of being forced to bury fallen comrades without the customary Muslim white cloth wrapping. Sometimes even salt was not available for months. According to Kargar, after extensive deliberations the local communist leaders admitted they could not defeat the enemy and decided to surrender to the mujahedeen after a long bloody battle in March 1991.[14] Like most Afghan communists, Kargar has done a lot of soul-searching about why their dream of creating socialist utopia in Afghanistan went sour.

'What happened on the 7th of Saur (April 27, 1978) was not a revolution, it was a military coup,' he recalled in an interview in Khost in 2011. 'Such coups can never achieve the aspirations of genuine revolutions. We were indoctrinated by the teachings of an alien ideology, which prompted us to call our military coup as a revolution. We then mistakenly established revolutionary goals for the regime formed after a military coup.

'Most Khaliqis and Parchamis had a very poor understanding of the alien political ideologies they were trying to imitate and implement after the Saur coup. It proved disastrous to force such notions on our society.

We developed an argument for building a military dictatorship, which was supposed to be a shortcut to establishing the communism's "dictatorship of the proletariat." But such a proletariat never existed in Afghanistan. Our country also lacked the kind of elite whose wealth and resources could have been redistributed. We hardly had any privately-owned industries that we could have privatised. Our land reforms badly backfired. We could have only distributed government-owned barren lands to the peasants and increased taxes for the wealthy landowners. But instead we snatched their arable lands by force. This was against Afghan norms because even the peasants who benefited from our land redistribution considered us infidels because we had usurped someone else's property and had given it to them.

'We opposed the mullahs, who were the most downtrodden section of our society, and punished them after labelling them as agents of the bourgeoisie. This showed that we had not worked among the masses and had failed to sell them our programme. We had hoped that the land redistribution will win us the backing of oppressed classes and they will defend our system. Instead, our measures backfired and they were the first to revolt against us. Finally, we became just another one of the Cold War's contests between the West and the Soviet Union. Everybody in the world who opposed the Soviet Union began opposing us. Pakistan led this effort and benefited tremendously from its fall out. It manipulated and interfered in our internal affairs openly and attempted to fashion our politics and society to its liking. On the other hand, instead of learning a lesson and trying to win over the public, the Khalqis and Parchamis adopted a more harsh approach towards Afghan masses. They imposed a dictatorship in which no opposition to the party was tolerated. The leaders and cadres of the two groupings were always at loggerheads with each other despite the fact that their differences had little material and political bases. Such differences grew into vendettas within the two factions. Moscow only fuelled the fire by alternately backing opposing sides. Thus, its presence was ultimately seen as occupation by most Afghans and outsiders.'[15]

While the communists have admitted their mistakes, they point to their adversaries among the mujahedeen and Taliban as even worse examples of working for foreign powers and being blinded by personal ambitions, rivalries and ideological commitment. Shahnawaz Tanai, the former defence minister who commanded Afghan forces during Operation Magistral, blamed his old nemesis Mawlawi Jalaluddin Haqqani for being responsible for most trouble in the Loya Paktia region after the demise of the Taliban regime in late 2001. He counts Islamabad's support for the ailing cleric as crucial in enabling him to sustain his large cadre of dedicated fighters. Tanai also believes the FATA's status as an economic and political backwater in Pakistan helped sustain the insurgency and contributed to insecurity in Loya Paktia. He regards the Taliban sanctuary in the FATA as a major factor that has blocked the return of peace to the region.[16]

Sulaiman Layeq, a former Parchami minister of tribal affairs, noted that the transformation in Loya Paktia and other Pashtun regions has been spearheaded by the changing role of the mullahs. He noted that mullahs were once popularly considered as inhabiting the lower rungs of society. They assumed a leadership role not because of their personal charisma, piety or popularity, but because of their access to arms, resources and foreign backing.[17]

The former communists made a limited comeback in Loya Paktia after the demise of the Taliban. The government in Kabul, composed of mujahedeen factions, was forced to call back communist-era security officials and professionals. But their comeback was not without controversy, and the divide between the mujahedeen and the communists has continued to foment instability in Loya Paktia. Local mujahedeen stalwarts have resented the return of the former communists to the military and the police forces. Perhaps more contentious was their employment in local forces that protected US special forces and acted as partners to the Americans in operations against the insurgents.[18] But the threat posed by Taliban-allied local families and their networks ultimately inspired a degree of unity among the former adversaries.

Jihad in Blood

In Loya Paktia, several large, extended families allied with the Taliban act as Pakistan's strategic ingress into Afghanistan. These families are also the main source of fighters who take up arms for the hard-line Islamist movement. Mawlawi Jalaluddin Haqqani, his sons and near kin constitute the largest such network. It has been dubbed the 'Haqqani Network' by the US-led international military coalition.

Haqqani joined the Taliban in 1995 and helped the movement overrun Kabul. A January 1997 diplomatic cable from the US Embassy in

Islamabad identified him as more 'liberal'—that is, not sharing the same views as the Taliban on issues such as how women should be treated. The cable described Haqqani as someone who played a minimal role in setting the Taliban's social and political agenda, but was central to their military affairs. The State Department was particularly worried about his ties to various radical Arab groups that he was alleged to be sheltering in exchange for money and weapons.[19]

As discussed previously, Haqqani's main base in North Waziristan was not targeted by the US military operation in Loya Paktia in late 2001 and early 2002. One Afghan lawmaker suggests that the family wanted to join the new political system, but their local rivals, particularly tribal arch-enemy Pacha Khan Zadran, opposed this and even persuaded the Americans to bomb a convoy of pro-Haqqani tribal leaders who were on their way to Kabul to express support for the new government.[20] Paktia locals believe Haqqani was reluctant to leave the region, but was pushed out after he was targeted twice by US air strikes. He was wounded in a US air strike while travelling between Gardez and Khost.[21] By 2006, the Haqqanis had consolidated a jihadist conglomerate in North Waziristan.

The network's expansion back into Loya Paktia was eased by its roots and contacts in the region. It was particularly aided by instability in the Zadran arch, which spans the provinces of Paktia, Paktika and Khost. Being Zadran tribesmen, it was not difficult for the Haqqanis to exploit local grievances and vulnerabilities. The network gradually extended its reach to the Afghan capital of Kabul and facilitated jihadist penetration into once-stable northern Afghanistan.

Remnants of the former Taliban regime from southern Afghanistan have remained in charge of the movement's overall political direction. But with an estimated 15,000 fighters, the Haqqanis became the Taliban's most potent military arm as the insurgency gathered momentum in 2005. Haqqani military operations have been led by Sirajuddin Haqqani, Mawlawi Jalaluddin Haqqani's eldest son, who is simply referred to as Siraj but is usually addressed as *Khalifa*, or the successor. His accession to power also signified the family's adoption of more extreme ideologies and a closer alliance with international jihadists.

The military ascendency of the Haqqanis has been underlined by their ability to strike targets in Kabul. Since 2008, the Haqqanis have employed a signature tactic of swarming important government, international and diplomatic targets with suicide bombers, who often engage in long firefights before detonating their explosives. Such attacks can cause massive damage and generate huge international attention. These tactics have had a large psychological impact on Afghan and international perceptions about the war.

In January 2008, a team of gunmen wearing suicide vests stormed the Kabul Sarena Hotel. The attack killed eight people, including two foreigners. The psychological impact was profound. The raid had targeted Kabul's most secure five-star hotel, located close to the presidential palace. The Haqqanis also launched an attack on President Karzai during the mujahedeen victory day parade on 27 April 2008. An attack on the Indian Embassy in Kabul on 7 July 2008, killed nearly fifty people, including the Indian defence attaché. In February 2009, Haqqani fighters stormed several government ministries, and in October 2009, carried out a deadly attack on a UN guesthouse. In 2010, Haqqani fighters again attacked government ministries and an army recruitment centre. The network's activities peaked in 2011, when it attacked Kabul's Intercontinental Hotel in July and besieged the US Embassy and the headquarters of the International Security Assistance Force (ISAF) in September.[22]

The attacks refocused attention on the Pakistani military's relationship with the Haqqanis. Kabul, New Delhi and Washington accused the ISI of being behind the attack on the Indian Embassy. In his last testimony before stepping down as chairman of the US Joint Chiefs of Staff, General Mike Mullen in September 2011, accused the ISI of helping the Haqqani Network conduct several high-profile attacks including the attack on the US Embassy. He called the Haqqanis a 'veritable arm' of the ISI.[23]

Pakistani military support for the Haqqanis has spanned more than four decades. But this support has evolved considerably during different phases of war in Afghanistan. After the overthrow of the Taliban in late 2001, the Haqqanis were central to what Islamabad saw as its key interests in Afghanistan. The network was used to undermine and attack Indian influence in Afghanistan. The Haqqanis kept the Loya Paktia tribes from assuming a role in Afghan politics, and acted as a firewall against the possible rebirth of Pashtun nationalism among tribes on both sides of the Durand Line. More crucially, the network has kept Loya Paktia destabilised to prevent its youth from joining the Afghan military. Residents of the region dominated Afghan military's officer corps before the disintegration of the Afghan military in 1992.[24]

The threat posed by the Haqqanis has generated a long and intense debate within US President Barack Obama's administration. On 7 September 2012, the US State Department designated the Haqqani Network as a foreign terrorist organisation. Critics of the move argued it would push the Haqqanis further away from any political settlement, and make the network vulnerable to even more Pakistani manipulation.[25]

The Haqqanis rise to become Afghanistan's most potent insurgent network was built on its extensive links and alliances with Al-Qaeda and Pakistani and Central Asian extremists. The network's literature showcases this relationship. In 2010, Sirajuddin Haqqani published a book entitled *Military Lessons for the Benefit of the Mujahedeen*. The 144-page Pashto-language book is an Al-Qaeda-influenced terrorist training manual. The book praises Al-Qaeda and supports beheadings and suicide bombings. It instructs operatives, presumably dispatched to strike targets in the West, to 'blend in, shave, wear Western dress, be patient'.

Much of the book's content—such as an explicit statement that men of immoral character can serve as commanders in jihad—goes against the philosophy of the Taliban, whose literature emphasises piety and strict adherence to Islamic moral principles.[26] Propaganda, such as DVDs produced by Al-Qaeda's media arm Al-Sahab, demonstrated the close working relationship between the Haqqanis and Al-Qaeda. Al-Sahab has released more videos of attacks in Loya Paktia than anywhere else in Afghanistan. Some of the suicide bombers who carried out these attacks were Arabs, Turks or citizens of Western countries.[27]

In Pakistan, the Haqqanis have provided sanctuary and encouraged the Islamic Movement of Uzbekistan and the Turkic Islamic Jihad Union to open offensives in Central Asia. These allies and other Taliban factions have a symbiotic relationship, particularly in northern Afghanistan, where the Taliban insurgency is keen on making inroads into ethnic Uzbek communities who consider themselves to have been marginalised since 2002. The killing of many senior government officials has significantly reduced security in the region.[28]

This situation has facilitated extremist fundraising. The Haqqani Network is at the apex of a mafia-like crime syndicate in Loya Paktia and parts of FATA. Its activities range from kidnapping for ransom to drug smuggling and protection rackets for criminals. Support from ideologues in oil-rich Gulf states and Pakistan has also been a perennial source of funding. The Haqqanis have invested capital in legal businesses such as real estate, construction and transport. The group is also involved in money-laundering. To this end, it has acquired large stakes in legitimate businesses in Loya Paktia, Waziristan, Kurram and Khyber Pakhtunkhwa.[29]

But Haqqani's extensive links with Pakistan and international jihadists have undermined his standing in Paktia. Pacha Khan Zadran, his main rival within his Zadran tribe, recalled how he tried to dissuade Haqqani from joining the Taliban. 'The Taliban were not masters of their views and thinking,' Zadran said in 2011. 'All their actions were guided by others.' He recalled sending a message to Jalaluddin Haqqani, through a mutual friend, to warn him against joining the hard-line movement in 1995. 'These people are not capable of governing Afghanistan and will ultimately create a regional problem for our country,' Pacha Khan Zadran's messenger told Haqqani. 'Today, the world is going in one direction and they are insisting on going in the opposite direction. It will be very difficult, even impossible, for them to succeed.'[30] Another Loya Paktia elder, Nazim Zadran, cites the political alienation Haqqani faced within his Gaman Khel clan. Nazim Zadran, a member of the regional peace council in Khost, said most Gaman Khel tribe members ended up backing the central government, including Haqqani's first cousin Miaki Khan, a member of the Khost provincial peace *shura*.

Both Pacha Khan Zadran and Nazim Zadran have been targeted for assassination multiple times, including by suicide bombers. Many members of their families have been killed by unknown assailants. Both men blame Haqqani and his Pakistani backers for the violence.[31] An Afghan parliament member from the region noted that almost all support Haqqani receives in Loya Paktia is due only to ideological commitments. He said tribal dynamics have played only a small role. The tribes resent Haqqani's alliance with Pakistan and blame him for the insecurity that plagues the region. They even blame him for provoking bombings and night raids by international security forces, according to the lawmaker, who requested anonymity.[32]

On a smaller scale, the Haqqani model of a Taliban-allied family is emulated by the Mansurs. The family gets its name from Mawlawi Nasrullah Mansur, a Deobandi cleric and head of his faction of the Harakat-e Inqilab-e Islami Afghanistan. He was killed by a roadside bomb in 1993. His brother Abdul Latif Mansur assumed the leadership of the family, which has controlled the strategic Zurmat district of Paktia Province. The family linked up with the Taliban as the militia advanced from Kandahar in 1995. Abdul Latif Mansur was appointed minister of agriculture in the Taliban cabinet. Zurmat became one of the most well-represented regions in the Taliban regime outside Kandahar. Nearly a dozen Taliban ministers, deputy ministers and senior officials came from Zurmat.

Saifur Rehman Mansur, the elder son of Nasrullah Mansur, emerged as deputy commander of the Taliban's 4th Division in Kargha, west of Kabul. In March 2002, he led nearly 1,000 fighters—including Arabs, Chechens and Central Asians—during two weeks of fighting in the mountains of the Shahikot Valley in Zurmat. The downing of a US helicopter and killing of seven American troops made Saifur Rehman Mansur a Taliban hero. Like the Haqqanis, the Mansurs returned to Loya Paktia in 2005. In subsequent years, their network dominated Zurmat and was responsible for operations in the nearby Logar and Ghazni provinces. The leaders of the Mansur family coordinated most of their combat activities from Pakistan.[33] The clout of such families has enriched them—but has undermined tribal solidarity.

Changing Tribal Landscape

Few conversations in tea shops, homes and *jirga*s in Loya Paktia are complete without a discussion about the root causes of the malaise in the region. Residents often retell the story of prominent tribal leader Abdullah Khan Zadran to illustrate what went wrong in Afghanistan. In one oft-repeated tale, it is said that in the summer of 1973, Abdullah Khan Zadran went to Kabul to pledge allegiance to Daud Khan. In line with the tradition of Afghan royal courts, participants were falling over each other to praise Daud Khan and glory in his wisdom and determination to end Afghanistan's backwardness. All were speaking with hope about a new beginning. Abdullah Khan Zadran, however, remained silent. Daud Khan noticed and asked: 'Abdullah Khan what have you to say?' The elderly Pashtun looked the feared Afghan leader in the eyes and replied: 'Afghanistan was like a tough fortress. Nobody dared to invade it. What you have done is similar to blowing open the door to this fortress. Now everybody will attempt to repeat your actions. This nation will never be able to stand on its feet again.' His warning proved correct. The tribes of Afghanistan have paid a heavy price for decades of political upheaval.

Following the demise of the Taliban in the winter of 2001, the tribes of Loya Paktia were ready for a new political life. It had been the only region where ordinary Afghans, rather than foreign forces, warlords or jihadi commanders, had overthrown the Taliban. Administration in the provinces of Logar, Paktia, Paktika and Khost fell to tribal *shuras*, or councils, on 14 November 2001, a day after Kabul had fallen to the Northern Alliance. The *shuras* mobilised young armed volunteers in *arbakis*, or tribal posses, to ensure security. The outside world, holding to the perception that the Taliban represented all Pashtuns, was oblivious to what had occurred. In a sign of things to come, American jets continued to bomb Gardez and other regions many days after the regime had crumbled and most Al-Qaeda and Taliban cadres had escaped into Pakistan or withdrawn to the mountains.[34]

That the Taliban are a supra-tribal and supra-ethnic Islamist organisation is obvious in Loya Paktia. Some tribes resisted and even fought the Taliban for encroaching on their way of life. The Taliban in general, and the individuals and networks associated with them, are deeply rooted in Pashtun culture and retain strong regional tribal and clan identities. It is within the Taliban that the balance between being Pashtun and being Muslim has changed. Islam has become the primary identity of the Taliban—and the price for this shift has been steep. The political, military and economic changes that have overwhelmed the region in the past three decades have been cataclysmic. The institution of *jirga*, central to implementing *Pashtunwali* and its codified customary laws called *narkh*, has been weakened. Even the term *jirga* is being replaced by the Arabic *shura*, and clerics and commanders have rarely been more powerful. In the words of one veteran observer, 'Might often trumps *Pashtunwali* and even Islamic law.'[35]

Haider Gul Mangal, a notable leader of the Mangal tribe, was part of a robust tribal initiative to be part of the 'new' Afghanistan after the demise of the Taliban. The Mangals held a large *jirga* in early 2003 to pledge support for Afghanistan's new government and the international reconstruction they hoped would be carried out. Haider Gul Mangal recalled the independent spirit of the *jirga*, which lasted for days. 'We wanted to resolve our problems,' he said in 2011. 'We did not want to have any problems with our neighbouring tribes or with the new government. We wanted to ensure that our people could live in peace.'

The gathering adopted a comprehensive *tarun*, or declaration, spelling out measures they hoped would guarantee peace. They raised an *arbaki*, consisting of hundreds of armed volunteers, to provide security, particularly along the strategic highway from Gardez to Khost. The Mangal elders enforced this declaration for nearly five years. As late as 2007, they were enforcing the declaration so strictly that Mangals burned the house of a man who was killed while planting a roadside bomb.[36] Haider Gul Mangal said that a lack of funding and government backing eventually forced the tribe to abandon the declaration and dismantle the *arbaki*.[37]

In another demonstration of solidarity, more than 1,000 tribal leaders and notables gathered in Khost in September 2006. The gathering was prompted by the killing of popular Paktia Province governor Hakim Taniwal in a suicide bombing.[38] When a second suicide bomber attacked Taniwal's funeral, killing seven and injuring more than forty, the anger of the Khost tribes escalated. There were no dissenting voices when the gathering adopted a comprehensive pledge to support the Afghan government and to condemn terrorism.[39] The document read:

1. The tribal leaders, *ulema*, intellectuals and notables of Khost Province's twelve districts and three administrative divisions fully back the government of the Islamic Republic of Afghanistan.
2. This gathering agrees that preserving the sovereignty of Afghanistan, loyalty to the government and preserving patriotic traditions, within the framework of Islamic teachings, is the national and Islamic duty of its participants.
3. The Muslim and patriotic people of Khost consider the recent pronouncements of Pakistani military dictator General Pervez Musharraf regarding Afghanistan's political and social conditions to be blatantly wrong and a clear example of interfering in our country's internal affairs.[40]
4. Musharraf's pronouncements in Brussels show that he and his country have failed to honour their international commitments. They have also failed to help the international community in its efforts against terrorism. By saying such baseless things, Musharraf is seeking to manipulate the international community.
5. The brotherly tribes of Khost pledge to put aside all differences and feuds to encourage peace and progress and to pave way for a bright future for coming generations. They will work to resolve their differences, using tribal, legal and Islamic traditions as guides.
6. The tribes of Khost pledge to protect their territories and not allow terrorists or troublemakers to foment disorder.

7. The *ulema*, tribal leaders and masses declare that suicide bombing attacks are clearly against the teachings of Islam and the traditions of our region and our country. We strongly condemn such attacks.
8. The *ulema* and tribal leaders consider suicide attacks, terrorist conspiracies and attacks on our country's security forces to be forbidden (according to Islamic teachings) and unjustifiable.
9. The participants of this forum demand that UN Secretary-General Kofi Annan and the international community investigate the external causes of the increasing insecurity in our country. We call on them to help the people of Afghanistan prevent this insecurity from spreading.
10. The tribal leaders, *ulema* and masses of Khost demand more support from the Afghan central government and international aid agencies for political, economic, social, cultural and educational development in our region. They must speed up the pace of reconstruction.

The tribes of Loya Paktia have been severely victimised by terrorist violence and intimidation. Many tribal leaders who openly opposed the Taliban have been targeted for assassination. Threats have forced other leaders to move to the relative safety of Kabul. Many communities have suffered from Taliban-imposed school and clinic closures. The Taliban has successfully capitalised on the failure of international forces to develop a sophisticated understanding of tribal dynamics. When it suits their goals, Taliban figures have shown themselves adroit at aggravating tribal disputes. The Taliban has sometimes gone on to later adjudicate such disputes—bringing them even more political clout and local influence.

The Afghan government, in contrast, has failed to adopt a tribal policy. The Ministry of Borders and Tribal Affairs has received little international funding. US special forces operations, which have often included night raids and arbitrary detentions, have backfired and made American troops unpopular with ordinary people. Indeed, US forces have sometimes been exploited, their firepower and authority manipulated to settle scores between rival families and groups. The US reliance on unsavoury local characters has also not endeared them to locals.[41]

Despite corruption and inefficiency that has hobbled reconstruction efforts, Loya Paktia has undergone a considerable transformation since the demise of the Taliban regime. By late 2012, Loya Paktia boasted a range of government offices, as well as three functioning universities and hundreds of rebuilt schools. During the Taliban stint in power, none of Paktika Province's twenty districts had even one government building. By early 2013, most districts had also been connected to the provincial capital Sharana by new roads that eventually link up with the national network. The most impressive achievement, however, has been the private construction projects funded, in many cases, by remittances sent home by diaspora labourers. With more than 25,000 shops, Khost has become a lively commercial centre. The city's frequent traffic jams testify to how far it has come since the 1980s, when it was a sleepy village of about 15,000 people.[42]

10

THE NEW TALIBAN IN LOY KANDAHAR

In February 2002, I took a flight in a small propeller plane to the vast dustbowl of Kandahar. It was my first visit to this venerable city, which lies on a plateau between rugged mountains. We were told shortly after landing that the airport was where Al-Qaeda fighters had made one of their last stands before fleeing Afghanistan. Under intense assault by US forces, hundreds of Arab fighters had died in trenches around the wind-swept airfield in December 2001.

A few kilometres from the airport, an arched gateway marked the entrance to the ancient city. Most shops and homes in Kandahar are made of clay bricks or mud. The old town is distinguished from newer settlements by the width of its streets. Narrow lanes contain the closely-knit urban communities in the old city, while affluent Kandaharis live along the wide lanes of Shar-e Nau, or New City neighbourhood.

Kandahar has been ravaged by the conflicts that have dominated its recent history. Parts of concrete buildings that once housed government departments were smashed during the Soviet occupation and have remained so. Other structures were distinguished by layers of old tyres piled on their rooftops—a bit of urban camouflage designed to fool American bombers. But such deception was rarely successful. Many Kandaharis were in awe of US bombs and missiles, which had hit Taliban installations with deadly precision.

With the bombardment at least temporarily over, life in Afghanistan's second largest city was slowly getting back to normal. Pedestrians dressed in long tunics, baggy trousers and colourful turbans strolled along the dusty streets. Boys flew kites and played football. Girls had already begun going back to school. Hard-line Taliban religious police working for the Department of Promotion of Virtue and Prevention of Vice had vanished, and music shops were again catering to Kandahari tastes. In nearly every taxi, one could hear songs by Obaidullah Jan Kandahari, the most popular Pashtun singer in southern Afghanistan.

But life was far from easy. In the subsequent months, I travelled extensively across southern Afghanistan. It was hard to escape the fact that many ordinary people were living in misery. In addition to the hardship of war, years of drought had pushed nomads and farmers to the extreme end of their survival strategies. A two-hour drive east of Kandahar, I found some 90,000 Pashtun farmers and nomads living in squalid displacement camps along the Pakistani border.

Loy Kandahar, or Greater Kandahar, spans the provinces of Kandahar, Zabul, Uruzgan, Helmand, Nimroz and Farah.[1] Home to an early human settlement, Kandahar, then called Arachosia, was founded by Alexander the Great in the fourth century B.C. Home to major Durrani and Ghilzai tribes, the region's Pashtuns speak a distinct dialect of Pashto and embody Kandahari culture. For centuries, Loy Kandahar has been contested by rival empires, bequeathing to the region's population a tradition of political canny and military prowess. The fertile soil of the region has made it an agricultural centre, and its proximity to Iran and Pakistan has made it a significant trading crossroads.

Modern Afghanistan is a rump state of Pashtun empires, established out of Loy Kandahar by the Ghilzai and Durrani dynasties in the eighteenth century. At its geographic peak, the empire extended deep into modern Iran and India. It is often said by Kandaharis that what happens in Loy Kandahar ultimately determines the destiny of Afghanistan. Wish Zalmayan, or Awakened Youth, emerged as a Pashtun reformist movement in the 1940s. It advocated a constitutional monarchy and the expansion of citizens' rights. Many of its members played significant roles in shaping twentieth-century Afghanistan. At the height of the civil war anarchy of the 1990s, the region was the crucible of the Taliban. It also shares geographic features and population characteristics with Pakistan's south-western Balochistan Province. This has increased the ability of Pakistani agents to penetrate Kandahar and promote Islamabad's policies. Since the early 1980s, Loy Kandahar has served as a key theatre for proxy wars.

Despite the poverty and political instability, the mood in Loy Kandahar was optimistic in 2002. At the time, Kandahar was the only major Afghan city without a night-time curfew. Kandaharis were pleased that Hamid Karzai, a royalist and pragmatic tribal leader from the region, had been selected to head the US-backed transitional administration. Many were hopeful that greater international engagement and investment would bring peace, rehabilitate communities and eventually help them rebuild their livelihoods. But residents were also worried that the *topakian*, or gunmen, had returned to power alongside Karzai. Members of these former anti-Soviet mujahedeen factions had claimed senior government positions after the collapse of the Taliban regime. Kandaharis were worried the *topakian* would revive their fratricidal power grabs, and that the region would slide back into chaos.[2]

A Dying Nation

Loy Kandahar remained relatively calm until the summer of 2003. The first signs of a renewed Taliban insurgency appeared in Zabul Province, when nearly 1,000 insurgents amassed in the mountainous Dai Chopan district. One of the militants' first early acts was to neutralise local Pashtun tribal leaders by intimidating them into submission.[3] As the insurgency spread across southern Afghanistan in subsequent years, the Taliban made the elimination of the tribal leadership a central goal. Powerful clan and tribal leaders, in particular, as well as government officials and clerics, were targeted.

The insurgents were well aware they would have little chance of triumphing in a conventional war against US-backed forces. They thus turned to asymmetrical warfare. A key feature of this strategy was assassination. The Taliban often labelled those they murdered as being supporters of the foreign occupation, and their elimination was justified in the name of *jihad*. The Taliban claimed responsibility for hundreds of assassinations, including the July 2011 killing of Ahmed Wali Karzai.[4] He was President Karzai's younger half-brother and was considered the most powerful political figure in southern Afghanistan. The high volume of targeted killings led to Kandahar being known as the 'assassination capital of Afghanistan'.[5]

The assassination campaign terrified the population, and was instrumental in helping the Taliban regain the upper hand. After the 2001 fall of the regime, most Pashtun tribal leaders were eager to resume their traditional role as a bridge between the government and clans. The Taliban, however, understood that this bridge had to be eliminated if the movement wanted to again capture power. Leadership among Pashtuns is often inherited through lineage, but it is developed and exercised through personal charisma. The existence of legitimate leaders is central to the working of social and political institutions.[6] The Pashto proverb, 'You may lose a hundred, but may not lose the one,' perhaps best summarises the importance of community leaders.[7]

By killing leaders, the Taliban sought to wound Pashtun tribal solidarity. In the long term, opposition from Pashtun communities still presents a greater strategic impediment to the return of the Taliban than all the firepower of the Afghan Army and its Western allies. The Taliban assassinations created a leadership vacuum, fostered an atmosphere of fear and demoralised ordinary people. The killings undermined trust and co-operation between residents and the government and foreign forces. The Taliban strategy was to prevent Durrani Pashtun leaders from becoming strong enough to stabilise southern Afghanistan and erect barriers to Taliban influence. The effort was largely successful. 'The Taliban now have a great impact on our tribal society,' said Kandahari intellectual Abdul Habib Khan. 'They oversee the funeral, birth and marriage rites, and have become the preferred authority for adjudicating disputes.'[8]

Al-Qaeda has helped provide justification for the assassination campaigns carried out by insurgents in both Afghanistan and Pakistan. According to Al-Qaeda's philosophy, killing is a legitimate punishment for Muslims accused of *takfir*, or apostasy.[9] In practice, *takfir* is cited by extremists seeking an excuse to justify the elimination of real or suspected opponents. The use of *takfir* killings also further undermined the traditional authority of families, clans and tribal elders in meting out punishments. Many Pashtuns speak of their illiterate youth being lured to the extremist cause by propaganda, cash or the promise of revenge for personal tragedies. Some of these same radicalised youth have later been linked to the killings of local leaders. This behaviour is in sharp contrast to the formal rules of conduct that the Taliban have established for members of the movement.

The Book of Rules

The Taliban insurgency in southern Afghanistan gathered momentum after the presidential elections of October 2004. The vote saw Hamid Karzai—who had been serving as the 'transitional' leader since early 2002—emerge as the first elected Afghan president. With Washington and its allies preoccupied with the war in Iraq, the Taliban faced little opposition as they gradually seized large swathes of territory in Loy Kandahar. By 2006, NATO had become aware of the threat and began to engage Taliban fighters in fierce battles. Some 1,500 Taliban squared off against thousands of Canadian and Afghan troops for nearly two weeks in the rural district of Panjwai, west of Kandahar City. NATO claimed to have killed more than 1,100 Taliban and captured more than 150. Operation Medusa, as NATO called the battle, underlined the extent of the Taliban renaissance in the southern homeland. It also highlighted a vulnerability: the Taliban comeback was being guided by leaders in hiding in neighbouring Pakistan.[10]

The Taliban Rahbari Shura,[11] or leadership council, based in Balochistan, was worried that some field commanders were becoming too independent. Commanders like Mullah Dadullah, for example, a popular figure in the southern insurgency who died in May 2007, were regarded by some Taliban leaders as wild cards. In response, they sought to consolidate their authority by issuing a rulebook. The pocket-sized Pashto-language publication, formally titled *Rulebook for the Mujahedeen of the Islamic Emirate of Afghanistan*, was released in the autumn of 2006. It included thirty prohibitions. When the next edition was released in May 2009, the number of prohibitions had increased to sixty-seven.

The most recent version of the rulebook, issued in May 2010, has fourteen chapters and eighty-five articles. Along with providing guidelines on how to discipline Taliban cadres, the manual sets down rules on how the movement should administer regions under its control. The book can be seen, at least in part, as a public relations exercise aimed at projecting a positive image of the Taliban, who are viewed by many Afghans as little more than uneducated thugs. Taliban leader Mullah Mohammad Omar is quoted on the back cover of the 2009 edition as telling his fighters that protecting the life and property of Afghan people is the main objective of the movement. 'Give a special place to your friends and your people in your hearts,' it reads. 'Extend a strong bond of loyalty and brotherhood to them, so that the enemy is unable to realise its objective of dividing you.'[12]

The rulebook portrays the Taliban as a centralised and hierarchical organisation. It asserts that the movement's primary aim is to expel international forces and overthrow the current Afghan political system. It details the Taliban's worldview and ideology, as based on the movement's interpretation of *sharia* law. It addresses internal organisational issues such as the chain of command, describes prohibited behaviours, offers advice on religious observance and ethical issues, suggests methods for adjudicating disputes between ordinary people and provides guidelines for dealing with the media. It instructs members on how to invite opponents into the movement and how to handle spies, prisoners, contractors and the spoils of war. To prevent the sexual exploitation of young boys, the rulebook bans 'beardless boys' from living with fighters in 'their military bases or lodgings'.[13]

The rulebook instructs leaders and cadres on how to operate within a rigid organisational framework consisting of provincial and district councils. The book outlines the functions and responsibilities of everyone from district leaders to the 'Imam', or supreme leader, Mullah Mohammad Omar. The various editions of the rulebook hint at the existence of a Taliban administration complete with governors, district administrators, judges and local councils. The responsibilities and limits of authority are spelled out. Those entrusted with leadership responsibilities should possess 'wisdom, bravery, piety and benevolence'. The rulebook warns against 'regional, ethnic, and linguistic' prejudices. It calls on Taliban cadres to 'represent the Islamic Emirate in such a way that all compatriots welcome them and extend their co-operation and help'.[14]

The rulebook has evolved through several editions, with harsh rhetoric noticeably softened in later editions. The later versions urge greater caution, and offer detailed instructions on how to deal with government officials, contractors and non-governmental organisations. The rulebook specifically bans torture and the severing of body parts. It says executions may only be carried out by shooting, and filming such acts is banned. This is in marked contrast to Al-Qaeda's penchant for spreading beheading videos. The rulebook says, 'When a convict is ordered to be executed, whether he is a spy or another criminal, he should be shot dead with a gun. Photographing such an incident is forbidden.' Only Mullah Omar and his deputies have the formal authority to order executions.[15]

Cadres are also warned against forcing confessions from detainees and offering false promises to suspected spies. Only senior leaders are authorised to decide the fate of spies. The rulebook also attempts to prevent field commanders from using *jihad* for personal profiteering. It prevents them from imposing fines, carrying out kidnappings for ransom, or collecting Islamic taxes such as *ushr* and *zakat* by force.[16] The rulebook urges fighters to concentrate on the battlefield and leave dispute resolution to local elders. Violators of the code of conduct are threatened with punishment.[17] Even smoking is prohibited.

The rules for carrying out suicide bombings are also laid out. 'Carry out suicide attacks only on high-value and important targets, so that the brave youth of the Islamic nation are not wasted targeting unimportant and ordinary targets,' the second part of article 57 reads. In the next part, suicide bombing volunteers are advised to 'pay great attention to preventing the killing and injuring of ordinary people'.

A Shadowy Organisation

Field research in southern Afghanistan suggests that Taliban ranks include three main types of fighters:

1) Those motivated by religious zeal;
2) Those who seek revenge for harassment, intimidation or perceived injustices by the government and foreign powers;
3) Those who are holdovers from the former Taliban regime, for whom 'climbing into the mountains'—a Kandahari euphemism for joining the insurgency—is a career path.

An example of the second type would be Mullah Abdul Ghani Baradar, a key architect of the insurgency who also served as Taliban military chief. 'Hamid Karzai freed Mullah Baradar in 2001 and even gifted him 25 guns in an effort to show that he posed no threat,' Kandahari intellectual Abdul Habib Khan recalled. 'Mullah Baradar then returned to his home in Uruzgan Province. Locals flocked to congratulate him on choosing a peaceful life. But within three months, his life was turned into hell. They raided his uncle's home one day, and his father's the next. Finally, he was forced to take up weapons and move to Pakistan.'[18]

Former police officer and Kandahari lawmaker Abdul Rahim Ayubi has observed that, in some cases, outrage over the government's systematic targeting of Taliban cadres has driven previously non-radicalised men to join the insurgency. Government incompetence and corruption has also pushed many Pashtuns into the arms of the insurgency. One Kandahari commentator observed, 'The Taliban are only responsible for one-third of the problems, while the weaknesses of the government created the remaining issues here.'[19]

Most Taliban in southern Afghanistan are local Pashtuns, including Mullah Omar. Pakistani jihadists, a sizeable number of whom are ethnic Punjabis, are also active in the region. The number of foreign militants has gradually declined as Al-Qaeda-affiliated Arab and Central Asian militant networks have been targeted by US drone strikes in Pakistan's Tribal Areas. The Taliban also began to distance themselves from foreigners who carried out acts of extreme violence.[20] The opening of jihadist fronts in Iraq, Yemen and Somalia, and more recently the unrest of the Arab Spring, have also prompted some international jihadists to exit the region.

The Taliban continues to rely on the religious credentials the movement established during its first stint in power. It continues to benefit from the widespread popular perception that Taliban leaders are not corrupt. Their simple lifestyle, accessibility to ordinary Afghans and commitment to rough, quick justice, has contributed to their stature.[21]

While often portrayed in the media as a monolithic force, 'Taliban' is actually an umbrella term used to describe networks with similar but varying interests. Taliban factions have broad agreement on strategic goals, such as ending the current political system and driving out foreign forces. They agree on working to implement an Islamic political system, But there are differences over tactical issues. The remnants of the old Taliban regime in Loy Kandahar, who call themselves the Islamic Emirate, enjoy a high degree of political legitimacy and are seen as less willing to use extreme violence. The Haqqani Network, rooted in Loya Paktia, are known for attacks that have claimed scores of civilian victims and claim less popular support. The Haqqanis are also seen as being closer to Pakistani intelligence operatives.

Taliban leadership contests have sometimes been fierce. The cohesion of the movement has always been threatened by the emergence of independent-minded field commanders, whose ultimate loyalties were not always clear.[22] At times, internal rivalries have also been inspired by personal, tribal and political differences. Mullah Omar and many Taliban fighters derive from both the Durrani and the Ghilzai tribal confederacies. But others come from less influential communities, such as the Kakar and the Tareen tribes.[23]

Like most residents of Afghanistan, the Taliban adhere to the Hanafi Madhab, or school of jurisprudence, a Sunni sect formally called Ahlus-Sunnah Wal-Jama'ah. Most Taliban leaders were educated in Deobandi madrasas in Pakistan, and the movement generally follows the outlook of Deobandis, who emphasise a puritanical interpretation of Islam. Unlike some extremist Deobandis in Pakistan, however, the Taliban viewpoint is not exclusively sectarian. They are tolerant of Salafis, Hanbalis and other sub-sects within Islam, and some followers of these schools are even part of the movement. 'Our major aim is to unite Muslims,' Taliban spokesman Zabihullah Mujahid said. 'This is the relationship we have with other sects, and it will remain so.'[24] The Taliban has exhibited a considerable degree of anti-Shi'ism. But the movement has not attempted to replicate in Afghanistan the Shia-Sunni sectarian conflict that, for example, continues to roil Pakistan. To the Taliban, no Islamic country in the contemporary world can be held up as a perfect example of the implementation of *sharia* law.[25]

Taliban finances are generated in a shadowy war economy that developed in the Pashtun borderlands during the 1980s. Taliban networks each have separate financing structures. For instance, the Haqqani Network has considerable economic interests in Pakistan. In southern Afghanistan, meanwhile, there is significant evidence the Taliban raise funds through the practice of Islamic taxation called *zakat*. They also impose the *ushr* tax on agricultural produce, including poppy cultivation. Criminality including kidnappings for ransom is a hallmark of most insurgencies worldwide.

The Taliban are formally opposed to poppy cultivation for the purpose of heroin production, and the movement does not have a controlling stake in the drug trade in southern Afghanistan. It is considered only a minor player in the illegal narcotics industry. Over the years, a large percentage of Taliban funds have been provided by private donors in Afghanistan, Pakistan and the wealthy Gulf states. It has never been clear to what extent the Taliban are directly bankrolled by the Pakistani security establishment. Foreign contractors, particularly those involved in security, logistics and building, have also proved a boon for Taliban fundraising. Some have resorted to making direct payments to field commanders in exchange for protection of their operations.[26]

Taliban Utopia

Most Taliban literature is in Pashto and can be described as either propaganda or earnest ideological exposition. The propaganda literature consists of CDs and cassettes of jihadi chants, poetry and DVDs lionising various attacks and battles. The Taliban website is regularly updated with news of battlefield successes, or used to refute and ridicule statements from the Afghan government and NATO troops. The more serious Taliban literature consists of essays, policy declarations, speeches and obituaries.

This literature seeks to establish the Taliban as an Afghanistan-focused group with few global aspirations. Understanding the movement's view of Afghanistan's history, present and future is a key to comprehending its strategy and ultimate goals. The Arabic-language *Al-Samood* magazine is a major Taliban publication that seeks to explain the movement's positions to the international community of Arab-speaking Islamists. Its 59th issue included an essay entitled 'The Afghanistan of Islam rejects pollution by democracy and Westernisation'.[27] The essay rejects the nearly century-old efforts of modernisation and democratisation in Afghanistan. It deplores King Amanullah Khan for being 'fascinated by the capitals of Europe'. It rejects Amanullah's emphasis on education and women's empowerment as 'imposing secularism and Westernization under the banner of engaging in democracy'.

The essay also justifies the rebellion against him: 'People charged him with unbelief, rebelled against him and expelled him from the country, nullified all of his Westernisation projects and forced him to flee to exile.' The article similarly rejects the cautious modernisation that occurred under the Musahiban dynasty, which assumed power after Amanullah.[28] It also condemns King Zahir Shah for introducing 'Western culture to the Afghan people, summoning Western educational experts to craft educational programmes suffused with Western spirit, and permitting Western countries and the Soviet Union to establish educational programmes and leftist and secular parties, which were working for Western democracy, and distancing people and groups from serious work for Islam and hindering the role of Islam in shaping society.'[29]

Some of the harshest criticism is reserved for the Soviet-backed communist regimes of the 1980s and the Western-backed government of President Hamid Karzai. It says the communist coup of 1978 ultimately resulted in Soviet occupation of Afghanistan. 'European ideas began to dominate this time under the guise of communism, represented by the People's Democratic Party of Afghanistan, which wanted to detach the Afghans from their Islamic religion and history, just as the communists have done before in the countries of Central Asia.'[30] The essay accuses the West of plotting against the Taliban regime as soon as it emerged. 'The West created an alliance against it, which included all the infidel powers in the East and the West, and attacked this Muslim country again to establish democracy in the country.' The essay doesn't seek to make a firm distinction between communism and Western democracy. It says, 'The Muslim Afghan people therefore have waged war against democracy and its system of ideas, whether in the form of communism or in its liberal secular form.'

The essay accuses the West of scheming to alter the Islamic character of the Afghan people. 'The Westernising and Christianising establishment focus their efforts on four axes: education, media, changing the structure of the social fabric of Afghan people and Christianising (proselytising) efforts among some minority sects and the remnants of communism in Afghanistan.' The article portrays the Western military presence in Afghanistan as part of an organised campaign of subjugation: 'In the realm of changing the structure of the social fabric, Western military forces and their civilian establishments have created hundreds of administrations to change Islamic tribal society into what is called a civil society through youth and women associations, councils, *shuras*, technical unions and political blocs in the cities, villages and countryside. Western establishments have begun to make available these new organisations cultural materials and are beginning to make them aware and Westernise them through conferences, seminars, classes, radio programmes and distribution of tapes and radio sets among the people.'

A relatively witty article that appeared on the Taliban website is useful for its summary of the movement's view of Afghan history. Entitled 'Announcement of fateha (funeral rites) for a martyr', the piece attacks the May 2012 signing of a Strategic Partnership Agreement between Kabul and Washington. It says three centuries of Afghan independence have been 'killed in a joint attack by a foreigner (Barack Obama) and a native (Hamid Karzai)'. The mock funeral announcement includes a list of Afghans who fought the British and Soviets. The list includes nineteenth- and twentieth-century Afghan and Pashtun war heroes, women, and a few living and deceased Taliban leaders. The most glaring omissions are secular and modernist Afghan figures such as King Amanullah and King Nadir Shah.[31]

The Taliban propaganda machine regularly releases detailed critiques of US and Afghan government policies. A Pashto-language essay called 'Another war is going on in Afghanistan' is an example. 'America has chosen democracy for Afghanistan,' it says. 'Under this system, humans are not weighed according to their wisdom, talent and piety. Instead they are merely counted like animals.' It goes on to say that the religion of Muslims 'outlines a comprehensive system and set of laws to enable them to live their lives under it. Thus, they do not need democracy and can never establish it in their society. [For Muslims] it is only possible to adopt democracy when, God forbid, they leave their religion.' It also criticises the Afghan constitution for preventing the implementation of *sharia* law. 'The current constitution considers the protection of democracy and support for human rights as the responsibilities of the state. It is clear that both democracy and the Universal Declaration of Human Rights are Western constructs. Their inclusion leaves no space for Islamic *sharia* law.'[32]

Important Taliban policy pronouncements have been released to mark the Islamic festivals of Eid-ul Fitar and Eid-ul Adha. Mullah Omar's Eid-ul Adha message of November 2010 specifies the Taliban's political goals:

> We are working for a strong Islamic and independent (political) system in the future. We want a system whose economic, security, legal, educational and judicial institutions are run in accordance with Islamic teachings. This system will be based on and move forward on consultations with knowledgeable and competent professional people. The system will protect all honest, experienced and professional cadres, irrespective of their political, ethnic and linguistic affiliation. They will be given administrative positions based on their competence and honesty. In addition, the rights that *sharia* accords to all people, including women, will be protected. We will enforce internal security and will prevent moral decadence, injustice and other *munkirat* [things banned by *sharia*] in light of the rulings of *sharia*. We will implement the law of accountability in government institutions to promote transparency.[33]

The Taliban appeared to soften its political stance after NATO unveiled its plans for a 2014 withdrawal from Afghanistan. 'Unlike the propaganda of our opponents, the Islamic Emirate does not have a policy of establishing monopoly over power,' Mullah Omar said in his August 2011 Eid-ul Fitar statement: 'Afghanistan is the home of all

Afghans and they all have a right to participate in protecting and running it. The coming transition should not be similar to the aftermath of the fall of communism, when our country lost everything and all government institutions were completely decimated.' The statement put forward the Taliban as a force for stability. 'The Afghans have a bright history of resolving internal differences in the absence of external interference,' it said. 'The Islamic Emirate is carrying out a struggle against the foreign occupation to defend our faith and homeland. The presence of invading military is the key reason behind this. If the international coalition ends its occupation, the Islamic Emirate is ready to maintain positive relations with countries in the region and the world at large.' The August 2012 Eid-ul Fitar statement set down the Taliban's bottom line: 'The independence of Afghanistan and the implementation of *sharia* are two fundamental issues that the Islamic Emirate can never compromise on.'

Taliban literature, however, has done little to dispel the almost universal belief in Afghanistan that most Taliban networks are ultimately loyal to Pakistan or are controlled by its security establishment. Most Taliban literature is oddly silent about the movement's relations with Pakistan. Criticism of Islamabad's role in Afghanistan, on the rare occasions it appears, is remarkably toned down. This is in sharp contrast to the rhetoric of the Tehreek-e Taliban Pakistan, Al-Qaeda and the Islamic Movement of Uzbekistan. These organisations have fought the Pakistani military and even declared the country's leaders and army to be *murtad*, or apostate, for being nominal US allies.

In September 2011, the chairman of the US Joint Chiefs of Staff, Admiral Michael Mullen, accused Pakistan's ISI agency of utilising the Haqqani Network as its 'veritable arm' inside Afghanistan. On 27 September the Taliban issued a detailed rebuttal denying any Haqqani cooperation with Islamabad. 'By lying, America wants to change the public image of a great jihadi figure and member of the Taliban leadership council, Al-haj Jalaluddin Haqqani,' the statement said. 'It wants him to be connected to other powers and separate from the Taliban. This is aimed at showing that the mujahedeen are divided and some of their leading personalities are related to foreign intelligence services.' It advised the Pakistani government to 'be attentive to its Islamic and national interests because America will not be satisfied until it robs all its material and spiritual wealth'.[34] Pakistani media gave voice to similar sentiments in the aftermath of Mullen's statement.

The Taliban, however, was restrained towards Pakistan even after the death in Pakistani custody of Mullah Obaidullah, the former Taliban defence minister and a deputy of Mullah Omar. Obaidullah was arrested in 2007 and died of heart disease in prison in Karachi in 2010. The Taliban refrained from directly condemning Islamabad, instead chiding it for failing to treat Obaidullah's condition.[35]

The Taliban's reliance on Pakistani sanctuaries has made the movement vulnerable to Pakistani manipulation. The Taliban leadership in Quetta was critical of, and even despised the role of, the Pakistani security agencies in Afghanistan. But the leadership understood that launching a new insurgency in Afghanistan would never be feasible without the acquiescence of the Pakistani intelligence services.[36] The Afghan Taliban also remained under the sway of Pashtun clerics affiliated with the Deobandi JUI political party in Balochistan and Khyber Pakhtunkhwa.

The assumption that the Taliban and Al-Qaeda constitute a united terrorist syndicate was never accurate. The Taliban and Al-Qaeda follow different sects and vastly different traditions within Sunni Islam, and co-operation between the two has sometimes been turbulent. After the Taliban established control over most of Afghanistan in 1996, Al-Qaeda fell under the influence of the regime. Osama bin Laden pledged a personal oath of loyalty to Mullah Mohammad Omar and sought to cultivate a personal friendship with the Taliban leader. But the Taliban's role in bin Laden's global *jihad* was never more than nominal. The Loy Kandahar Taliban never planned or participated in major attacks in the West. They were Islamists concerned only with Afghanistan. The Haqqani clan, on the other hand, has had longstanding relations with Arab extremists.

The US intervention in Afghanistan after 11 September 2001, and Washington's treatment of Al-Qaeda and the Taliban as a single terrorist alliance, only pressured the two groups to strengthen their ties. Both viewed NATO's presence in Afghanistan as an occupation, and displayed a degree of unity in fighting against it. NATO's systematic targeting of Taliban leaders often led their younger replacements to rely more on Al-Qaeda personnel and techniques. The two groups also depended on sanctuaries in Pakistan for their survival. Despite such co-operation, however, the agendas of the two groups remained distinct. Unlike Al-Qaeda and its Central Asian and Pakistani affiliates, the Afghan Taliban have never flirted with joining the fight against the Pakistani military.[37]

Making Peace with the Taliban

A basis for peace can be found in the fact that Taliban ambitions are limited to Afghanistan. President Hamid Karzai knew this, even as he dodged Taliban bullets in the mountains of Uruzgan Province in December 2001. After he was named interim leader, Karzai was sympathetic to the idea of allowing the Taliban to exist peacefully if they abandoned militancy. Karzai was well familiar with the wounds Afghanistan continued to suffer from cycles of revenge and retribution. Some key Taliban leaders, including Mullah Obaidullah and Mullah Baradar, wrote Karzai a letter in late 2001 offering to accept the legitimacy of his administration in exchange for amnesty.[38]

But this initiative was vetoed by Washington, where officials ruled out reconciliation with any movement allied to Al-Qaeda. At the time, 'reconciliation' wasn't part of the vocabulary of the 'Global War on Terrorism', and many US officials believed the Taliban was already a spent force. Karzai's allies among the former Northern Alliance and Pashtun mujahedeen commanders in southern Afghanistan also opposed reconciliation. In the early years of the Karzai administration, some Taliban figures even participated in elections. Others were appointed to government posts, including governorships, but a majority was forced to move into Balochistan, where they plotted their insurgency.

As the Taliban insurgency gained momentum, Karzai pressured the Bush administration to enlist Pakistan in a new peace effort. The result was a meeting in Kabul of some 700 Afghan and Pakistani leaders and officials in 2007. The three-day event culminated in the release of a joint declaration describing terrorism as a 'common threat to both countries', and recommending that the war against terrorism be an integral part of national security policy. The document also pledged that the 'government and people of Afghanistan and Pakistan will not allow sanctuaries/training centres for terrorists'.[39]

The *jirga*, however, did not deliver peace. Angry speeches by Pashtun leaders against Pakistan's Afghan policy unsettled the regime of President General Pervez Musharraf, and the Pakistani government began to backpedal from its stated commitments.[40] Chaos triggered by the December 2007 assassination of Pakistani former Prime Minister Benazir Bhutto pushed an Afghan settlement even further down Islamabad's agenda.

In 2008, Karzai initiated another peace effort. He wrote to Saudi King Abdullah Bin Abdul Aziz, calling on the monarch to use his clout and influence to spur the Taliban to talks. The Saudi and Taliban sides held a few meetings in the holy city of Mecca, but a breakthrough remained elusive. In Kandahar, Karzai enlisted his younger half-brother, Ahmad Wali Khan, to reach out to Mullah Baradar across the border in Quetta. Like the Karzais, Baradar was a member of the Durrani Popalzai tribe, which eased the process of making contact. Again, however, the talks got no further than an introductory stage.[41]

Hopes for a breakthrough were renewed after Barack Obama was elected US president and took office in early 2009. After a major review of the war, Obama announced a new strategy that made reconciliation among Afghans a key goal. 'In a country with extreme poverty that's been at war for decades, there will also be no peace without reconciliation among former enemies,' Obama said. 'These Afghans must have the option to choose a different course. And that's why we will work with local leaders, the Afghan government, and international partners to have a reconciliation process in every province.'[42]

By this point, however, the Taliban were in no mood for compromise. 'The invading Americans want to use the negotiations as an excuse for the *mujahedeen* to surrender,' Mullah Omar said in his 2009 Eid-ul Adha statement. 'This is out of the question.'[43]

At an international conference on Afghanistan in London in January 2010, the international community announced a new Afghan Peace and Reintegration Trust Fund, budgeted at $140 million. The initiative was aimed at reintegrating Taliban foot soldiers into mainstream society by providing jobs and security.[44] But the initiative soon suffered a setback when Pakistani intelligence agents arrested Mullah Baradar in Karachi in February 2010. Pakistani agents had apparently been told of Baradar's contacts with Karzai and the Saudis. Pakistani military leaders have always rejected direct negotiations involving the Taliban and Washington, insisting that Islamabad be the main broker of any settlement. More Taliban leaders were rounded up in Pakistan after Baradar's arrest.[45]

In June 2010, Karzai hosted some 1,600 prominent Afghans in a peace *jirga* in Kabul. The meeting was aimed at showing his reconciliation efforts had popular backing. The Taliban, however, demonstrated their disapproval by sending suicide bombers and firing rockets at the meeting venue. Later that year, in September, Karzai unveiled a seventy-member peace council to reach out to the Taliban. He named ethnic Tajik Islamist leader and former President Burhannuddin Rabbani to be its head.

German officials eventually hosted the first direct meeting between the Taliban and US officials. The contacts were by no means negotiations, but they led to a series of confidence-building measures and gave the two sides insight into each other's thinking.[46] Washington later acted on long-standing Afghan demands to remove some Taliban figures from United Nations sanctions lists.[47] The Taliban responded by softening their stance. This included using different words in their statements to subtly signal a willingness to engage in a negotiating process.[48] But the insurgents viewed peace as still far in the future.

In October 2010 the former Taliban foreign minister, Wakil Ahmad Muttawakil, told me that negotiations would be a tedious and intricate process. He argued that bringing about a durable, fair settlement must consist of three steps. 'Firstly, there has to be reconciliation among Afghans,' he said. 'Secondly, peace needs to be established between Afghans and the Americans, or NATO at large. And lastly, a settlement among regional states is required.' To facilitate a peace process, Muttawakil added, a Taliban contact office should be established in a neutral country.[49]

While the Taliban and Western officials attempted to keep their contacts secret, their interaction was eventually reported in the media and generated much speculation. The Taliban were compelled to formally acknowledge that talks had taken place. 'The contacts we have established with various quarters for freeing prisoners cannot be labelled comprehensive negotiations,' Mullah Omar said in his 2011 Eid-ul Adha statement. 'As an organised political and military organisation, the Islamic Emirate has a determined and independent agenda in this regard, which will be made public at an opportune time.'

In September 2011 a suicide bomber killed High Peace Council Chairman Rabbani, dealing a fresh blow to prospects for negotiations. The Taliban opened a political office in Qatar in January 2012, but the militia's hopes for a high-profile prisoner exchange with Washington never materialised. This prompted the Taliban to suspend contacts in March 2012. The militants accused the US of changing its position and backing out of a deal to swap five Taliban inmates held at Guantanamo Bay in exchange for the only American soldier they held. In July 2013 the Taliban formally opened their office in Qatar but it was soon closed after President Karzai criticized the hoisting of the movement's flag and a plaque with their formal name (The Islamic Emirate of Afghanistan) as efforts to recreate a parallel Taliban state in Afghanistan. The Taliban viewed the exercise as a failure. It ended up strengthening hard-liners wanting to position the militants for another takeover of Afghanistan after the planned withdrawal of NATO-led combat forces in 2014.[50]

The Nationalist Card

The Taliban have said little about how, should they return to government, they would work to maintain harmony among Afghanistan's patchwork of ethnicities. Most Taliban rank-and-file are ethnic Pashtuns, and the movement relies on the Pashto language as its sole means of communication. Their Pashtun identity is also obvious from their dress and individual behaviour. These traits have led many inside and outside Afghanistan to view them fundamentally as 'Pashtun nationalists', whose main aim is to revive a centralised Pashtun-dominated state. During their rule in the 1990s, however, the Taliban failed to satisfy any segment of Afghan society, including Pashtuns. The regime's rigid policies and close links to Pakistan prevented it from attracting wide support. Taliban hostility to Pashtun political elites who were part of earlier Afghan governments undermined the movement's legitimacy and capacity to govern.[51]

The Taliban have shown little affinity for engaging in traditional tribal politics. While *andiwali* (Pashto for friendship) has remained a cornerstone of their organisation, and some Taliban elements have embraced tribal solidarity and the code of *Pashtunwali*, the Taliban in south-eastern Afghanistan and elsewhere have opposed important aspects of local *narkhs*, or Pashtun customary law.[52] This attitude is one reason why few Pashtuns consider the Taliban to be their representatives or a movement fighting for their rights.[53]

The Taliban has always adhered to its core goal—to establish an Islamic *sharia* state, or an 'Islamic Emirate', in Afghanistan. Under the formal Taliban model, pan-Islamist solidarity supersedes tribalism and nationalism. Article 85 of the Taliban rulebook quotes a *hadith*, or saying of the Prophet Mohammad, declaring that Islam does not endorse the use of ethnic, regional or tribal biases. The *hadith* says that anybody who dies for separatist causes will be dying for *jahiliayah*, or the period of 'darkness' that existed before the seventh-century emergence of Islam in Arabia. Since the 1980s, Pakistan has helped strengthen this concept by supporting Islamist factions and bankrolling Islamist parties. Islamabad did this not because it hoped the Taliban would succeed, but rather because the first goal of the Pakistani leadership was to undermine secular Pashtun nationalism.

Some of Mullah Omar's political positions do, however, resemble those of Pashtun nationalists. The Taliban, for example, had a military stake in preventing the formation of local police in southern Afghanistan after US-led forces broke the Taliban stranglehold in rural areas. But the words Omar used to describe the Taliban's opposition suggested a broader ethno-nationalist motivation. 'The [Afghan] communists created tribal and ethnic militias when they were on the threshold of defeat, to foment rivalries, hatred and ethnic divisions,' he said in his November 2009 Eid-ul Adha statement. 'They used these groups to take revenge from the people for their defeat. Now the Americans are on the verge of defeat and they want to repeat the same failed experiment.'

Omar's response to debates about decentralisation, or creating an Afghan federation, was even more direct. 'Those planning the division of Afghanistan should know well that the Islamic Emirate, with the support of the people, will not allow this plan to succeed,' Omar said in his 2012 Eid-ul Adha statement. 'We will not allow our country to be divided in the name of regions or ethnicities.' The Taliban also blamed US intervention for deepening ethnic divisions, citing American support for the Northern Alliance, the Taliban's nemesis. 'With their arrival, they [the US] incited some corrupt nationalist factions in Northern Afghanistan to fight against the Pashtun tribes,' said a Taliban analysis.[54] 'Some Pashtun tribes were forced to leave the region. Their lands were grabbed and even their honour was violated... Such acts hastened rivalries and broke the bonds among the ethnic groups comprising Afghan society.'[55]

PART FOUR

CONCLUSION

11

CRAFTING A PEACEFUL PASHTUN FUTURE

I have the power to conquer war.
And oh, war! I shall begin
To drive you from the face of earth.
I now declare full war on war,
A challenge I have drawn from birth.
The god of war has not withstood
The valour of my Pashtun blood.

– Ajmal Khattak[1]

An imposed war in my homeland kills me over and over,
Strangers reap its benefits, imposed by outsiders, it kills me over and over.

My attire torn, my being shattered, I am being killed again and again,
What a deadly skill, kills me with my own, I am being massacred over and over.

Whether Peshawari or Kabuli, the Pashtun is a single spirit,
One is my sweetheart, the other my beloved, I am being assassinated over and over.

Our streets are coloured by my beloved blood, every day I watch them burn,
The war is alien, the guns are foreign, I am being killed over and over.

Oh, peace loving people of the world, stop these warmongers,
This is my doomsday, end of my world, I am being killed over and over.

– Rehmat Shah Sayel[2]

The prospects for peace in the Pashtun homeland remain uncertain. Pashtun civilians continue to constitute the majority of victims of terrorist attacks and military operations in Afghanistan and Pakistan. NATO announced the withdrawal of its combat forces from Afghanistan by the end of 2014, but violence appears certain to persist until at least then. Many Afghans have been disturbed by the West's decision to pull out without first guaranteeing even a modicum of peace and stability. With all sides hedging their bets pending NATO's withdrawal, regional co-operation remains a distant dream.

Afghan government institutions have remained fragile. Key pillars of the state, including the judiciary, legislature, executive and security institutions, continue to be dominated by powerful figures controlling patronage networks. These men are intimately connected to the mayhem of Afghanistan's recent past. Afghan security forces have grown enormously in numbers, but their capacity to provide real protection for the citizenry remains limited. Creating or sustaining additional such structures could prove problematic.

The peace and reconciliation process has failed to gain much traction amid an environment of regular violence. Uncertainty has led some powerbrokers and commanders in northern and western Afghanistan to rearm their supporters. In this atmosphere of ambiguity, there have even been moves towards fomenting a Shia-Sunni sectarian war. The most dangerous scenario for many Afghans is a rerun of the proxy war of the 1990s, along ethnic lines. Many informed Afghans feel confident that the modest progress seen after 2001, and exhaustion from more than three decades of conflict, will prevent a return to all-out civil war. But they are aware that meddling by outsiders could still spawn a new generation of horror.

Pakistan has its own gargantuan problems—and the crisis that would arise from the collapse of the nuclear-armed state would dwarf by many degrees the predicament of Afghanistan. Pakistan's relations with the West in general, and Washington in particular, have continued to deteriorate over Islamabad's tolerance of extremist sanctuaries on its soil. Pakistan's reputation as the preferred hideout for international terrorists was only strengthened when US special forces found and killed Osama bin Laden in the north-western military garrison town of Abbottabad on 2 May 2011. In the wake of bin Laden's demise, Islamabad has become more isolated internationally. Even traditional allies such as China and Saudi Arabia have expressed disapproval. Hostility between Pakistan and India, meanwhile, is moving into its third generation and shows little sign of abating.

Pakistan's military has lowered its public profile, but it continues to dominate the political system and foreign policy decision-making. The 'deep state' of the security establishment continues to overshadow Pakistan's anaemic democracy. The Pakistani nuclear arsenal has become an albatross, a paradoxical symbol of the country's insecurity and the government's failure to provide even basic infrastructure for its citizens. The arsenal is often portrayed as a threat to international security; most Pakistanis consider the entire country unsafe. From north to south, sectarian and ethnic conflicts are festering. Separatism in Balochistan has only been strengthened by a harsh crackdown. A sizeable number of international and Pakistani jihadists that the military nurtured during the 1980s and 1990s now consider the state itself to be apostate. Jihadi attacks have destabilised Pakistan and created an unprecedented climate of fear. More than 10 million Pakistanis have been displaced by fighting and natural disasters since 2004. The Pakistani economy is best likened to a patient permanently hooked on life support. According to US intelligence estimates, both Pakistan and Afghanistan face a high risk of 'state failure' by 2030.[3]

Uncle Sam in Pashtunistan

Few nations would be more threatened by such failures than the United States. In the aftermath of the 11 September 2001 attacks, Washington launched what has become the longest war in US history. It is a conflict that has been fought predominantly in Pashtun towns and villages on both sides of the Durand Line. The war has added the names of remote villages and communities—such as Shkin, Marjah, Tora Bora and Waziristan—to American battlefield lore. A generation of US soldiers, journalists and diplomats will spend the next decades recounting their experiences in these regions. By the autumn of 2013, more than 2,200 US soldiers had been killed and some 18,000 wounded in Afghanistan since 7 October 2001.[4] By that time, Washington had spent nearly $650 billion on the war in Afghanistan alone.[5]

The litany of Washington's blunders in this theatre is enormous. As I discussed in the initial chapters, Washington's disinterest in providing development aid and a security umbrella in the 1950s pushed Afghanistan's Pashtun rulers into the Soviet sphere. Another golden opportunity was squandered when Washington again lost focus after the Soviet withdrawal in 1989. That failure was critical in turning Afghanistan into an epicentre of international terrorism. After declaring war against Al-Qaeda and its Taliban hosts, the administration of President George W. Bush focused on narrow military goals that could be sold at little risk to sceptical American politicians and the public. His administration's war in Iraq proved a disastrous distraction from Afghanistan.

President Barack Obama likewise sought to lower expectations. Obama's Afghan-Pakistan strategy, released in November 2009, concluded: 'This approach is not fully resourced counterinsurgency or nation building, but a narrower approach tied more tightly to the core goal of disrupting, dismantling and eventually defeating al-Qaeda and preventing al-Qaeda's return to a safe haven in Afghanistan and Pakistan.'[6]

The narrow focus necessarily meant that Washington was forced into making bad political choices. The Bush administration, for example, was reluctant to support the deployment of large numbers of international peacekeepers after the Taliban was toppled in late 2001. Adequate security at that crucial moment could have helped generate the political goodwill and economic rebirth needed for the growth of a new democracy. Initial US support for Northern Alliance militia commanders, who had allied their forces with Washington against the Taliban, later resulted in these warlords enriching themselves at the expense of state institutions and the welfare of ordinary Afghans. Washington can also be blamed for constructing a simplistic narrative of allies and enemies. Anyone remotely associated with the Taliban was viewed by the US with suspicion and hostility. This pushed many Taliban leaders to move to Pakistan—contributing a great deal to the Taliban's re-emergence as an insurgency.

Francesc Vendrell, a former United Nations and European Union envoy to Afghanistan, concluded that Washington's early mis-steps helped create the conditions that would lead to the next decade of war. 'Bad governance, large-scale corruption and impunity became the order of the day,' Vendrell wrote in November 2011. 'Afghans, who had mostly welcomed the international intervention, became increasingly cynical about its motives and alienated from the new regime which, by and large, had no clear policy nor did it seem to offer an appealing alternative to the Taliban. These feelings were even more pronounced among the Pashtuns, the largest minority in the country and long accustomed to ruling Afghanistan, who perceived themselves as the losers in the new order.'[7]

America's greatest failing was in its relationship with Pakistan. While Islamabad ostensibly became a frontline ally in the war on terrorism, Pakistan remained the preferred sanctuary for global jihadists. After 11 September 2001, Washington showered Pakistan with more than $25 billion in military and economic assistance. President Bush declared Pakistan a non-NATO ally in 2004, and the Pakistani military received US weapons, including F-16 fighter jets, maritime patrol and transport aircraft, Cobra helicopters and advanced missile systems.[8] But even as the aid poured in, Al-Qaeda and the Taliban were receiving safe haven in Pakistan. Washington's failure to persuade Pakistan's security establishment to dismantle extremist networks threatened progress in Afghanistan and sustained the terrorist threat. The US was late to recognise the importance of pushing political reforms and development in the Pashtun borderlands. As a result, its declared enemies were able to rejuvenate.

Washington has succeeded in preventing complete chaos in Afghanistan, and the feeble Afghan state it helped create shows signs of life even after more than eleven years of fighting. After a summit in January 2013, Presidents Obama and Karzai agreed on a roadmap for Afghanistan's future. Both 'reaffirmed shared commitments to US and Afghan strategic objectives: advancing peace, security, reconciliation, and regional co-operation; strengthening Afghanistan's democratic institutions; and supporting Afghanistan's long-term economic and social development'.[9] A month later, in his State of the Union address, Obama announced plans to withdraw 34,000 American soldiers from Afghanistan in 2013—reducing the US deployment by more than half.[10] The remainder of US troops are scheduled to leave by the end of 2014. Washington is now firmly banking on the ability of Afghan troops it has trained and equipped to prevent the country from again slipping into anarchy.

None of these objectives, however, have a hope of success without sustained US engagement for many more years. America failed in its attempt to build a new Afghanistan in the first decade of the twenty-first century. It now must help to create an environment in which Afghans can do their own nation-building. This can be only done if Washington aligns its interests with those of Afghanistan and treats Kabul as a long-term partner—something it has pledged to do in several official agreements. The transition years of 2013 and 2014 will test the US commitment to Afghanistan, and Washington can little afford to fall short. It would be another mistake, however, if the US insisted on fashioning Afghan politics to its liking. Such attempts ended in disaster for the Soviet Union, and have already contributed considerably to Washington's debacles in Afghanistan since 2001.

Support for Afghan nation-building must go hand-in-hand with structural changes in Washington's approach to Pakistan.[11] Specifically, a strong international alliance should devote itself to ensuring that Pakistan takes action to permanently end the use of the Pashtun borderlands as terrorist sanctuaries. Drone attacks on these havens, however precise, will not alone guarantee immunity from terrorist attacks. Washington must also use its influence to persuade Kabul and Islamabad to develop a bilateral relationship independent of their relations with India. This will involve encouraging Afghanistan and India to effectively address, respectively, Pakistani security concerns related to the Pashtun and Baloch border regions and Kashmir. Instead of focusing merely on aid, the US and its allies should provide incentives for Pakistan and Afghanistan to develop modern, interconnected economies.

Washington can only make headway when all its institutions work in unison. Since the 1950s, the US has oscillated between being the most generous foreign benefactor of Pakistani military dictators, to sanctioning Islamabad for developing nuclear weapons and even threatening it with being declared a state sponsor of terrorism.[12] In the long term, US policy should continue to be based on support for a democratic Pakistan, despite the inevitable setbacks that will accompany such a policy. The withdrawal of US forces from Afghanistan should improve Washington's bargaining power, as NATO will no longer be dependent on Pakistani supply routes.[13] But overall, after its troops are largely gone, US leverage is unlikely to increase in either Afghanistan and Pakistan.

A Democratic Pakistan

The Pakistani electorate dealt a severe blow to fundamentalist Islamist parties in the 2008 parliamentary elections, when moderate secularists fared surprisingly well. The Pakistan People's Party-led civilian government had a mixed record in fighting terrorism, tackling debilitating energy shortages, providing services and ensuring transparency and accountability. But it succeeded in ridding the constitution of some provisions that inhibited democracy.[14] This, coupled with a renewed consensus among the political class that the military should be phased out of its traditional king-maker role, helped the civilian government complete its five-year term for the first time in history.[15]

Pakistani politicians ensured the continuity of the democratic process when parliamentary elections were held in May 2013. The elections, however, were marred by violence. The ANP was targeted by Taliban attacks that killed dozens of its workers, and the party went on to lose the vote by a big margin.[16] The defeat will have far-reaching consequences for peace in the Pashtun homeland. The elections, however, marked the first time that a Pakistani elected civilian administration completed its full term and peacefully handed power over to another batch of elected leaders.

The new Prime Minister, Nawaz Sharif, has inherited all the old problems, along with an intensifying clamour among ordinary Pakistanis for concrete reforms. His Pakistan Muslim League-Nawaz won a majority in the federal parliament and Punjab Province, but was forced into a coalition in Balochistan.[17] In Khyber Pakhtunkhwa and the Sindh, the Tehreek-e Insaf (Movement for Justice) and the Pakistan People's Party formed the provincial administrations. Both are part of the opposition in Islamabad.

One of Sharif's primary domestic challenges will be to move away from his image as a Punjabi leader. He will need to form a working relationship with smaller ethnic groups to deliver results within Pakistan's federal constitutional arrangements. However, just months after assuming office, his administration already appeared ineffective in Balochistan, where the military continued its policy of violently suppressing Baloch separatism. Similarly, his administration has talked about ending terrorist violence, but has been slow to act. Sharif has promised to revive the economy and end the power shortages that badly affect many areas. But he must be careful to ensure equitable development and the fair distribution of resources across the country. Prosperity in Punjab alone is likely to aggravate the sense of alienation among smaller ethnic groups.

Of course, Sharif's biggest challenge will be to manage the civilian government's relationship with the military, making sure that the role of the generals in political life remains limited. Ironically, the steel magnate was once the favoured son of the military establishment, which assisted his rise to power in the 1980s and 1990s. But, having learned hard lessons when he was removed in a military coup in 1999, Sharif is a seasoned and wily player and remains Pakistan's best hope for a civilian saviour. Reorienting Pakistan's foreign policies, particularly towards its neighbours, is a major task. But Sharif has yet to sell the idea of a grand rapprochement with India to the generals. More significantly, he will also have to rein in those who would like to again 'conquer Kabul', or have untrammelled influence over events Afghanistan, as Islamabad did following the fall of Najibullah in 1992, when Sharif was serving his first term as prime minister.

There have been some signs that the military is changing its outlook. In January 2013, the Pakistani military revised its decade-old military doctrine. In its annual Green Book, it added a new chapter on 'sub-conventional warfare'. The chapter noted that Islamist radical groups operating from within Pakistan pose a bigger threat to the country's security than traditional rival India.[18] The statement represented a remarkable reversal. The 1994 edition of the Green Book, for example, stated that 'the existence and survival' of Pakistan depended on the complete implementation of Islamic ideology. 'If the ideology is not preserved,' it read, 'then the very existence of Pakistan becomes doubtful.'

The changes were in line with the thinking of General Ashfaq Parvez Kayani, Pakistan's military chief. In a major policy speech on 14 August 2012, Kayani noted that 'the most difficult task for any army is to fight against its own people'. He went on to say that 'no state can afford a parallel system of government and militias, and that extremism is the gravest threat to Pakistan'. Kayani defined an extremist as a person 'who believes his opinion to be the final verdict'. He added that extremists turned into terrorists when they used guns to try to enforce their opinions. 'Islam does not allow anyone to claim to be a know-it-all and flirt with divinity,' he concluded. With such words, the military has allowed democracy breathing space. But to complete the process, the military must also cease interference in politics and stop offering covert and overt support to jihadists.[19] It must accept the supremacy of law and respect the constitution in letter and spirit.[20]

An opportune place to test the military's new commitment would be the western Pashtun regions, where a decade of military operations has so far failed to eliminate the militant threat. A first step would be to push the civilian administration to scrap the 2010 'Actions in Aid of Civil Power' law. This measure granted sweeping powers to the military in some regions of Khyber Pakhtunkhwa Province and the adjacent FATA. Politicians, tribal leaders and legal experts have assailed it as unconstitutional for provisions allowing security forces to detain suspected militants for prolonged periods. It also empowers military and civilian officials to hand down severe punishments without due process. Such laws have undermined efforts to reform the antiquated border regime and contribute to a paralysing climate of uncertainty and fear.[21]

A genuine change in the military's thinking would create room for locally-tailored initiatives that promote stability and development. The modest reforms introduced in the FATA in August 2011 have created grounds for optimism. The promised reforms include measures that will increase political participation, and modifications to the harsh FCR regime. These changes suggest progress towards more accountability and some conformity with contemporary human rights standards. Implementing the reforms and creating a consensus roadmap for absorbing FATA into the national mainstream will not be easy. But the greater risk is to allow the region to persist as an extremist sanctuary. Likewise, Islamabad's continued insistence on the use of force to 'restore order' in the Tribal Areas will only further alienate the government from ordinary people.[22] It needs to respond to popular sentiment in favour of peace. Improving the general welfare of the vast majority of citizens would be a far more effective strategy to counter extremism than focusing on reaching a settlement with a tiny minority of militants.

There is much for Pakistan to learn from the Arab Spring revolts and the evolution of Turkey. Like Pakistan, Turkey has a history of military interference in politics. It was economically dependent and had troubled relations with its neighbours. But under the leadership of Prime Minister Recep Tayyip Erdogan, Turkey has emerged as a democratic-leaning role model. It has spurred economic growth and maintained firm ties with the West through alliances with Washington and its membership in NATO. Turkey's governing Justice and Development follows a foreign policy that aims at 'zero problems with the neighbours'. The Turkish model seeks to balance tradition with modernity, democracy and economic development. Arab Islamists, including Egypt's Muslim Brotherhood and Tunisia's Al-Nahda (Renaissance Movement), have indicated they look to Turkey as a guide.[23] Most Islamist leaders in Pakistan, meanwhile, have recognised the dangers posed by the radical ideologies of Al-Qaeda and the Pakistani Taliban. Their challenge will be to reinvent themselves so they are seen as independent and not the pawns of the security establishment. They can only claim a genuine niche in the country's crowded political marketplace if the electorate deems them able to deliver practical and pragmatic solutions.

The Future of Afghanistan

Afghans face a stark choice: either they will find a way to resolve their differences, or the country is likely to descend once more into civil war after the departure of NATO-led forces. While the Taliban continues to publicly rule out compromise with Western-backed authorities, the movement has recently made what must be considered pragmatic statements. In his Eid-ul Adha statement of October 2012, Mullah Omar sought to offer assurances about Taliban intentions, while not budging from the movement's fundamental goals:

> Regarding the political future of the country, I would like to repeat that we are neither looking for establishing a monopoly over power, nor are we thinking about sparking a civil war. We support the determination of the political future of our country by Afghans free of interference from global powers and our neighbours. This [future] political system should be Islamic and Afghan in character. With the help of Allah, after the independence of the country [following the departure of foreign forces] we will establish a *sharia*-based national political system. We will establish a single central authority free of discrimination and biases. We will establish security, protect the territorial integrity of our country, implement *sharia* law and promote meritocracy in appointments to [government] jobs. We will rebuild the economic foundations [of our nation]. We will guarantee the rights of men and women and strengthen social foundations. We will provide education to all citizens in the light of our national interests and Islamic principles. We will carry out academic and cultural affairs efficiently. With the help of our brave people, we will never allow anybody to provoke a civil war or cause the partition of Afghanistan. Nobody should consider the Afghan nation so simple-minded they can be easily persuaded to break the deep religious, cultural, social and historical bonds among the fraternal ethnic groups. The former Soviet Union wanted to implement this hated formula of disintegration and as a result it finally broke down. We want to establish good relations with all those who would respect Afghanistan as an independent Islamic country and would not seek to dominate it or establish an imperial relationship. In my view, this is what every independent Muslim Afghan wants.[24]

The statement reflects an attitude common among tribal Afghans. Longstanding feuds in rural areas, particularly in Pashtun regions, are in many cases resolved amicably after the belligerents realise that they cannot continue fighting indefinitely. Such realisations prompted many figures and factions involved in the civil war of the 1990s, and the anti-Soviet mujahedeen war of the 1980s, to come together to work in the Karzai administration. The Taliban are aware of changing sentiments among Afghans. This may create an incentive for them to pursue reconciliation. It remains to be seen, however, whether the Taliban is capable of putting compromise and pragmatism ahead of their ideology and worldview.

The Taliban also faces uncertainty. Atrocities carried out by the movement have driven many rural Pashtuns to opposition. Local uprisings, such as the one in central Ghazni Province in 2012, were partly provoked by the presence of Pakistanis in Taliban ranks.[25] The Kandahari leadership in exile in Balochistan cannot hope to promote itself as part of a potential national leadership while facing popular resistance in their main recruiting base. Kandahari Taliban seeking a place in the legitimate power structure recognise the threat to the movement's image from the Haqqani alliance with Al-Qaeda and links to Pakistani extremists and the military establishment.

A bigger challenge for the Taliban, however, is a looming leadership struggle. Years of war have reduced the ranks of the original leadership. Mullah Omar, the spiritual founder, has been seen by very few of his followers since he disappeared from Kandahar in December 2001. Statements issued in his name are understood to have been written by the Taliban political committee in Quetta. There are strong doubts about Omar's ability to resume public command. Though the Taliban has shown remarkable unity compared to other Afghan organisations, the movement has not set out a clear line of succession. This is a great strategic vulnerability.[26]

The Taliban has also changed enormously since its emergence in the 1990s. The movement has experienced exile and exposed itself to the ideologies of more radical Islamists. It has been forced to adapt to new technologies to respond to an Afghan population that is increasingly connected to the outside world thanks to a largely free media. Taliban cadres must also grapple with an Afghan economy that has been transformed by international intervention. Most Afghans can no longer be lured by promises of justice alone. They want improved living conditions and a more responsive government—something most realise the Taliban cannot achieve on its own. In late 2012, the Taliban publically reversed its stance with an announcement that militants would refrain from attacking teachers and health workers. It also announced that the movement was no longer opposed to the teaching of mathematics and science.[27]

The Taliban's relationship with its principal foreign backer, Pakistan, has also undergone a metamorphosis. Despite the Taliban dependence on sanctuaries in Pakistan, many among the Kandahari core view Islamabad with great suspicion. Like the Pashtun mujahedeen factions of the 1980s, Kandahari Taliban leaders are likely to turn against their erstwhile benefactors once they return to Afghanistan. Many former Taliban leaders, incarcerated by Islamabad since 2001, share the popular Afghan perception of Pakistan as a troublemaker.[28] Islamabad's relations with the Haqqani clan are independent of the Kandahari branch and are likely to continue, but even the Haqqanis cannot afford to reject a comprehensive peace settlement among Afghans, should one take shape. At the end of 2012, senior Kandahari Taliban leaders signalled for the first time that they were prepared to publicly renounce Al-Qaeda and agree to measures aimed at preventing the return of international jihadists to Afghanistan. They expressed a willingness to accept a ceasefire, and were even open to a limited US military presence.[29]

Former Taliban diplomat Mullah Abdul Salam Zaeef says a sincere effort will be required to broker peace. In December 2012, Zaeef took part in an informal Paris meeting of Afghan factions, including the Taliban, representatives of the Afghan peace council and members of anti-Taliban factions. He wrote afterwards that the meeting left him with the impression that most Afghans are in agreement on a few essential points. These include the desire to replace current policies centred on conflict with a strategy of achieving peace; the need to form an inclusive government; and the need for unified Afghan national security institutions. He noted that Afghans want the restoration of full sovereignty and a new constitution. Zaeef argued that all Afghans agree that *sharia* should be the law of the land.[30]

Taliban insistence on implementing *sharia*, however, is certain to lead to disagreement. The Taliban and other extremists maintain that *sharia* is a set of non-negotiable specific rules, such as the strict criminal code known as *hudood*.[31] Others argue *sharia* is only an ethos behind a complicated tradition, subject to differing interpretations. The Afghan constitution already affirms Islam as the state religion and requires all laws to be consistent with Muslim doctrines. But the Afghan supreme law also guarantees the observance of the Universal Declaration of Human

Rights and other global human rights conventions. The Taliban would need to demonstrate to Afghans why their vision of *sharia* is better than what the drafters of the constitution understood as *sharia*. The movement would have to convince a majority of Afghans that their vision is largely consistent with the internationally-recognised conception of human rights. An insistence on strict adherence to *hudood* is unlikely to be received well by Afghans who remember the Taliban's gruesome implementation of such laws in the 1990s.[32]

President Karzai's administration has succeeded in attracting unprecedented international support for Afghanistan. The Bilateral Security Agreement with Washington could provide the basis for a long-term strategic alliance with the West, which should contribute to Afghan stability, promote regional cooperation and prevent blatant interference from belligerent neighbours. Karzai, and future leaders, must put this support to good use by making state- and nation-building a top priority. One major issue is ensuring a sustainable future for Afghanistan's rebuilt security forces, which numbered some 350,000 at the end of 2012.[33] Washington has promised to support these forces through to 2017, but the Afghan government should aim to move beyond funding. It must define the future role of these troops, ensure that they are seen as national security forces and not private militias, and prevent them from turning into marauders.

An immediate challenge for the government will be to guarantee security as Afghanistan regains full sovereignty after the departure of NATO troops. The scheduled April 2014 presidential elections will be an early test. Security concerns kept a significant number of Pashtuns away from the polls in the 2009 presidential contest and the 2010 parliamentary vote, undermining both elections. An opportunity for all voters to participate in 2014 would promote national unity. A peaceful, democratic transfer of power will give Afghans a stake in the future and set a valuable precedent.[34]

Karzai has pledged to step down after the election. He should use his remaining time in office to move beyond deal-making and patronage, and implement genuine reform, including building up a meritocratic class of civil servants. Improvements in top-level governance will filter down to towns and villages. The 2004 constitution envisioned elected district *shuras*, or councils, but these local bodies have not yet been established. Devolving power and decision-making from Kabul to the provinces and districts is necessary for equitable regional development and promoting national unity. Justice has been historically central to Afghan notions of good governance and legitimacy. A reformed judiciary will be welcomed by Afghans who have suffered for too long from corruption and backroom dealing.

Future governments would also be wise to invest in preserving Afghanistan's cultural heritage and promoting regional cultures and languages. Moves should be made towards gradually adopting English as an official language. The international community's engagement with the country since 2002 has already made English an integral part of bureaucratic and business life. Promotion of this global language can play a role in putting an end to the rivalry between Pashto and Dari. It will also go a long way towards modernising Afghan education.[35]

A Permanent Peace

True stability will not be possible without a comprehensive settlement between Afghanistan and Pakistan. The division of Pashtuns into two states remains an open wound, severely affecting economic growth and social development. Without a resolution to this question, the region will never rise to its potential as a land bridge between South Asia and Central Asia on the one hand, and the Middle East and China on the other. President Karzai has long been aware of the urgency of making peace with Pakistan. 'Pakistan is a brother of Afghanistan. Pakistan is a twin brother. We're conjoined twins, there's no separation,' Karzai told journalists alongside Pakistani Prime Minister Yusuf Raza Gilani in March 2010.[36]

Sooner or later, the two countries will have to come to terms over the question of the Durand Line, which has vexed relations for nearly seventy years. A Pashto language proverb says: 'You cannot separate water with a stick.' This is as true as ever in regards to the Durand Line, an artificial border that has created more instability and strife between the neighbours than any other issue. Successive generations of political leaders have tried to ignore the problem, declare it a non-issue, or to 'fix' it by advancing impractical, costly proposals to fence or mine the line. Israel and Uzbekistan have recently engaged in similar fence-building measures, but they have failed to deliver peace or regional co-operation in the Middle East and Central Asia.[37]

Pakistan has held since the 1947 partition that the Durand Line, as delineated in a 1893 treaty, is 'a valid international boundary subsequently recognised and confirmed by Afghanistan on several occasions'.[38] This is rejected by Kabul, which maintains that since 1947, it has never recognised the colonial-era demarcation as its eastern border. The unresolved question is seen by Afghans as the principal motivation for Pakistani interference in Afghan affairs and Islamabad's effort to create a pliant hard-line Afghan Islamist regime.[39]

There is little evidence to support such fears. Afghanistan's government, since 2001, has consistently resisted championing the Pashtun and Baloch causes in Pakistan. Indeed, Kabul has indicated that resolving the Durand Line issue can wait until stability and security conditions improve. Abdul Karim Brahui, Afghanistan's minister of border and tribal affairs, confirmed in April 2006 that the government does not recognise the line as an international border. But he told the lower house of parliament that Kabul does not even believe it currently has a mandate to negotiate the issue. He suggested, however, that reaching a consensus on the question could potentially be achieved in a national *loya jirga*.[40]

Declaring the Durand Line to be a closed transaction has proved unacceptable to many Pashtuns, particularly among the Afghan political and intellectual elite. Kabul reacted dismissively to Washington's description of the issue as non-existent. In an interview with Afghan television in October 2012, Marc Grossman, the US special representative for Afghanistan and Pakistan, reaffirmed longstanding US policy that recognises the Durand Line as an international border. The Washington-allied Afghan foreign affairs ministry issued a curt statement noting that Kabul 'rejects and considers irrelevant any statement by anyone about the legal status of this line'. The status of the Durand Line, the statement added, was a matter of 'historic importance' for the Afghan people.[41]

A future Afghan government will likely have to modify Kabul's hard-line position on the Durand Line to reach an accommodation with Islamabad. There have been encouraging signs. Despite consistently blaming Pakistan for allowing extremist sanctuaries and supporting militant operations, President Karzai's administration has sought to keep Islamabad engaged on questions of Afghan stability. A significant segment of Afghans, including many Pashtuns, privately hold that the moment is nearing to talk to Islamabad about resolving all issues. But Afghan leaders will first need to encourage public debates about what is to be gained and lost from a permanent resolution with Pakistan.

Regarding the border, Kabul could show goodwill by indicating to Islamabad it is ready to consider an historic compromise.

Kabul and Islamabad should embark on a peace process that includes serious talks about permanently opening the border. The aim would be to establish, finally, a recognised and mutually agreed frontier. The economic and social benefits of the free exchange of people and goods across the border would be immediate. To those who would reject an open border, citing security concerns, an appropriate response would be that the past decades of restricting movement have led only to bloodshed, the growth of extremism, great power intervention and the expenditure of tens of billions of dollars. Opening the border could hardly lead to a worse state of affairs.

The two governments must have confidence in their populations to make a settlement work. Millions of Afghans have lived in Pakistan since the 1980s. Similarly, hundreds of thousands of Pakistanis have worked in Afghanistan since 2001. Daily cross-border traffic runs into the tens of thousands of people. Such contacts, if they are allowed to develop in an environment of peace and security, will strengthen trust among ordinary people and make them stakeholders in the stability of the region. Carried out under the right conditions and crafted in a way that gains the support of most Pashtuns, an open border regime is certain to benefit future generations.

Since the creation of Pakistan in 1947, there has been no major violent Pashtun secessionist movement. Senior Pashtun ethno-nationalist leaders such as Abdul Ghaffar Khan, his son Abdul Wali Khan and Abdul Samad Khan Achakzai have participated only in mainstream Pakistani pro-democracy and anti-dictatorship parties. These leaders and their various political parties and movements have always struggled for representative rule. Despite often being at the receiving end of state oppression, their demands never went beyond calling for provincial autonomy within a federal Pakistan. All the major Pakistani Pashtun parties still prefer ballots over bullets.

There are compelling domestic reasons for Pakistan to pursue change. The fighting since 2003, along with economic stagnation, has forced many hundreds of thousands of Pashtuns to migrate to Karachi and the Gulf region. Karachi, in particular, has been haunted by instability and ethnic and political violence since the 1980s. It is sometimes called 'Mini-Pakistan' for being home to all of Pakistan's ethnicities. Karachi's population of nearly twenty million includes at least four million Pashtuns—making it one of the largest urban concentrations of Pashtuns outside their homeland. Moves by Islamabad to sideline Pashtuns in Karachi have not delivered stability. Pashtuns hold investments in Karachi transport, real estate and trade. They also comprise a large number of skilled and unskilled labourers in this major port city and commercial hub. The full integration of Pashtuns into economic and political life would help stabilise the troubled megalopolis and prevent it from turning into another Beirut or Baghdad. In the long-run, however, the establishment of stability in the Pashtun homeland would reduce migration to Karachi. This would relieve population pressures and reduce competition over resources. The successful integration of Pashtuns would also stimulate separatist-minded Baloch to pursue a peaceful track.

Pakistan has begun a tentative process of reform of its foreign and military policies. However, an acceleration of this effort is needed if Islamabad seeks real change. The government should abandon, once and for all, its covert efforts aimed at controlling Afghan regimes. Pashtun leaders have warned of the futility of such efforts for decades. Politician Afrasiab Khattak spoke for many when he wrote in November 2011, 'Policymakers in Pakistan must realise they cannot support Afghanistan by befriending a single group. We should be open to friendship with the entire Afghan nation. We should have a benign policy modelled after China's [approach to friendship with Pakistan]. Secondly, we also need to focus on the political and economic aspects of our relationship with Afghanistan, instead of getting bogged down in the Cold War-like fixation with the geo-strategic.'[42]

A permanent Afghan-Pakistan settlement would deliver profound political and economic benefits. It would reduce ethnic tensions and strengthen national unity in both states. It would resolve the fraught question of Pashtun citizenship rights. A new deal between Kabul and Islamabad could enable some Pashtuns in the borderlands to legitimately seek dual citizenship. Such measures would go a long way towards ending the historic isolation of some borderland communities. They would open a new horizon for Pashtuns and other ethnic groups, encouraging them to communicate and develop economic and cultural links in a spirit of co-operation.[43]

President Karzai has touted Afghanistan as a potential 'Asian Roundabout' that could become a trade hub between China, the Middle East,

South Asia and Central Asia. These regions are home to one-third of the world's population. This 'land bridge' can only materialise, however, if Pakistan commits to developing its half. Pakistan's exports to Afghanistan grew from $221 million in 2001 to $2.5 billion in 2013. The volume is expected to reach $5 billion in the next few years. In 2010, Washington helped broker the Afghanistan-Pakistan Transit Trade Agreement, which improved Afghan access to China, India and the sea.[44] However, implementation of the agreement has been hampered by poor infrastructure, insecurity and bureaucratic inefficiency. Successful implementation of the agreement could pave the way for realising the dream of a 'New Silk Road'.[45]

Afghanistan and Pakistan each possess natural resources that provide realistic incentives for future investment. US surveys in Afghanistan have indicated the existence of more than $1 trillion in estimated untapped mineral deposits.[46] China and India have already made multibillion dollar investments in copper and iron ore extraction projects. Water is another key resource. Parts of Central Asia, Iran and lowland Pakistan depend on water from Pashtun zones for agriculture and electricity generation. Four of the five major river basins in Afghanistan irrigate territories in Central Asia, Iran and Pakistan—making water a potential driver of conflict.[47] Again, it will require regional co-operation and diligent planning to ensure that water is used for mutually beneficial purposes.

Pakistan and Afghanistan are young countries with rapidly growing populations. More than half of their combined populations—or some 100 million people—are under the age of thirty. This youth bulge could easily become cannon fodder for decades of ethnic and sectarian war, or conflicts over control of resources. The challenge for today's policymakers is to find workable solutions that will prevent the problems of the past from returning as the conflicts of the future. After the atrocities and mayhem of the past thirty-four years, the youth of the region deserve to inherit a clean slate. The Pashtuns of the twenty-first century should have the opportunity to work towards economic and cultural development, instead of perpetuating the wars of their fathers. This would be the most valuable legacy the current generation could leave. The continued exploitation of the Pashtuns, aimed at keeping them weak and tormented, may serve the short-term interests of powerful governments. But such policies will only prevent the region from rising to its potential, and may yet again prove self-defeating.

NOTES

1. TWENTY-FIRST CENTURY PASHTUNS: CONTINUITY AMID CATASTROPHE

1. Dari is the Afghan dialect of Farsi or Persian, an Indo-European language written in the Arabic script. Dari and Pashto are the two official languages of Afghanistan, but Dari is the lingua franca of the country.
2. From coverage of Karzai's speech on state-run Radio Television Afghanistan and the private Ariana Television Network on 28 September 2010. The speech was widely covered by Afghan and international media and variously interpreted.
3. Woodward, Bob, *Obama's Wars*, New York: Simon and Shuster, 2010, p. 10.
4. Pashtun is also pronounced 'Pakhtun' in the northern hard dialect of Pashto spoken in north-western Pakistan and eastern Afghanistan. In Pashto, the word is written as پښتون (PAXTUN), which can be pronounced in both major dialects of Pashto.
5. The Durand Line is the 1893 demarcation between British India and the Kingdom of Afghanistan. It is the modern-day border between Afghanistan and Pakistan, but Kabul has never recognised it as an international border.
6. The Afghan population figure is based on the Afghan government's *Statistical Yearbook 2009–10*, http://cso.gov.af/yearbook.zip. Afghanistan's current population is estimated at thirty million. Pakistani figures are from the Population Census Organisation, http://www.census.gov.pk/MotherTongue.htm.
7. Some 2,500 kilometres long, the Amu Darya is the longest river in Central Asia.
8. During the recent decades of war, Pashtun diaspora communities have grown in the Gulf, Southeast Asia, Europe, north America and Australia. Many of these Pashtuns have remained connected to their homeland through travel and modern communication technologies. A large number of Pashtuns have been integrated into various regions of the subcontinent, including a sizable Pashto-speaking community in Indian-administered Kashmir. 'Pathans' rank as a higher caste in the stratified societies of South Asia.

9. Qais is not mentioned in Arab history. The authenticity of Mughal genealogies is considered suspect because they were written in Mughal courts amid the Pashtun rivalry with Mughals.
10. Most Pashtun communities are characterised by the prevalence of what anthropologists call 'segmentary lineage'. This model structures societies in hereditary, tree-like hierarchies based on male descent. In the Pashtun case, smaller lineages, or *zais* and *khels*, are merged into larger tribes and tribal confederations.
11. The Durranis are considered perhaps the most important political confederacy. The Durrani monarchy (1747–1978) derived from the Popalzai and Barakzai branches. The Durranis are divided into two branches: the Zirak and the Panjpai. The Popalzai, Alokozai, Barakzai and Achakzai are important Zirak tribes. The Noorzai, Alizai and Ishaqzai are important Panjpai tribes.
12. The Ghilzais established empires in India in the fifteenth and sixteenth centuries (Lodi dynasty and Suri dynasty). In the early eighteenth century, the Hotakis established their empire by conquering most of Iran and today's south-western Afghanistan.
13. For a somewhat dated but detailed discussion of Pashtun genealogies, see Caroe, Olf, *The Pathans 550 B.C.A.D.–1957*, London: Macmillan, 1958.
14. *Badal* can be best described as a complex system of reciprocity.
15. Rubin, Barnett and Abubakar Siddique, 'Resolving the Afghanistan Pakistan stalemate', *Special Report 176*, United States Institute of Peace, October, 2006. The overall amount invested in successive wars in the Pashtun homeland since the late 1970s adds up to more than one trillion dollars.
16. Ibid.
17. The international deployment began as a small force in Kabul in 2002, but was gradually extended across Afghanistan. The number of foreign troops peaked in 2010, after President Barack Obama ordered a 'surge' of tens of thousands of troops in a bid to deal a crippling blow to the Taliban insurgency.
18. Altitude of 1,800 metres.
19. More than four million people call Kabul home, but the majority of original Kabuli families long ago fled the city. Most of its population is now composed of migrants from villages, or Afghans who have returned to re-establish themselves after years of exile in Pakistan or Iran.
20. There is a sizeable number of Pashai people in Nangarhar and Laghman, while various Nuristani communities are resident in Nuristan. Many among them are bilingual and speak fluent Pashto.
21. Bin Laden disappeared from Tora Bora during the US onslaught. The United States said US forces killed him during a raid on his compound in Abbottabad, Pakistan on 2 May 2011.
22. The majority Pashtun Hizb-e Islami originated as a pan-Islamist political party, but turned into an armed organisation. It later split into the Khalis and Hek-

matyar factions named after their respective leaders, Mohammad Younas Khalis and Gulbuddin Hekmatyar. Khalis died in 2006, while Hekmatyar went on to lead remnants of his organisation in the insurgency.

23. Greater Paktia is called P2K in US military slang. Paktia remained unchanged in the 1964 reforms, when the fourteen provinces were divided further into twenty-eight. Paktia was split into three provinces: Paktia, Khost and Paktika, in the 1980s. Afghanistan today has thirty-four provinces, nearly half of which have majority Pashtun residents. But the country remains a patchwork of ethnicities, like a colourful carpet.
24. Habibullah Kalakani, a Tajik from the Shomali plains north of Kabul, bestowed himself the title Amir Habibullah II. He is commonly known as *Bacha-yi Saqao*, or son of the water carrier, in admiration or mockery of his humble origins.
25. The core leadership of the Haqqani Network is composed of his extended family and is closely associated with Al-Qaeda. Based in the North Waziristan tribal district, across the border in Pakistan, it has also served as a conduit for extremist organisations in South Asia and Central Asia. With the elder Haqqani reportedly on his deathbed, his son Sirajuddin Haqqani has managed the network.
26. Nimroz is a Baloch majority province, but most Baloch in southern Afghanistan are trilingual and speak Pashto and Dari. Unlike in Iran and Pakistan, there is no separatist Baloch ethno-nationalist movement in Afghanistan.
27. Some arms traders and enthusiasts from Pakistan's Tribal Areas told me it would not be difficult to buy advanced Chinese weapon systems, such as long-range anti-tank missiles that allegedly could hit targets within a sixteen-kilometre range.
28. The northern, cooler districts of Pakistan's south-western Balochistan Province are Pashtun-populated. Ten out of Balochistan's thirty districts have a Pashtun majority. Pishin, Qila Abdullah, Qila Saifullah, Harnai, Sherani, Ziarat, Zhob, Musakhel, Loralai and the provincial capital Quetta all have a Pashtun majority.
29. The narrative of Punjabi domination of the Pakistani state—meaning that institutions, particularly the military, are controlled by ethnic Punjabis—is equally popular among the leaders of other minority ethno-nationalist movements in Pakistan.
30. Deobandi is an Islamic revivalist movement that arose from the Darul Uloom Deoband, an anti-colonial Islamic seminary established in northern India in the nineteenth century. It is a puritanical orthodox movement which follows the Hanafi school of Sunni Islam. Today, various political parties, militant movements and seminaries across South Asia share the identity, but their political objectives, worldview and strategies differ markedly.
31. Formerly called Fort Sandeman, after the British colonial officer Robert Sandeman. Sandeman was a late nineteenth-century British colonial officer who evolved his own theory of tribal control by advocating the 'peaceful penetra-

tion' of Pashtun and Baloch tribal territories. He advocated the gradual absorption of the tribes by offering them jobs and by bribing and cajoling tribal leaders. His strategy was more successful among the Baloch, where tribal chiefs exerted greater control, while it failed among the more egalitarian Pashtuns.

32. This was part of nineteenth- and twentieth-century British policies for the Pashtun regions and entailed very limited or no contact between various Pashtun regions, while also curtailing their independent contacts with the wider world. This policy is still visible in the isolation of Pakistani Tribal Areas.
33. As a young anthropologist in the 1990s, I made several memorable bus journeys between the two regions and witnessed first-hand how imperial British policies of dividing the Pashtuns are still in place. What should have been a mere one hour journey used to take six hours in dry river beds. Passengers aboard the rickety, overcrowded, and brightly coloured bus joyously belted out traditional Pashto songs, providing some respite from the furnace-like weather.
34. FATA is sometimes referred to simply as the 'Tribal Areas'.
35. FATA is divided into seven agencies, or administrative units, which from north to south are Bajaur, Mohmand, Khyber, Orakzai, Kurram, and North and South Waziristan. A few more frontier regions adjacent to the settled districts of Peshawar, Kohat, Dera Ismail Khan, Bannu and Tank are also part of FATA.

2. FROM PEACEFUL BORDERLANDS TO INCUBATORS OF EXTREMISM

1. Caroe, Olaf, *The Pathans: 550 B.C.–A.D. 1957*, London: Macmillan and Company, 1958, pp. 151–67.
2. Babur's campaigns against Pashtuns included building pillars from their severed heads. 'Those our men brought in as prisoners were ordered to be beheaded and a pillar of their heads was set up in our camp,' he was quoted as saying about a campaign against the Bangash tribe near Kohat, in today's Khyber Pakhtunkhwa Province. See *Babur Nama (Memoirs of Babur)*, translated from the original Turki text of Zahir al-Din Muhammad Babur Padshah Ghazi, by Beveridge, Annette Susannah, Vols. I and II, New Delhi: Oriental Books Reprints Cooperation, reprint 1979, p. 232.
3. Masud, Saifur Rehman, *Pir Roshan and the Roshnya Revolution* (in Pashto: *Pir Roshan Ao Roshani Inqilab*), Peshawar: University Book Agency, 1998, pp. 130–5.
4. Masud, Ibid.
5. *Tauheed* refers to the oneness of God or monotheism in Islam. It is the most fundamental tenet of Islamic faith.
6. Mahsud, Mir Wali Khan, *Maqsud-al-Mu'Minin of Bayazid Ansari*, English translation with introduction and commentary, Peshawar: Khyber Printers, 1980, p. 64.

7. Caroe, *The Pathans*, p. 246.
8. This translation is from Raverty, Henry George, *Selections from the Poetry of Afghans*, (1880) reprinted as *Selections from Pashto Poetry*, Lahore: Al-Biruni, 1978. Raverty, a nineteenth-century linguist and British colonial officer, translated this poem as an 'Ode to Spring'. The Pashto version is from, *The Collection of Khushal Khattak* (in Pashto: *Dey Khushal Khattak Kolyat*), Kabul: Afghanistan Academy of Sciences, Pashto Department, 1990. A shorter version of this poem is translated in Howell, Evelyn and Olaf Caroe, *The Poems of Khushal Khan Khattak*, Peshawar: Pashto Academy, University of Peshawar, 1963.
9. Shah Waliullah (1703–62) was a religious scholar and Sufi who saw himself connected to the sixteenth-century revivalist Shaikh Ahmad Sirhindi Faruqi, who is more commonly known by his title, Mujaddid Alf-e Thani. They were among the pioneering leaders of orthodox revivalist Sunni Islam, which later had a generational influence on Islamic movements in the Pashtun regions where most clerics define themselves as Deobandi. See Roy, Olivier, *Islam and Resistance in Afghanistan*, Cambridge: Cambridge University Press, 1986, p. 55.
10. Elphinstone, Mountsuart, *An Account of the Kingdom of Caubaul and its Dependencies in Persia, Tartary and India*, London: Longman, Hurst, Rees, Brown, Orme and Brown, 1819.
11. Dost Mohammad declared himself *amir-ul momineen*, or commander of the faithful, for his jihad against the Sikhs. See Noelle, Christine, *The State and Tribe in Nineteenth-Century Afghanistan: The Reign of Amir Dost Muhammad Khan (1826–1863)*, Surrey: Curzon Press, 1977.
12. Haroon, Sana, *Frontier of Faith: Islam in the Indo-Afghan Borderland*, London: Hurst & Company, 2007, p. 41.
13. Roy, Olivier, *Islam and Resistance in Afghanistan*, Cambridge: Cambridge University Press, 1986.
14. During the uprising, some 4,000 Pashtuns died in eight days of battles in an unsuccessful attempt to take the Malakand and Chakdara garrisons. They fought under the leadership of Sadullah, known as Mullah Mastan. See Lindholm, Charles, *Jealousy and Generosity: The Swat Pakhtuns of Northern Pakistan*, New York: Columbia University Press, 1982, p. 41.
15. For a detailed study of Hadda Mulla see Edwardes, David, *Heroes of the Age: Moral Fault Lines on the Afghan Frontier*, Berkeley: University of California Press, 1996.
16. Caroe, *The Pathans*, p. 406.
17. Some of the concepts in this chapter first appeared in Rubin, Barnett and Abubakar Siddique, 'Resolving the Afghanistan Pakistan stalemate', *Special Report 176*, United States Institute of Peace, October 2006.
18. 'Loss of the lives of fifteen thousand men (loss of camp followers not known);

destruction of fifty thousand camels … loss of a least £ 13,000,000 [now estimated from £ 17,000,000 to 20,000,000]', *Report of the East India Committee on the Causes and Consequences of the First Afghan War*: Dupree, Louis, *Afghanistan*, Princeton: Princeton University Press, 1980, p. 400.

19. Under the treaty, the Afghan ruler agreed to give up several frontier districts, including Khyber, Michni and Kurram in the north and Pishin and Sibi in the south. The territories ceded to the British in the south were later named 'British Balochistan', undermining their predominantly Pashtun character. The territories still form the northern Pashtun-populated districts of Pakistan's south-western Balochistan Province.
20. There was no single decisive military victory for the Afghans in the Second Anglo-Afghan War. Louis Cavagnari, the British high official in Kabul, and his staff were killed in 1879. In July 1880, a British force was decisively defeated in Maiwand near Kandahar, with nearly 1,000 of 2,500 British and Indian soldiers killed.
21. The demarcation was decided by Anglo-Russian commissions with little Afghan input. Britain controlled Afghanistan's foreign affairs from 1879 to 1919.
22. Mohmand was created in 1951, while the Bajaur and Orakzai agencies came into being in 1973. See Ahmed, Akbar S., *Social and Economic Change in the Tribal Areas; 1972–1976*, Karachi: Oxford University Press, 1977, p. 23.
23. In the mid-twentieth century, the settled districts of NWFP replaced the river Indus as the outer ring of the threefold frontier.
24. Embree, Ainslie (ed.), *Pakistan's Western Borderlands: The Transformation of a Political Order*, Karachi: Royal Book Company, 1979 (New Delhi: Vikas Publishing House, 1977), pp. 10–40.
25. Trives, Sebastien, 'Afghanistan: tackling the insurgency, the case of the southeast', *Politique Entrangère*, January 2006.
26. Marwat, Fazal-ur-Rahim, *The Impact of the Great Game on the Pashtuns/Afghans*, Peshawar: Baacha Khan Research Centre, 2009, pp. 50–5.
27. Rubin and Siddique, 2006.
28. Haqqani, Hussain, *Pakistan: Between Mosque and Military*, Washington: Carnegie Endowment For International Peace, 2005, pp. 28–9.
29. Perhaps due to remorse for participating in crushing a Baloch uprising, Nawab Akbar Bugti turned against Pakistan's security establishment and eventually became a key leader of the Baloch insurgency that began in 2004. Bugti was killed in a Pakistani military operation on 26 August 2006.
30. To the present day, Kabul and Islamabad frequently trade allegations of support for each other's opponents.
31. Coll, Steve, 'The stand-off', *The New Yorker*, 13 February 2006.
32. Rubin and Siddique, 2006.
33. Abdullah Azzam was killed in Peshawar in November 1989.

34. Haqqani, *Pakistan Between Mosque and the Military.*
35. Some Pashtun leaders also wanted to see a united province for all Pashtuns living east of the Durand Line. The proposal called for the creation of a province that would include the NWFP, some districts of Balochistan and the tribal agencies.

3. THE TALIBAN IN POWER

1. Details of Muttawakil's biography are from my interview with him in October 2010. His Pashto-language short autobiography, *Afghanistan and the Taliban* (*in* Pashto: *Afghanistan Ao Taliban*), Kabul: Baryalai Pohanyoon, 2005, also sheds light on his life and thinking.
2. Ibid.
3. Reflecting on his education, Muttawakil told me he now believes that clerical education should feature less emphasis on philosophy and logic, and that subjects such as natural and computer sciences should be added to the curriculum.
4. Hanafi, or Hanfiya, is one of the four schools of the Islamic religious law or *fiqh* within Sunni Islam. It is named after the eighth-century theologian Imam Abu Hanifah (Abu Hanifah Annuman Ibn Thabit). The majority of Hanafis live in the non-Arab Muslim nations of Turkey, Central Asia and South Asia.
5. Deobandis, formed from a nineteenth-century Indian movement, are essentially a South Asian sect within Sunni Islam. The thrust of the Deoband movement was to resist British imperialism by training cadres of conservative clerics who would adhere to what they viewed as puritanical Islam. Today, the meaning of Deobandi Islam in India is considerably different from its meaning in Pakistan and Afghanistan. The current leaders of Deoband in India do not endorse the Taliban. See Donovan, Jeffrey and Abubakar Siddique, 'Taliban's spiritual fathers denounce terror. Could Taliban be next?', *Radio Free Europe/Radio Liberty*, 19 November 2009, http://www.rferl.org/content/Talibans_Spiritual_Fathers_Denounce_Terror_Could_Taliban_Be_Next/1350341.html
6. Harakat-Inqilab-i-Islami (Islamic Revolutionary Movement). This was one of the seven Afghan Sunni jihadi groups recognised by Islamabad and generously bankrolled by the West and Gulf Arab autocrats. Its leader, Mawlawi Mohammad Nabi Mohammadi, was a religious teacher with strong links among the mullahs on both sides of the border. Though described as a traditionalist, Mohammadi's vision essentially was that of an Afghanistan run by Sunni clerics.
7. A village fifty kilometres north-west of Kandahar, which serves as the district centre of Maiwand District. A large plain in Maiwand was the scene of a major British defeat during the Second Anglo-Afghan War in July 1880.
8. Author interview with Abdul Salam Zaeef, Kabul, October 2010. For a detailed discussion of the rise of the Taliban, see Zaeef, Abdul Salam, *My Life with the Taliban*, New York: Columbia University Press, 2010.

9. Spin Boldak is a sprawling truck stop across the border from the Pakistani town of Chaman.
10. Author interview with Muttawakil, Kabul, October 2010
11. Jamiat Tulaba Islam (JTI) refers to the student wings of the Jamiat Ulam-e Islam (JUI) political party, which is now divided into multiple factions.
12. Haji Bashar Noorzai, a famous jihad-era figure from Kandahar, is now serving a life sentence in New York City for drug smuggling.
13. Davis, Anthony, 'How the Taliban became a military force', in Maley, William (ed.), *Fundamentalism Reborn? Afghanistan and the Taliban*, London: Hurst & Co, 1998. Davis offers the most complete military history of the Taliban in the early years of the movement.
14. Ibid.
15. Rashid, Ahmed, *Taliban, Militant Islam, Oil and Fundamentalism in Central Asia*, London: Yale University Press, 2000, pp. 183–95.
16. Observers suggest that Najibullah's close ties with India after the Soviet exit from Afghanistan in 1989 did not endear him to Islamabad and the fundamentalist Afghan factions operating out of Pakistan.
17. Mozhdah, Waheed, *Afghanistan Under Five Years of Taliban Control* (In Dari, *Afghanistan Va Panj Sala Salta-e Taliban*), Kabul: Maiwand Publications, 2001.
18. Muttawakil, 2005.
19. Interviews with former Taliban leaders, Kabul, October 2010. These leaders insist that the Taliban never aimed to rule for a long time and that their main objective was to unite and pacify Afghanistan. They argue this never would have occurred peacefully, forcing them to turn to violence and Islam to achieve their patriotic goals.
20. At one point, senior Taliban leaders pressed Omar to stop using the Taliban name to describe the movement, citing concerns about politicising a segment of the society traditionally marginal to the running of the state and thus immune from corruption associated with power. Mullah Omar also resisted the inclusion of non-Taliban figures into the government, citing concerns about opening Taliban ranks to politicisation. Discussions with former senior members of the Taliban regime, Kabul, October 2010.
21. Mozhdah, *Afghanistan Under Five Years of Taliban Control*. I am grateful to the author for providing an unpublished English language translation. The quote is from page 19 of the translated version.
22. Kakar, Hassan, *Journey to the Homeland: The Taliban and Islamic Fundamentalism* (in Pashto: *Watan tha yo safar, Taliban Ao Islami Bansatpalana*), Peshawar: Danish Publication House, 2004, p. 195.
23. Ibid, p. 197.
24. A short form of *Amar Bil Maroof Wa Nahi An al-Munkar*.
25. Official Gazette No. 77, Kabul, Ministry of Justice, 2001. The forty-eight-page

document lays out hundreds of similar rules and is perhaps one of the strictest moral laws of modern times.

26. Unpublished version of the Taliban constitution. 'The Constitution of the Islamic Emirate of Afghanistan.' The preface of the document says it was approved in July 1998. The document was obtained from Kandahar in 2010.
27. Gutman, Roy, *How We Missed the Story: Osama bin Laden, the Taliban, and the Hijacking of Afghanistan*, Washington DC: United States Institute of Peace, 2008, p. 233.
28. For a detailed discussion see Rubin, Barnett and Abubakar Siddique, 'Resolving the Afghanistan Pakistan stalemate', *Special Report 176*, United States Institute of Peace, October 2006.
29. Ibid. In British India and later in Pakistan, Pashtun nationalists were in alliance with elements of the Deobandi movement. Many Deobandi *ulema* were part of Abdul Ghaffar Khan's Khudai Khitmatgar movement. Again, though, the alliance fractured over questions of modernity and ideology. The Soviet invasion of Afghanistan finally pushed the two sides into opposing camps.
30. Ibid.
31. Discussion with Senator Afrasiab Khattak, Islamabad, April 2010. I have heard Khattak express similar views in public meetings in Peshawar in the 1990s. Mahmood Khan Achakzai and his Pashtunkhwa Milli Awami Party had been publically projecting similar views since the emergence of the Taliban in 1994.
32. Rashid, *Taliban, Militant Islam, Oil and Fundamentalism in Central Asia*. Former senior members of the Taliban movement downplay Islamabad's influence and reject the idea that Taliban salaries were paid by Islamabad.
33. Ahmed Rashid's book is one of the best sources on Pakistan's relationship with the Taliban because of the author's access to senior Pakistani leaders.
34. Rubin and Siddique, *Resolving the Afghanistan Pakistan stalemate*.
35. Colonel Imam was kidnapped by Punjabi extremists in March 2010, and killed by their Pakistani Taliban allies in January 2011.
36. Zaeef's views were corroborated by a retired Pakistani diplomat who was part of such deliberations. The diplomat requested anonymity.
37. Hussain, Zahid, *Frontline Pakistan: The Struggle with Militant Islam*, New York: Columbia University Press, 2007, pp. 39–40.
38. The letter is discussed in Zaeef, Mullah Abdul Salam. *My Life with the Taliban*. The quotes are from Judah, Tim, 'The Taliban papers', *Survival*, 44, 1 (Spring 2002).
39. Azzam, Abdullah, *Join the Caravan* (original in Arabic, *Ilhaq bil-qawafilah*), 1987. English translation: http://www.religioscope.com/info/doc/jihad/azzam_caravan_1_foreword.htm
40. Azzam, Abdullah, 'Defence of the Muslim lands: the first obligation after Iman', undated but written and published in the 1980s. English translation: http://www.religioscope.com/info/doc/jihad/azzam_defence_1_table.htm

41. Bin Laden was essentially forced out of Sudan.
42. Bin Laden's oath of allegiance to the Taliban leader is from Waheed Mozhdah. See Siddique, Abubakar, 'Study says window for Afghan peace is closing quickly', 8 February 2011, Radio Free Europe/Radio Liberty.
43. Coll, Steve, *Ghost Wars: The Secret History of the CIA, Afghanistan, and bin Laden, from the Soviet Invasion to September 10, 2001*, New York: Penguin Press, 2004.
44. See the full text of World Islamic Front Statement 'Jihad against Jews and Crusaders', http://www.fas.org/irp/world/para/docs/980223-fatwa.htm
45. Author's personal communication with a former Pakistani diplomat who requested anonymity.
46. Coll, *Ghost Wars*, p. 510.
47. van Linschoten, Alex Strick and Felix Kuehn, 'Separating the Taliban from Al-Qaeda: the core of success in Afghanistan', New York University, Center on International Cooperation, February 2011.
48. Author interview, Kabul, October 2010.
49. Muttawakil, 2005, pp. 23 and 42.
50. Mozhdah, *Afghanistan Under Five Years of Taliban Control*, p. 84 of the unpublished translation.
51. Author interview with Muttawakil, October 2010.
52. Text of UN Security Council Resolution 1193, adopted on 28 August 1998, http://unama.unmissions.org/Portals/UNAMA/Security%20Council%20Resolutions/28%20August%201998.pdf
53. Text of UN Security Council Resolution 1214, adopted on 8 December 1998, http://unama.unmissions.org/Portals/UNAMA/Security%20Council%20Resolutions/8%20December%201998.pdf
54. In June 2011, a separate Taliban Sanctions Committee was established after the UN Security Council adopted Resolution 1988.
55. Text of UN Security Council Resolution 1333, adopted on 19 December 2000, http://daccess-dds-ny.un.org/doc/UNDOC/GEN/N00/806/62/PDF/N0080662.pdf?OpenElement
56. Schmemann, Serge, 'U.S. ATTACKED; president vows to exact punishment for "Evil"', *The New York Times*, 12 September 2001.
57. Bearak, Barry, 'Prospect of US attack raises fears in Afghanistan', *The New York Times*, 12 September 2001.
58. Text of UN Security Council Resolution 1378, adopted on 14 November 2001, http://unama.unmissions.org/Portals/UNAMA/Security%20Council%20Resolutions/14%20November%202001.pdf
59. Text of UN Security Council Resolution 1386, adopted on 20 December 2001, http://unama.unmissions.org/Portals/UNAMA/Security%20Council%20Resolutions/20%20December%202001.pdf

4. WAR IN WAZIRISTAN

1. I am indebted to a wide array of local sources for their help in understanding the dynamics of the Tribal Areas. Many of them requested anonymity over fears of being targeted for assassination or other reprisals.
2. Rashid, Ahmed, *Descent into Chaos: The United States and the Failure of Nation Building in Pakistan, Afghanistan, and Central Asia*, New York: Viking, 2008 p. 270.
3. Pakistani forces first clashed with Al-Qaeda militants around Wana in June 2002 and again in a village west of Wana in October 2003.
4. The group's influence was represented by Qari Hussain Mehsud, who was educated at an anti-Shia madrasa in Karachi. See Wolfe, Brian, 'The Pakistani Taliban's suicide bomber trainer: a profile of Qari Hussain Mehsud', *AEI Critical Threats*, 25 May 2010, http://www.criticalthreats.org/pakistan/gearing-long-awaited-offensive-north-waziristan-june-1–2011
5. The Urdu-language pamphlet entitled 'The first step toward the Sharia system' was distributed in North Waziristan in the spring of 2010. It contains a directive calling for the implementation of *sharia* for the Mehsud (TTP) Taliban.
6. Miram Shah is also called Miran Shah. Miram Shah is closer to the local Waziri pronunciation, Miroom Shah.
7. The Urdu-language pamphlet 'Happy Announcement' was distributed in North Waziristan towards the end of September 2006.
8. The undated note was hand-written on a letterhead bearing the printed name of Hakimullah Mehsud as the leader of the TTP. Written in the Urdu language, the note was distributed in North Waziristan in December 2009.
9. The Urdu-language edict is entitled 'Warning—honorable tribal Muslims'.
10. Urdu-language 'Public announcement' dated 8 August 2008, was distributed in North Waziristan. Flatbread made from wheat flour is a staple food in Waziristan. However, the arid region does not produce enough wheat to meet demand and its import is regulated by political agents. They tax its transportation, which is allowed only by permission. Thus, permission papers called 'permits' are highly sought after.
11. The Urdu-language 'Announcement for arms traders' was printed on the official letterhead of Hafiz Gul Bahadar and distributed in November, 2007.
12. Undated Urdu-language pamphlet entitled 'An important message for the brothers visiting from the Arab world.' The pamphlet is issued from Mujahedeen Waziristan in Mehsud Regions, suggesting it was issued before the formation of the TTP in 2007.
13. The Urdu-language statement dated 25 March 2011 was issued on various jihadi websites. Following Al-Qaeda's footsteps, the TTP declared Colonel Imam an 'apostate'. Colonel Imam was the *nom de guerre* of Amir Sultan Tarar, a former Pakistani military brigadier general. He was an officer of the Inter-Services Intel-

ligence Agency in the 1980s and claimed responsibility for the training of thousands of Afghan guerillas, including Taliban leader Mullah Mohammad Omar, in Pakistan's south-western Balochistan Province. Colonel Imam served as a Pakistani diplomat to the Taliban regime, but was widely seen as their mentor. He was kidnapped in North Waziristan in March 2010, and killed nearly a year later.

14. Crile, George, *Charlie Wilson's War: The Extraordinary Story of the Largest Covert Operation in History*, New York: Grove Press, 2003, p. 473.
15. For details of the Haqqani Network see Ruttig, Thomas, 'Loya Paktia's insurgency: the Haqqani Network as an autonomous entity', in Giustozzi, Antonio, (ed.), *Decoding the New Taliban*, London: Hurst and Company, 2009. Also Dressler, Jeff, 'The Haqqani from Pakistan to Afghanistan', Afghanistan Report 6, Institute For the Study of War, October, 2010, and Dressler, Jeff, 'The Haqqani Network: A Strategic Threat', Afghanistan Report 9, Institute For the Study of War, March 2012.
16. Mawlavi Jalaluddin Haqqani interview with *The News*, 20 October 2001.
17. Christia, Fotini and Michael Semple, 'Flipping the Taliban', *Foreign Affairs*, July/August 2009.
18. Rashid, *Descent into Chaos*, pp. 243–4. Such raids became a routine in later years but resulted in capturing few Haqqanis.
19. The Pashto language hand-written document is dated 18 *Rabi ul Thani*, 1427 (A.H.) [17 May 2006]. It is signed by an unnamed Mr. President, Usmani Sahib [presumably the former Afghan Taliban commander Mullah Akhtar Mohammad Usmani] and Bakhta Jan, a key Haqqani confidant. It was distributed in Waziristan in the summer of 2006.
20. The Haqqanis detest the term and see themselves as part of the Islamic Emirate of Afghanistan, the official name of the Afghan Taliban organisation headed by Mullah Muhammad Omar.
21. Sattar, Madiha, 'ANP leaders said military protected Haqqanis, other militants', *Dawn*, 23 May 2011.
22. Sanger, David, *The Inheritance: The World Obama Confronts and the Challenges to American Power*, New York: Harmony Books, 2009, pp. 248–55.
23. Mullick, Haider Ali Hussain, *Al-Qaeda and Pakistan: Current Role and Future Considerations*, Institute for Social Policy and Understanding Report, October 2010. For Loya Paktia's role in Afghan military see Rashid, Ahmed, 'Obama must keep his eye on the Afghan Eexit', *The Financial Times*, 5 October 2010, http://www.ft.com/cms/s/0/df0d6f9a-d06b-11df-afe1 00144feabdc0,s01=2.html#axzz1SB0RrVjJ
24. Zehra, Nasim, interview with Javed Ashraf Qazi, *Dunya TV*, 2 July 2011.
25. A complete translation of the letter is available on the website of the Combating Terrorism Center at West Point, http://www.ctc.usma.edu/wp-content/

uploads/2010/08/CTC-AtiyahLetter.pdf. Atiyah Abd al-Rahman was reportedly killed in a CIA drone strike in August 2011. He was considered Al-Qaeda's leader at the time of his death.

26. An Islamic concept meaning innovation in religious practice and beliefs.
27. Abandoning one's homeland in the footsteps of the Prophet Muhammad's seventh-century migration from Mecca to Medina is considered a sacred sacrifice for the cause of Islam.
28. Again Ansar refers to the Prophet Muhammad's hosts and companions in Medina.
29. Mujahedeen here refers to Al-Qaeda radicals.
30. *Shirk* is an Islamic concept and applies to people who, while claiming to be Muslims, engage in associating false gods with Allah. *Shirk* is the first stage of *kuffar* (disbelief in the religion of Allah; Islam) and can be roughly translated into polytheism.
31. Farooq, Ustad Ahmad, 'A sword in one hand and the Quran in the other' (in Urdu: *Nawa-e Afghan Jihad*, July 2010. This Al-Qaeda linked magazine is available in print in Pakistan and electronically on the internet. According to many jihadi websites and magazines, Ustad Ahmed Farooq is in charge of Al-Qaeda's media operations in Pakistan.
32. Cruickshank, Paul, *The Militant Pipeline: Between the Afghanistan-Pakistan Border Region and the West*, Washington DC: New America Foundation, July 2011. This paper provides a detailed account of all the major plots against the West until 2011.
33. Ibid.
34. Office of Public Affairs, Department of Justice, 'Najibullah Zazi pleads guilty to conspiracy to use explosives against persons or property in US, conspiracy to murder abroad and providing material support to Al-Qaeda', 22 February 2010, http://www.justice.gov/opa/pr/2010/February/10-ag-174.html
35. Ibid.
36. Farrell, Stephen, 'Video links Taliban in Pakistan to C.I.A. attack', *The New York Times*, 11 January 2010.
37. Lashkar-e Jhangvi later formed an international branch called Lashkar-e Jhangvi Al-Alami.
38. Siddique, Abubakar, 'IMU's evolution branches back to central Asia', Radio Free Europe/Radio Liberty, 6 December 2010.
39. Siddique, Abubakar, 'IMU takes root in increasingly insecure northern Afghan provinces', *Radio Free Europe/Radio Liberty*, 8 December 2010.
40. Cruickshank, *The Militant Pipeline*, pp. 47–8.
41. The tally is from the *Long War Journal*. Based on monitoring of Pakistani and international media, the website keeps an updated tally of reported drone strikes. Given the lack of access to attack sites, the data cannot be independently veri-

fied, http://www.longwarjournal.org/pakistan-strikes.php. The New America Foundation maintains a similar database at: http://counterterrorism.newamerica.net/drones

42. Bergen, Peter and Katherine Tiedemann, 'Washington's phantom war: the effects of the US drone program in Pakistan', *Foreign Affairs*, July/August 2011. For a good overview of the effects of drone strikes in Waziristan, see Shah, Pir Zubair, 'My drone war', *Foreign Policy*, 27 February 2012.
43. Rashid, *Descent into Chaos*.
44. Khattak, Afrasiab, 'Hiding behind Pakhtun tribes?', *Dawn*, 10 May 2003.
45. 'Pakistan pays tribe al-Qaeda debt', *BBC News*, 9 February 2005. http://news.bbc.co.uk/2/hi/south_asia/4249525.stm
46. The quotes are from the text of the original Urdu-language agreement.

5. VANISHING TRIBES

1. *Khateeb* is a term used for the Islamic prayer leader delivering the sermon during the *juma*, or Friday afternoon prayers.
2. Omar, Rageh, 'Battle for Pakistan's soul', *New Statesman*, 12 July 2007, http://www.newstatesman.com/international-politics/2007/07/red-mosque-pakistan-state
3. Fatwa is a religious decree or ruling issued by Islamic scholars or *ulema*.
4. Text of the original Urdu language fatwa, 'The unanimous edict of Pakistani ulema about Wana operation', *Nawa-e Afghan Jihad* magazine, July 2010.
5. The virtue campaign reached its zenith in June, when a Chinese massage parlour was stormed. Six Chinese women and a man working at the clinic were kidnapped. The incident disturbed officials in Beijing, Islamabad's supposed 'all-weather friend'. Chinese officials let it be known they were concerned about what an Islamist takeover in Pakistan could mean to China's strategic and economic interests.
6. Abdul Rashid Ghazi interview with Geo TV, 10 July 2007.
7. Massod, Salman, 'Musharraf defends raid that ended Red Mosque siege', *The New York Times*, 12 July 2007, http://www.nytimes.com/2007/07/13/world/asia/13pakistan.html?scp=5&sq=Red%20Mosque&st=cse
8. The Associated Press, 'Al-Qaida: wage Holy War against Pakistan', 11 July 2007.
9. Bin Laden is believed to have issued the message from his compound in Abbottabad, near Islamabad. This was the house in which bin Laden was killed by US forces in May 2011.
10. 'Sharia or martyrdom', *Nawa-e Afghan Jihad*, July 2010.
11. Kakar, Abdul Hai, 'Who is Maulvi Faqir?', *BBC Urdu Online*, 1 November 2006.
12. Kakar, Abdul Hai, interview with Maulvi Faqir Muhammad, *BBC Urdu Online*, 1 November 2007.

13. The peace *lashkars*, or peace committees, were amorphous organisations mostly consisting of local volunteers. They were often attacked by the Taliban.
14. Malik, Sajjad and Hasbanullah Khan, 'Security forces declare final victory in Bajaur', *Daily Times Lahore*, 3 March 2010.
15. Interview with Maulvi Faqir Muhammad, *BBC Pashto Online*, 3 June 2011, http://www.bbc.co.uk/pashto/afghanistan/2011/06/110603_faqeer-iv-03.shtml
16. Orakzai, Rifatullah, 'Maulvi Faqir supports negotiations with the government', *BBC Urdu Online*, 6 March 2012.
17. Rogio, Bill, 'Sidelined Pakistani Taliban commander back in good grace', *The Long War Journal*, 31 January 2013.
18. Rosenberg, Mathew and Jawad Sukhanyar, 'Top member of Taliban in Pakistan is captured', *The New York Times*, 19 February 2013.
19. Rashid, Haroon, 'Can Bajaur prove to be an island of peace', *BBC Urdu Online*, 18 January 2013.
20. Shah, Pir Zubair and Jane Perlez, 'As government backs off, Taliban take control in Pakistan tribal areas', *The New York Times*, 14 July 2008. Over the years, Pulitzer Prize-winner Pir Zubair Shah has contributed outstanding reports on the conflict in Pakistan's Pashtun regions.
21. 'Mohmand elders, tribal elders ink peace accord', *The News*, 27 May 2008.
22. Namdar established the Taliban-style *Amar Bil Maruf* and *Nahi Anil Munkir*, or Promotion of Virtue and Prevention of Vice in 2003. These were vigilante squads that forced locals to observe Islamic rules and meted out harsh punishments to violators.
23. Barelvis are a moderate Sufi sect of Sunni Islam in eastern and southern Pakistan. The movement was pioneered by Ahmed Raza Khan Barelvi, a nineteenth-century Sunni cleric in India, in reaction to Salafi influences in South Asia which were critical of the traditional beliefs and practices associated with Islam in the subcontinent.
24. Fatah, Sonya, 'FM mullahs', *Columbia Journalism Review*, July/August 2006.
25. *Jizya* is a tax that early Islamic rulers demanded from their non-Muslim subjects as a mark of submission and for allowing them to practise their religion.
26. Orakzai, Rifatullah, 'Lashkar-e Islam existence in danger', *BBC Urdu Online*, 18 April 2011.
27. Hadi, Abdul, 'How to choke crusader supplies through Pakistan', *Nawa-e Afghan Jihad*, March 2010.
28. Orakzai, 'Lashkar-e Islam existence in danger'.
29. Siddique, Abubakar, 'Pakistan's Islamist militia and its fight for influence', *Radio Free Europe/Radio Liberty*, 29 January 2013.
30. Mir, Amir, 'Intra-TTP rift led to Commander Afridi's murder', *The News*, 17 February 2013.
31. Siddique, Abubakar, 'Peace in one Pakistani tribal valley offers hope', *Radio Free Europe/Radio Liberty*, 28 February 2011.

32. Two brothers of Jalaluddin Haqqani, Ibrahim Omari and Haji Khalil Ahmad Haqqani were active in behind-the-scene manoeuvring in Kurram.
33. Munir, Asad, 'Explaining Fazal Saeed's "Defection" in Kurram', *Express Tribune*, 8 July 2011. The quotes are from AFP, 'Taliban commander Fazal Saeed leaves TTP', 27 June 2011.
34. Taj, Farhat, *Taliban and Anti-Taliban*, Newcastle upon Tyne: Cambridge Scholars Publishing, 2011, pp. 121–49.
35. For example: 'Waziristanis (who come mostly from the Wazir and Mehsud tribes) have repelled outsiders for centuries. Marauding down onto the plains of northern Punjab—now North-West Frontier Province (NWFP)—their long-haired warriors would rape, pillage and raise a finger to the regional imperialist, Mughal or British, of the day. No government, imperialist or Pakistani, has had much control over them. "Not until the military steamroller has passed over [Waziristan] from end to end will there be peace," wrote Lord Curzon, a British viceroy of India at the turn of the 19th and 20th centuries.' 'Waziristan: the last frontier', *The Economist*, 394, 8663 (28 January 2010).
36. Bangash, Mumtaz Ali, 'Political and administrative development of tribal areas—focus on Khyber and Kurram', unpublished PhD dissertation, University of Peshawar, 1996.
37. Human Rights Commission of Pakistan, 'FCR—A Bad Law Nobody can Defend', Lahore, 2005.
38. Since the 1950s, the FCR has been frequently challenged in court. In 1954, prominent Pakistani jurist Alvin Robert Cornilius described the FCR as 'obnoxious to all recognised modern principles governing the dispensation of justice'. Hussain, Faqir, paper presented in a 2008 workshop on FATA reforms in Islamabad.
39. Amnesty International, 'As if Hell Fell on Me': *The Human Rights Crisis in Northwest, Pakistan*, 2010.
40. Amnesty International, 'The Hands of Cruelty': *Abuses by Armed Forces and Taliban in Pakistan's Tribal Areas*, December 2012.
41. 'Is Pakistan failing the FATA?', *Jane's Islamic Affairs Analyst*, 18 December 2008.
42. Author's interview with Farhatullah Babar, October 2010.
43. Siddique, Abubakar, 'Pakistan's tribal area reforms too little, too late', *Radio Free Europe/Radio Liberty*, 20 August 2011.
44. Rubin, Barnett and Abubakar Siddique, 'Resolving the Afghanistan Pakistan stalemate', *Special Report 176*, United States Institute of Peace. October, 2006.
45. In March 2013, officials reported that the Taliban had blown up some 1,300 schools in Pakistan's Pashtun regions. In the Tribal Areas, some 500 schools were destroyed, while another 800 were blown up in Khyber Pakhtunkhwa Province. See 'Targeting education: 1,300 schools destroyed in six years', *BBC Urdu Online*, 8 March 2013.

46. Or even 100 per cent, seasonally, if remittances and migrant labour are not counted. Rubin and Siddique, 'Resolving the Afghanistan Pakistan stalemate'.

6. TERROR IN PAKHTUNKHWA

1. Renamed Khyber Pakhtunkhwa Province in 2010.
2. Paracha, Nadeem, 'When the mountains were red', *Dawn*, 1 August 2013.
3. Abdul Wali Khan, Khair Baksh Marri, Mir Ghaus Baksh Bizenjo and Attaullah Mengal were some of the prominent NAP leaders detained in Hyderabad. For an insightful history of the NAP see Kutty, B.M., *Sixty Years In Self Exile: No Regrets, a Political Biography*, Karachi: Pakistani Study Centre, University of Karachi, 2011.
4. 'Bin Laden urges support for Taliban,' *BBC News Online*, 10 April 2001. And Yousafzai, Rahimullah, 'Deoband moot ends condemning US hegemony', *The News*, 12 April 2001.
5. *The News Hour with Jim Lehrer*, 30 April 2002.
6. Rashid, Ahmed, *Descent into Chaos: The United States and the Failure of Nation Building in Pakistan, Afghanistan and Central Asia*, New York: Viking, 2008, pp. 157–8.
7. Khan, Ismail, 'From idealism to pragmatism', *Dawn*, 6 July 2003.
8. Rashid, Ahmed, 'Pashtuns want an image change', *BBC News*, 5 December 2006, http://news.bbc.co.uk/2/hi/6198382
9. The cable was written in March 2006, and was made public by WikiLeaks in 2010. Asfandiyar Wali Khan and Afrasiab Khattak visited Washington in the spring of 2006 to present a Pashtun perspective on the situation in western Pakistan.
10. Zareef, Adil, 'ANP rejoices with restraint', *Dawn*, 24 February 2008.
11. Ustad Fateh seems to be a Jihadist *nom de guerre*.
12. Interview with Ustad Fateh, military leader of Tehreek-e Taliban Swat, Al-Sahab, July 2009. The Urdu-language transcript appears to be translated from Pashto.
13. The name translates as the 'Movement for the Implementation of Muhammad's Sharia'.
14. Siddiqui, Irfan, 'First detailed interview with Maulana Sufi Muhammad leader of Tehreek-e Nifaz-e Shahriat-e Muhammadi', *Takbeer Magazine*, 19 January 1995.
15. For profiles of Sufi Muhammad and TNSM, see Ali, Imtiaz, 'Militant or peace broker? A profile of the Swat Valley's Maulana Sufi Muhammad', *Terrorism Monitor*, 7, 7 (26 March 2009). And Abbas, Hassan, 'The black-turbaned brigade: the rise of TNSM in Pakistan', *Terrorism Monitor*, 4, 23 (30 November 2006).
16. I am indebted to Shaheen Buneri, a journalist from the region, for explaining this to me.

17. Ibid.
18. The quote is from a Pashto-language broadcast recording obtained from Swat. The references to military operations and the government appear to be from late 2007 or early 2008.
19. Buneri, Shaheen, 'Dancing girls of Swat Valley', Pulitzer Center on Crisis Reporting, 13 September 2011.
20. Kakar, Abdul Hai, 'Government tolerates a Taliban comrade (in Urdu: *Taliban Ka Pyara, Hakumat Ko Gawara*)', *BBC Urdu Online*, 28 April 2009. Sayed Muhammad Javed was removed from his post in April 2009, when a security operation against the Taliban became imminent. He was dismissed from the civil service in 2011 for Taliban links.
21. Perlez, Jane and Pir Zubair Shah, 'Taliban enlist an army of Pakistan's have-nots', *The New York Times*, 27 April 2009.
22. Abdul Hai Kakar, interview with Sirajul Haq, December 2010.
23. Pir Samiullah's execution also negates the theory that the Taliban emergence was a manifestation of class struggle revolving around peasant grievances against the landed gentry or the *khans* in Swat. Pir Samiullah was a Gujjar—traditionally, the downtrodden caste in the region. His ascendency to the leadership of anti-Taliban factions suggests that the militancy in Swat was not a class or caste struggle.
24. Aamir, Najib, 'Faith trumps fear for anti-Taliban politician in Pakistan', *Radio Free Europe/Radio Liberty*, 3 February 2009.
25. Rahman, Tariq, 'Talibanization of Pakistan', *Dawn*, 2 April 2009.
26. Kakar, Abdul Hai, interview with Wajid Ali Khan, December 2010.
27. Kakar, Abdul Hai, interview with Aftab Sherpao, December 2010.
28. Kakar, Abdul Hai, Interviews with Amir Haider Khan Hoti, December 2010.
29. Stout, David, 'Clinton delivers rebuke to Pakistan', *The New York Times*, 22 April 2009.
30. Wright, Tom, 'Pakistan WSJ ad unlikely to change narrative', *The Wall Street Journal*, 13 September 2011, http://blogs.wsj.com/indiarealtime/2011/09/13/pakistan-wsj-ad-unlikely-to-change-narrative/. Café Pyala, 'Trust us even if we don't trust ourselves', 14 September 2011, http://cafepyala.blogspot.com/2011/09/trust-us-even-if-we-do-not-trust.html
31. Rashid, *Descent into Chaos*, pp. 219–40.
32. Riedel, Bruce, 'Obama and Romney must address the Pakistan problem', *The Daily Beast*, 21 October 2012.
33. Siddique, Abubakar, 'Pakistan: armed with power, perks, and privileges', *Radio Free Europe/Radio Liberty*, 4 June 2011, http://www.rferl.org/content/pakistani_military_is_armed_with_power_perks_and_privileges/24215518.html. For a detailed study of the issue, see Siddiqa, Ayesha, *Military Inc: Inside Pakistan's Military Economy*, Karachi: Oxford University Press, 2007.

34. Siddique, Abubakar and Abdul Hai Kakar, 'Islamization a catch-22 for Pakistani military', *Radio Free Europe/Radio Liberty*, 3 July 2011, http://www.rferl.org/content/islamization_a_catch-22_for_pakistani_military/24254110.html
35. See Hoodbhoy, Pervez, 'Can Pakistan work? A country in search of itself', *Foreign Affairs*, November/December 2004. And Khan, Aamer Ahmed, 'International community fed up with the policy of alliances with the extremists (in Urdu: *Shidat Pasando Sey Ittehad Ke Policy Par Aalami Paimana Sabr Labrez*)', *BBC Urdu Online*, 29 September 2011, http://www.bbc.co.uk/urdu/columns/2011/09/110929_militancy_analysis_aak_zs.shtml
36. Al-Sahab interview with Ustad Fateh, 2009.
37. Kakar, Abdul Hai, 'General Kayani should save the military's standing', *BBC Urdu Online*, 29 January 2009, http://www.bbc.co.uk/urdu/pakistan/story/2009/01/090129_lal_kiani_meet_rh.shtml
38. Whitmore, Brian and Abubakar Siddique, 'RFE/RL interview: US Vice President Joe Biden', *Radio Free Europe/Radio Liberty*, 23 October 2009, http://www.rferl.org/content/RFERL_Interview_US_Vice_President_Joe_Biden/1859703.html
39. Zardari, Asif Ali, 'Pakistan did its part', *The Washington Post*, 3 May 2011.
40. Siddique, Abubakar, 'Which way for Pakistani leadership?', *Radio Free Europe/Radio Liberty*, 4 May 2011, http://www.rferl.org/content/which_way_for_pakistan_leadership/24091584.html
41. 'Mullen accuses Pakistan of exporting violence to Afghanistan', *Radio Free Europe/Radio Liberty*, 22 September 2011, http://www.rferl.org/content/pakistan_mullen_violence/24337069.html
42. Ibid.
43. Riedel, Bruce, 'A new Pakistan policy: containment', *The New York Times*, 14 October 2011.
44. Ijaz, Mansoor, 'Time to take on Pakistan's Jihadist spies', *The Financial Times*, 10 October 2011. The op-ed also mentions a secret memo sent by Pakistani civilian leaders to the US leadership asking for help in preventing a military coup in the aftermath of bin Laden's killing. The op-ed eventually became the source of a huge political scandal in Pakistan called 'Memo-gate'. It eventually cost Husain Haqqani, the Pakistani ambassador to the US, his job. In Pakistan, the debate remained focused on the memo Ijaz claimed to have delivered. There was little discussion about his allegations about ISI's support for extremism.
45. A draft counterterrorism manual in 2013 gave the CIA a major exemption in Pakistan from the administration's rules for targeted killings. See Miller, Greg, Ellen Nakashima and Karen DeYoung, 'CIA drone strikes will get pass in counterterrorism "Playbook", officials say', *The Washington Post*, 19 January 2013.
46. The ancient city of Peshawar is located between a fertile river valley and the Khyber Pass. In 2012, it was a drastically changed place from just a few years

before. The military's war in the Pashtun lands had led hundreds of thousands of Pashtuns from the Tribal Areas and Malakand to seek shelter in Peshawar. Meanwhile, Peshawar's wealthy had fled to Islamabad and other more secure cities because they had become a main target for Taliban attacks. Police and security checkpoints were ubiquitous in Peshawar. Khattak lived in a secure part of town, behind blast walls and multiple barricades. The measures restricted his movements somewhat, but he continued to make a point of staying in contact with the outside world.

47. The party has lost more than 700 members, including its senior provincial minister Bashir Ahmad Bilour, who was killed by a suicide bomber in December 2012.

7. SIMMERING BALOCHISTAN: A TALIBAN HAVEN

1. Rashid, Ahmed, 'Afghanistan and Pakistan—safe haven for the Taliban', *Far Eastern Economic Review*, 9 October 2003.
2. Ibid.
3. Fighters from the Baloch Marri tribe fought for the PDPA regime in southern Afghanistan in the 1980s.
4. Hasan, Syed Shoaib, 'Rare Taliban praise for Pakistan's Maulana Abdul Ghani', *BBC News*, 27 October 2011, http://www.bbc.co.uk/news/world-south-asia-15479758
5. Some Pashtun residents of the region call this region Southern Pashtunkhwa or the southern Pashtun homeland.
6. Rubin, Elizabeth, 'In the land of the Taliban', *The New York Times*, 22 October 2006.
7. Koelbl, Susanne, 'Headquarter of the Taliban', 26 November 2006, http://www.spiegel.de/international/spiegel/0,1518,450605,00.html
8. Gall, Carlotta, 'At border, signs of Pakistani role in Taliban surge', *The New York Times*, 27 January 2007. I am also grateful to many locals for explaining nuances and helping me follow up on key issues and events. Most of them requested anonymity.
9. Ibid.
10. Kuchlack is also called Kuchlagh by local Pashtuns.
11. Khan, Ilyas, 'The Afghanistan Pakistan militant nexus', *BBC*, 5 February 2013. Many Balochistan residents have confirmed this to me.
12. Moreau, Ron, 'With friends like these', *Newsweek*, 31 July 2010.
13. Ibid.
14. Moreau, Ron, 'The Taliban after Bin Laden', *Newsweek*, 15 May 2011.
15. JUI is divided into various factions. Fazalur Rahman is the biggest faction.
16. Mohammad Khan Sherani has served as a lawmaker in both the houses of Pak-

istani parliament many times and was also serving as the head of the Islamic Ideological Council, a government body tasked with ensuring that all legislation in Pakistan follows Islamic principles.

17. Kakar, Abdul Hai interview with Maulana Muhammad Khan Sherani, December 2010.
18. Kakar, Abdul Hai interview with Maulvi Asmatullah, December 2010.
19. Ibid.
20. Kakar, Abdul Hai interview, December 2010.
21. Some observers assert that Pakistan never militarily crushed the Baloch and the two sides fought to a stalemate in all the conflicts.
22. Recknagel, Charles and Abubakar Siddique, 'Gwadar: a port for China, a tinderbox for Balochistan', *Radio Free Europe/Radio Liberty*, 28 February 2013.
23. 'Pakistan, Iran leaders inaugurate pipeline project', *The Associated Press*, 12 March 2013. The overall cost of the project was estimated at $7.5 billion in 2010.

8. OLD AND NEW ISLAMISTS IN LOY NANGARHAR

1. Author interview with Abdul Rashid Waziri, March 2012.
2. Quotes are from a video recording of his speech on 16 February 1989. Many participants have confirmed the authenticity of the recording.
3. Coll, Steve, *Ghost Wars: The Secret History Of the CIA, Afghanistan, and Bin Laden, from the Soviet Invasion to September 10, 2001*, New York: The Penguin Press, 2004, pp. 190–5.
4. Waziri interview, 2012. Also see Fineman, Mark, 'Afghan leadership mellowing—but can it last?', *Los Angeles Times*, 30 April 1989.
5. Coll, *Ghost Wars*, p. 193.
6. Burns, John F., 'Jalalabad shows its recovery as siege by rebels dwindles', *New York Times*, 13 September 1989.
7. See Burke, Jason, *Al-Qaeda: The True Story of Radical Islam*, London: I. B. Tarus, 2004, pp. 81–2. Bergen, Peter, *The Osama Bin Laden I know: An Oral History of the Al-Qaeda Leader*, New York: Simon and Schuster, 2006, pp. 87–91. Anonymous (Scheuer, Michael), *Through Our Enemies' Eyes: Radical Islam and the Future of America*, Washington: Potomac Book Inc., 2006, pp. 110–2.
8. Tomsen, Peter, *The Wars of Afghanistan: Messianic Terrorism, Tribal Conflicts and The Failure of Great Powers*, New York: Public Affairs, 2011, p. 306.
9. Misdaq, Nabi, *Afghanistan: Political Frailty and External Interference*, London: Routledge, 2006, p. 150.
10. Roy, Olivier, *Islam and the Resistance in Afghanistan*, Cambridge: Cambridge University Press, 1986. pp. 112–8.
11. Ibid.
12. Ibid.

13. Roy, *Islam and the Resistance in Afghanistan*, p. 72.
14. Mawlawi Habibur al-Rehman and Ghulam Mohammad Niazi were other pioneering leaders of the Afghan Islamist movement.
15. Roy, *Islam and the Resistance in Afghanistan*, p. 70.
16. Edwards, David B., *Before Taliban: Genealogies of the Afghan Jihad*, Berkeley: University of California Press, 2002, pp. 247–9. Minhajuddin Gahez was the editor of Afghanistan's only Islamist newspaper, *Gahez* (Pashto for morning).
17. Ibid.
18. Roy, *Islam and the Resistance in Afghanistan.*
19. Tomsen, *Messianic Terrorism*, pp. 304–5.
20. Healy, Melissa, 'Reagan lauds United Afghan resistance', *Los Angeles Times*, 13 November 1987.
21. Tomsen, *Messianic Terrorism*, p. 306.
22. Khalis, Mohammad Younas, Letter to the Mujahidin Shura, 1989, printed in *Tora Bora Magazine*, Summer 2010. This magazine is a propaganda publication arm of the Tora Bora Front.
23. Interview with *Gorbat Magazine* (Pashto), June/July 2000. Reprinted in Ghastalai, Hafizullah, *One Mirror and Thirteen Faces* (Pashto), Kabul: Danish Publication, 2010.
24. Interviews in Nangarhar, summer 2011 and spring 2012. This observation in reinforced by Nangial, Shuhrat, 'Leader Khalis: Nabi Khel poet, the aspects of life of a fanatical mullah', *Dawat Magazine* (Pashto), Summer 2006.
25. Mujahid was released in November 2012. Yousafzai, Rahimullah, 'Afghan Taliban leader freed by Pakistan finally reaches home', *The News*, 17 November 2012.
26. I am grateful to Rohullah Anwari, a journalist in Kunar, for explaining this to me.
27. Van Der Schriek, Daan, 'Nuristan: insurgent hideout in Afghanistan', *Terrorism Monitor*, 3, 10 (26 May 2006).
28. Ibid. Mawlawi Afzal returned to Afghanistan after the demise of the Taliban regime. He supported the new political order and was considered a little-known jihadist leader who supported President Karzai until his death in 2011.
29. Interviews with tribal leaders and lawmakers from eastern Afghanistan, summer 2012. Jamil ur-Rahman's real name was Mohammad Hussain.
30. The fact that the Salafis of Kunar and Nuristan referred to themselves as Salafis in the 1980s is remarkable evidence of globalisation.
31. Rubin, Barnett, *The Fragmentation of Afghanistan: State Formation and Collapse in The International System*, New Haven: Yale University Press, 2002, pp. 242, 263.
32. Afghanistan's fragmented Salafist currents have never posed a serious threat to the Taliban, as the Salafis of the east kept a distance from Abdul Rab Rasul's

Sayaff's Ittehad-e Islami Bary-e Azadi-e Afghanistan, which fought against the Taliban and allied with their enemies in the Northern Alliance. The Taliban enlisted some Salafi cadres from the east, but never expressed any interest in adopting Salafism.

33. Haji Rohullah Wakil's participation in the Cyprus process is confirmed by his 'Detainee assessment' at Guantanamo, made public by WikiLeaks in 2011.
34. Similar accusations are made by Abdul Rahim Muslim Dost and Ustad Badar Zaman Badar. The two brothers were members of the Jamil ur-Rahman faction but developed strong differences with Haji Rohullah Wakil. They even accuse him of conspiring in their incarceration in Guantanamo Bay from November 2001 to April 2005. See Dost, Abdul Rahim Muslim and Ustad Badar Zaman Badar, *The Broken Shackles of Gunatanamo* (in Pashto: *Da Guantanamo Matay Zolanay*), Peshawar: Khilafat Publishing Society, 2006.
35. In their formal statement about the accession of the Jamaat al-Dawa al-Quran wa-Sunah, the Taliban acknowledged him to be the leader of the group.
36. Moore, Michael and James Fussell, *Kunar and Nuristan: Rethinking U.S. Counterinsurgency Operations*, Institute for the Study of War, July 2009.
37. Ibid.
38. Ruttig, Thomas, 'On Kunar's Salafi insurgents', *The Afghanistan Analyst Network*, 14 January 2010.
39. Rubin, Alissa J., 'U.S. forces close post in Afghan "Valley Of Death"', *The New York Times*, 14 April 2010. See also Rubin, Elizabeth, 'Battle company is out there', *The New York Times*, 24 February 2008. Junger, Sebastian and Tim Heterington's 2010 documentary *Restrepo* also documents the combat in Korengal.
40. Gall, Carlotta and Eric Schmitt, 'Taliban breached NATO base in deadly clash', *The New York Times*, 15 July 2008. See also, Shanker, Thom, 'Report cites firefight as lesson on Afghan war', *The New York Times*, 3 October 2009.
41. Kuz, Martin, 'Six months after pullback, U.S. goes back in to contest Pech Valley', *Stars and Stripes*, 4 August 2011.
42. Tenkel, Stephen, 'Lashkar-e-Taiba: from 9/11 to Mumbai', *Developments in Radicalization and Political Violence*, The International Centre for the Study of Radicalization and Political Violence, ICSR King's College London, April/May 2009.
43. Rehman, Zia Ur, 'Militants striking both sides of the Afghanistan-Pakistan border to disrupt security cooperation', *Terrorism Monitor*, IX (22 July 2011).

9. TRIBES, COMMUNISTS AND GENERATIONAL JIHADISTS IN LOYA PAKTIA

1. Author's communication with Farooq Waziri, spring 2012. His father Mir Habib, a district governor at the time, was an eye-witness to Faiz Mohammad's killing.

Author's communication with Abdul Rashid Waziri, a close friend and colleague of Faiz Muhammad who witnessed his career.

2. Mawlavi Jalaluddin Haqqani is a cleric from the powerful Zadran tribe who had studied at the Haqqania Madrasa in Akora Khattak Pakistan. He maintained close ties to the country's intelligence community and was emerging as one of the leading commanders of the nascent armed resistance. Reuters, 'Afghan cabinet official reported slain by villagers', *The New York Times*, 15 September 1980.
3. In 1965, the People's Democratic Party of Afghanistan was formed with the goal of working towards the establishment of a Marxist-Leninist society. By 1967, divisions among its top leaders had led to the emergence of two distinct factions: The Khalq (Masses) and Parcham (Banner). Ideological differences, personal rivalries and the disparate backgrounds of top leaders kept the two factions at loggerheads.
4. Sayyed Mohammad Gulabzoi was one of the key officers who participated in the July 1973 coup. Gulabzoi interview with *Gorbat* magazine (Pashto), June-September 2005. Reprinted in Ghastalai, Hafizullah, *One Mirror and Thirteen Faces*, (Pashto), Kabul: Danish Publication, 2010.
5. Waziri, 2012.
6. See Gregg, Tom, 'Caught In The Crossfire: The Pashtun Tribes of Southeastern Afghanistan', Policy Brief for the Lowy Institute For International Affairs, October 2009. Trives, Sebastien, 'Afghanistan: tackling the insurgency, the case of the southeast', *Politique Etrangère*, January 2006. The tribes of Loya Paktia did pay some taxes, such as giving one cattle per every forty.
7. Sher Mohmmad Karimi, head of the Afghan National Army under President Hamid Karzai, is a native of Khost. He is one of the few Afghan officers who attended Britain's Royal Military Academy at Sandhurst.
8. Amir Baheer interviews with tribal leaders in Khost, summer of 2011. Misdaq, Nabi, *Afghanistan: Political Frailty and External Interference*, London: Routledge, 2006.
9. Ibid. See also Edwardes, David, *Before Taliban: Genealogies of the Taliban*, Berkeley: University of California Press, 2002, p. 260.
10. Loya Paktia and Loy Nangarhar are the two major regions with considerable natural forests in Afghanistan. Both regions have suffered major deforestation during the past three decades.
11. Haji Mohammad Chamkani, an interim leader in 1986–87, was also from the region. He is considered more a tribal figure than a communist partisan.
12. Factions and members of the Afghan communists were involved in many successful and abortive coups. The Parchamis were responsible for Daud Khan's 1973 coup. The Khalqis killed Daud Khan and his extended family on 27 April 1978 in what they called the 'Saur Revolution'. Two Khaqi ideologues fell out

with each other and, as a result, Hafizullah Amin secretly executed Nur Mohammad Tarakai in October 1979. Amin was killed by Soviet special forces on 27 December 1979. Karmal was replaced by Najibullah after opposition to his rule mounted within the Parchamis in late 1986. Najibullah survived a coup by his Khalqi Defence Minister Shahnawaz Tanai in March 1990, but lost his grip on power in April 1992. Significant members of his Parcham faction had joined the mujahedeen and prevented him from going to India. The coup also dealt a mortal blow to a UN plan for a peaceful transfer of power.

13. Feifer, Gregory, *The Great Gamble: The Soviet War in Afghanistan*, New York: HarperCollins Publishers, 2009, pp. 233–8. Also see Grau, Lester W., *The Bear Went over the Mountain: Soviet Combat Tactics in Afghanistan*, Washington D.C.: National Defense University Press, 1996, pp. 60–5.
14. Amir Baheer, interview with Amir Shah Kargar, Khost, summer 2011.
15. Ibid.
16. Mohmand, Hameed, interview with Shahnawaz Tanai, Kabul, autumn 2010.
17. Author interview with Sulaiman Laiq, Kabul, October 2010. Among the PDPA leaders, Laiq perhaps had the best understanding of the power of Islamic clerics because his father was a religious cleric and devotee of Sheikh Ahmed Sirhindi. He was the only senior PDPA leader who was educated in a madrasa. A fluent Arabic speaker, he studied Islamic studies at Kabul University. Laiq said that as a cabinet member in the 1980s, he conducted an informal survey which determined that there were 220,000 mosques across Afghanistan. He observed that this made the mullahs perhaps the largest network in the country, with deep penetration at the grassroots level.
18. Ruttig, Thomas, 'Loya Paktia's insurgency: the Haqqani Network as an autonomous entity', in Giustozzi, Antonio (ed.), *Decoding the Taliban: Insights from the Afghan Field*, London: Hurst and Company, 2009, pp. 87–8.
19. A redacted version of the cable is available on George Washington University's National Security Achive, 'Afghanistan: Jalaluddin Haqqani's emergence as a key Taliban commander', 7 January 1997, http://www.gwu.edu/~nsarchiv/NSAEBB/NSAEBB295/doc05.pdf
20. Author's interview with a lawmaker from Paktia Province, October 2010.
21. Local sources suggest he received medical treatment and remained in hiding in the Tanai district on the Pakistani border. Amir Baheer, interviews in Khost, summer 2001.
22. Dressler, Jeffery, 'The Haqqani Network: A Strategic Threat', Afghanistan Report No. 9, Institute for the Study of War, March 2012. See also, Binnie, Jeremy and Joanna Wright, 'Network warriors, Al-Qaeda and the Haqqani Network', in *Relationships and Rivalries: Assessing Al-Qaeda's Affiliate Networks*, Jane's Consulting, October 2010.
23. Bumiller, Elisabeth and Jane Perlez, 'Pakistan's spy agency is tied to attack on U.S. Embassy', *The New York Times*, 22 September 2011.

24. Siddique, Abubakar, 'Questions raised about Haqqani Network ties with Pakistan', *Radio Free Europe/Radio Liberty*, 23 September 2011. Rashid, Ahmed, 'Obama must keep his eye on the Afghan exit', *Financial Times*, 5 October 2010.
25. van Linshchoten, Alex Strick and Felix Kuehn, 'A pointless blacklisting', *The New York Times*, 11 September 2012.
26. Moreau, Ron and Sami Yousafzai, 'Dueling manifestoes', *The Daily Beast*, 14 November 2011.
27. Binnie, Jeremy and Joanna Wright, 2010. Stenersen, Ann, *Al-Qaeda's Allies: Explaining the Relationship Between Al-Qaeda and Various Factions of the Taliban After 2001*, Counterterrorism Strategy Initiative Policy Paper, New America Foundation, April 2010.
28. Siddique, Abubakar, 'In Afghanistan, IMU-Taliban alliance chips away at the stone', *Radio Free Europe/Radio Liberty*, 9 June 2011.
29. Peters, Gretchen, *Haqqani Network Financing: the Evolution of an Industry*, Harmony Program, Combating Terrorism Center at West Point, July 2012.
30. Baheer, Amir interview with Pacha Khan Zadran, Paktia, summer 2011.
31. Baheer, Amir interview with Nazim Zadran, Khost, summer 2011. Both Pacha Khan Zadran and Nazim Zadran were among the senior mujahedeen commanders in Loya Paktia during the 1980s. Like Haqqani, both were based in North Waziristan.
32. Author's interview with a lawmaker from Paktia province, Kabul, October 2010.
33. Ruttig, Thomas, 'Loya Paktia's insurgency', pp. 78–83. See also Yousafzai, Rahimullah, 'Battle creates a new Taliban legend', *Time Magazine*, 7 March 2002.
34. Clark, Kate, '2001 ten years on: the fall of Loya Paktia and why the US preferred warlords', Afghan Analyst Network, 24 November 2011, http://aan-afghanistan.com/index.asp?id=2269
35. Ruttig, Thomas, *How Tribal Are the Taliban: Afghanistan's Largest Insurgent Movement Between its Tribal Roots and Islamist Ideology*, Afghan Analyst Network Paper, June 2010.
36. Osman, Mohammed Tariq, *Tribal Security System (Arbaki) in Southeast Afghanistan*, CSRC Occasional Paper No. 7, 2008.
37. Baheer, Amir interview with Haider Gul Mangal, Khost, summer 2011.
38. Hakim Taniwal was a native of Khost. He was a sociologist at Kabul University and was among the moderate Afghan intellectuals in Peshawar during the 1980s. Taniwal returned to Khost from exile in Australia in 2002.
39. Translated from the original Pashto text.
40. Speaking to the Foreign Affairs Committee of the European Parliament in September, 2006, Pakistani military dictator Pervez Musharraf warned that the resurgence of the Taliban could spark a Pashtun civil war. His comments angered

Pashtun leaders in Afghanistan and Pakistan, who accused the Pakistani intelligence services of fomenting the insurgency. See Lobjakas, Ahto, 'Afghanistan: Taliban could spark Pashtun "National War"', *Radio Free Europe/Radio Liberty*, 12 September 2006.

41. Gregg, *Caught in the Crossfire*.
42. Baheer, Amir interview in Khost, summer 2011.

10. THE NEW TALIBAN IN LOY KANDAHAR

1. Nearly half the population of Nimroz is ethnic Baloch. Most Baloch in Afghanistan are trilingual and speak both Pashto and Dari.
2. For a detailed account of southern Afghanistan during the first years after the fall of the Taliban, see Chayes, Sarah, *The Punishment of Virtue: Inside Afghanistan after the Taliban*, New York: Penguin Press, 2006.
3. Guistozzi, Antonio, *Koran, Kalashnikov and Laptop: The Neo-Taliban Insurgency in Afghanistan*, London: Hurst & Company, 2007.
4. The motives and perpetrators of such murders are rarely clear. Ahmed Wali Karzai, for example, was killed by Sardar Mohammad, who had been a trusted Karzai family guard for years. Personal and family feuds and tribal rivalries, sometimes predating the Taliban emergence, have played a role in some murders. The Afghan government's failure to investigate any of the scores of murders of high-profile leaders has helped to further obscure the motives behind such killings.
5. Azami, Dawood, 'Kandahar: assassination capital of Afghanistan', *BBC World Service*, 29 October 2012.
6. Siddique, Abubakar, 'Taliban violence is creating a social revolution among Pashtuns', *Radio Free Europe/Radio Liberty*, 23 July 2010.
7. Azami, *Kandahar*.
8. Rashtinai, Mohammad Sadiq, interview with Abdul Habib Khan, Kandahar, summer 2011.
9. *Takfir* is the act of passing the verdict of *kufar* (deviation from fundamental Islamic beliefs) on an individual or community whose acts or words openly manifest deviations from, or opposition to, fundamental Islamic beliefs. In summer 2011, a Taliban spokesman contacted by my researcher Abdul Hai Kakar denied the employment of *takfir*.
10. Rashid, Ahmed, 'NATO's top brass accuse Pakistan over Taliban aid', *The Daily Telegraph*, 6 October 2006.
11. The Taliban leadership council was commonly referred to as Quetta Shura because they were seen as being based in Quetta, Balochistan.
12. Siddique, Abubakar, 'New Taliban rulebook aims to win Afghan hearts and minds', *Radio Free Europe/Radio Liberty*, 31 July 2009.

13. Pashto language text of the *Dey Afghanistan Islami Emirate Da Mujahideeno Lapara Layeha*, or *Rulebook for the Mujahedeen of the Islamic Emirate of Afghanistan*, 29 May 2010. Available on the Taliban website and distributed as a paperback.
14. Ibid, article 78.
15. *Rulebook*, article 21.
16. *Zakat* is one of the five pillars of Islam. It means that a certain portion of the wealth is collected from the rich and given to the poor. *Ushr* means tithe. It is a tax that involves taking one-tenth of agricultural produce from farmers.
17. Clark, Kate, 'The Layha: calling the Taliban to account', *Afghanistan Analyst Network*, July 2011.
18. Rashtinai, Sadiq, interview, 2011.
19. Rashtinai, Mohammad Sadiq, interview with Mohammad Omar Satay, Kandahar, summer 2011.
20. Rashtinai, Mohammad Sadiq, interview with Ahmad Shah Spar, Kandahar, summer 2011.
21. Rashtinai, Mohammad Sadiq, interview with Mawlawi Abdul Hadi Hammad, Kandahar, summer 2011.
22. van Linschoten, Alex Strick and Felix Kuehn, *Lessons Learnt:* 'Islamic, Independent, Perfect and Strong': Parsing the Taliban's Strategic Intentions, 2001–2011, Arts and Humanities Research Council, *Public Policy Series No. 3*, January 2012.
23. Rishtinai, interviews, Kandahar, summer 2011.
24. Mujahid responded to questions sent to him through my researcher Abdul Hai Kakar, summer 2011.
25. Ibid.
26. Rishtinai, interviews, Kandahar, summer 2011.
27. Kabuli, Abdul Wahhab, 'The Afghanistan of Islam rejects pollution by democracy and Westernisation', 6 June 2011. English translation available on www.ansar1.info website: htto://www.ansar1.infor/showthread.php?t=33963. last accessed Jul. 2011.
28. Amanullah was declared a 'Ghazi' for declaring a *jihad* against the British soon after assuming power in 1919. Ghazi is an Islamic term honouring an individual for participating in a holy battle.
29. Kabuli, 'The Afghanistan of Islam'.
30. Such criticism is a recurring theme in the writings of anti-communist *mujahedeen* during the 1980s.
31. Habib, Qari, 'Announcement of fateha for a martyr', 28 May 2012. Available on the Taliban website and circulated to journalists.
32. 'Another war is going on in Afghanistan', 29 April 2012. Available on the Taliban website: www.alemara1.com
33. The quotes are from original Pashto-language texts available on the Taliban web-

site: www.alemara1.com Insiders said the statements were supervised by the leadership council and drafted by the Taliban Political Committee. They went through many drafts.

34. 'Islamic Emirates' statement about America's latest allegations', 27 September 2011. Issued to journalists and available on the Taliban website: www.alemara1.com
35. Pashto-language statement, 'Martyr Mullah Obaidullah, a bright example of Afghan pride', 5 March 2012.
36. Rashid, Ahmed, *Pakistan on the Brink: The Future of America, Pakistan, and Afghanistan*, New York: Viking, 2011, pp. 113–36.
37. Siddique, Abubakar, 'Study says window for Afghan peace is closing quickly', *Radio Free Europe/Radio Liberty*, 8 February 2011.
38. Gopal, Anand, 'The battle for Afghanistan: militancy and conflict in Kandahar', New America Foundation, November 2010.
39. Text of Pak-Afghan Peace Jirga Declaration, *Daily Times*, 13 August 2007.
40. Discussions with senior Pashtun politicians, November 2007.
41. Rashid, *Pakistan on the Brink.*
42. The White House, 'Remarks by the president on a new strategy for Afghanistan and Pakistan', 27 March 2009.
43. The quotes are from original Pashto-language texts available on the Taliban website: www.alemara1.com
44. The reintegration funds were eventually increased to $250 million. But few Taliban fighters and commanders joined the initiative.
45. Siddique, Abubakar, 'Mystery of Taliban military leader's capture deepens', *Radio Free Europe/Radio Liberty*, 17 February 2012.
46. Rashid, *Pakistan on the Brink.*
47. The UN sanctions list aimed at enforcing a travel ban and asset freeze was established in 1999. There were more than 100 Taliban leaders among the more than 400 names on the list. A majority were Al-Qaeda members. The UN began removing reconciled Taliban leaders from the list in 2010. In June 2011, the UN Security Council separated the Taliban and Al-Qaeda sanctions committees, which made it easier to remove reconciled Taliban figures from the list.
48. Rashid, *Pakistan on the Brink.*
49. Siddique, Abubakar, 'Former Taliban leaders in Afghanistan see peace as a long way off', *Radio Free Europe/Radio Liberty*, 3 November 2010.
50. Siddique, Abubakar, 'Prospects for Afghan peace deal with the Taliban dim, but not dead', *Radio Free Europe/Radio Liberty*, 25 October 2012.
51. They opposed the nationalist mainstream of the old royalist regime and, unlike the communists, had no worldly focus on material development as a means of progress. Many Pashtun *mujahedeen* commanders fought against the Taliban for years.

52. For a detailed discussion of ethnic issues in Afghanistan see Siddique, Abubakar, 'Afghanistan's ethnic divides', Barcelona Centre for International Affairs, January 2012.
53. Based on extensive interviews with a cross-section of society in southern Afghanistan and other Pashtun regions.
54. 'Another war is going on in Afghanistan', 2012.
55. This refers to the forceful eviction of some Pashtuns from northern Afghanistan after the demise of the Taliban regime in late 2001. I met some of them in displacement camps near Kandahar in February 2002. Community leaders complained of being driven out of their homes by forces loyal to Abdul Rashid Dostum.

11. CRAFTING A PEACEFUL PASHTUN FUTURE

1. For a detailed discussion of Khattak's life, see Dupree, Louis, 'Ajmal Khattak—revolutionary Pashtun poet', American University Field Staff Reports, South Asia Series, XX, 9 (May 1976).
2. Sayel, Rehmat Shah, *How the Heart Fares on the Flames of Blood* (in Pashto: *Zarah Da Weeno Pa Lambo Sanga Khkari*), Peshawar: 2006.
3. National Intelligence Council, *Global Trends 2030: Alternative Worlds*, December 2012.
4. For details of US casualties, see http://icasualties.org/OEF/Index.aspx
5. Cordesman, Anthony, 'The US cost of the Afghan war: FY2002–FY2013, cost in military, operating expenditures and prospects for "Transition"', Center for Strategic and International Studies, 14 May 2012.
6. Woodward, Bob, *Obama's Wars*, New York: Simon & Schuster, 2010, p. 387.
7. Vendrell, Francesc, 'A decade of mistakes', *Foreign Policy*, 3 December 2011.
8. Reidel, Bruce, 'Dr. Afridi's warning: Pakistan's hatred of the United States', *The Daily Beast*, 12 September 2012.
9. The White House, 'Joint statement by President Obama and President Karzai', Office of the Press Secretary, 11 January 2013.
10. President Barack Obama, State of the Union Address (official transcript), 12 February 2013.
11. Tomsen, Peter, *The Wars of Afghanistan: Messianic Terrorism, Tribal Conflicts, and the Failure of Great Powers*, New York: Public Affairs, 2011.
12. Reidel, Bruce, *Deadly Embrace: Pakistan America and the Future of Global Jihad*, Washington: Brookings Institution, 2011.
13. Editorial, 'Time to pack up', *The New York Times*, 13 October 2012.
14. Gedmin, Jeffery and Abubakar Siddique, 'Watering Pakistan's nascent democracy', *International Herald Tribune*, 29 June 2010.
15. The government of Prime Minister Zulfiqar Ali Bhutto had an uninterrupted

term in the 1970s, although it chose to hold elections before its term was complete.

16. The electorate in the ANP's Peshawar Valley base had been unhappy with the party's five-year stint in office, seeing its administration as corrupt and ineffective. But ANP leaders told me that another reason for the party's defeat was that the Pakistani security establishment wanted to keep them out of power during the Western military withdrawal from neighbouring Afghanistan.
17. The Pakistan Muslim League-Nawaz formed an alliance with the nationalists, Pashtunkhwa Milli Awami Party and National Party in an effort to reach out to Pashtun and Baloch nationalists.
18. Mir, Amir, 'As army changes its doctrine, TTP decides to target India', *The News*, 13 January 2013.
19. Hoodbhoy, Pervez, 'Negotiate with the TTP', *The Express Tribune*, 14 January 2013. Pashtun public opinion and intelligentsia blamed the Pakistani military for creating, strengthening and sustaining Islamist radicals in their homeland.
20. Sattar, Babar, 'Law and the army', *The News*, 18 June 2011.
21. Siddique, Abubakar, 'Securing peace and promoting stability in western Pakistan', in Muggah, Robert (ed.), *Security and Development: States of Fragility Studies, Studies in Conflict, Development and Peacebuilding*, Oxford: Routledge, 2013.
22. Ibid.
23. Rashid, Ahmed, *Pakistan on the Brink: The Future of America, Pakistan, and Afghanistan*, New York: Viking, 2011, pp. 204–5.
24. Translated from the Pashto-language text of the Mullah Omar Eid-ul Adha message, 24 October 2012.
25. Moreau, Ron, 'Villagers in Afghanistan's Ghazni Province rise up against the militants', *The Daily Beast*, 24 June 2012.
26. Seibert, Sam, 'Has Taliban leader Mullah Omar lost his mind?', *The Daily Beast*, 15 October 2012.
27. Semple, Michael et al., 'Taliban perspectives on reconciliation', Briefing Paper, Royal United Services Institute, September 2012.
28. Yousafzai, Sami and Ron Moreau, 'Taliban commanders say they were tortured by Pakistani intelligence', *The Daily Beast*, 12 January 2013.
29. Semple et al., 'Taliban perspectives on reconcilliation'. It is important to remember that these were the views of individual Afghans. The Taliban have never officially adopted such positions and have in fact, rejected any reports attributing such pronouncements to their leaders.
30. Zaeef, Abdul Salam, 'Six fundamental facts for establishing peace', statement e-mailed to Abubakar Siddique, 12 January 2013.
31. *Hudood* is a strict Islamic criminal code. Punishments ordained under *hudood* include the amputations of limbs for theft, stoning to death for adultery and lashes for alcohol consumption.

32. Siddique, Abubakar, 'Stoning of Afghan couple for adultery sparks debate on sharia law', *Radio Free Europe/Radio Liberty*, 17 August 2010.
33. Department of Defense, Report on Progress Toward Security and Stability in Afghanistan, December 2012.
34. Most Afghan leaders were either killed or forced into exile during the twentieth century.
35. Siddique, Abubakar, *Afghanistan's Ethnic Divides*, Barcelona Centre for International Affairs, January 2012.
36. Anthony, Augustine, 'We don't want proxy wars in Afghanistan, Karzai says', *Reuters*, 11 March 2010.
37. In 2005, Pakistani military dictator Pervez Musharraf proposed to fence and mine the Durand Line. The offer came in response to allegations that the Taliban were using sanctuaries in Pakistan to support the Afghan insurgency. Kabul strongly opposed the proposal.
38. Pakistan's formal position further entails: 'The drawing of this international border terminated any Afghan sovereignty over the territory or influence over the people east of [the] Durand Line. Pakistan as a successor state to British India derived full sovereignty over this region and its people and has all the rights and obligation of a successor state. In addition, the question of self-determination for Pashtuns was foreclosed by the British supervised plebiscite held in 1947 in NWFP in which 99 per cent of votes cast were in favour of joining Pakistan. The Tribal Areas too expressed their assent through special Jirgas.' Embree, Ainslie (ed.), *Pakistan's Western Borderlands, the Transformation of a Political Order*, Karachi: Royal Book Company, 1979, (1st edn, New Delhi: Vikas Publishing House, 1977), p. 134.
39. Afghans also point out that, by nurturing rebels on Afghan soil, Islamabad has violated the border far more frequently than Afghans ever have.
40. Rubin and Siddique, 'Resolving the Afghanistan Pakistan stalemate'.
41. Siddique, Abubakar, 'Border talk crosses the line in Afghanistan', *Radio Free Europe/Radio Liberty*, 24 October 2012.
42. Khattak, Afrasiab, 'Stalemate in Afghanistan', *Dawn*, 15 November 2011.
43. Rubin and Siddique, 'Resolving the Afghanistan Pakistan stalemate'.
44. Khan, Tahir, 'Trade problems irk Afghan businessman', *The Express Tribune*, 19 January 2013.
45. Robert D. Hormats, the US undersecretary for economic, energy and agricultural affairs, defined the concept in 2011 as: 'The basis for the New Silk Road vision is that if Afghanistan is firmly embedded in the economic life of the region, it will be better able to attract new investment, benefit from its resource potential, and provide increasing economic opportunity and hope for its people. We also believe that the New Silk Road Initiative will be of particular importance to Pakistan, and can be an important way for Pakistan to further develop its

economy and provide jobs for its people.' See Hormats, Robert D., 'The United States' "New Silk Road" strategy: What is it? Where is it headed?', Address to the SAIS Central Asia-Caucasus Institute and CSIS Forum, Washington DC, 29 September 2011, http://www.state.gov/e/rls/rmk/2011/174800.htm

46. Risen, James, 'US identifies vast mineral riches in Afghanistan', *The New York Times*, 13 June 2010.
47. Mashal, Mujib, 'What Iran and Pakistan wants from the Afghans: water', *Time World*, 2 December 2012.

INDEX